# A PIONEER HISTORY
# OF THE
# COUNTY OF LANARK

# A Pioneer History of the County of Lanark

*Jean S. McGill*

Distributed by

Clay PUBLISHING COMPANY LIMITED
BEWDLEY, ONTARIO
"The House of Helpful Books"

First printing, March 1968
Second printing, January 1969
Third printing, April 1970
Fourth printing, August 1974
Fifth printing, July 1979

ISBN 0-9690087-1-6

Printed and Bound in Canada by
T. H. Best Printing Company Limited
Toronto

# PREFACE

This book aims to set down in readable form records that have been available concerning the beginnings of Lanark County and the lives of the people who pioneered it.

Many people have assisted the work by supplying information or finding others who could. The author wishes to acknowledge with appreciation all those who shared their family records or provided other material pertaining to the early history of Lanark. These include: Miss Helen Rodger, Mrs. Harry Wilson, Mrs. E. Hilliard, Mrs. Meda McRae, Mrs. Frank Rodger, Mrs. Viola Reid, Mrs. Keith Armstrong, Miss Jessie Scott, Mrs. Frank Paul, Mrs. Nelson Sadler, Mrs. Alice Hughes, Miss M. Lowe, Mrs. Verna Ross McGiffin, Waldo McCrea, H. Moulton, Mrs. H. Lowry, Miss Barbara Hutchison. Special thanks are due librarians Miss Elizabeth Kelly, Almonte, and Mrs. Keith Walsh, Carleton Place; E. C. Beer, Archivist, Douglas Library, Kingston; the staffs of the Toronto Public Library, the Public Archives of Canada, and the Ontario Archives for their cooperation in making historical material available; and to Miss Frances Halpenny of the University of Toronto Press for editorial suggestions and advice.

Special appreciation is extended to Edwin C. Guillet, author of many fine books on Canadian history, who gave time and energy to bringing this manuscript to publication, offered valuable advice and criticism, and edited the final typescript.

Illustrations have been obtained from a wide variety of sources. Some of the best are reproduced from the work of famous travelling artists like James Pattison Cockburn, W. H. Bartlett, and Thomas Burrowes; while woodcuts from historical atlases, and photographs or sketches of buildings which still remain, provide other representations of the past.

The author is particularly indebted to Mr. and Mrs. R. A. Stewart of Pakenham, whose encouragement and support have made possible the publication of this book.

March 1, 1968. Jean S. McGill

To my mother and father

## INTRODUCTION

The County of Lanark, long without adequate coverage of its local history, is the subject of Jean McGill's careful research and writing. Well back from the front line of settlement in Ontario, the region was yet early occupied by Scottish and Irish immigrations, some of them state-conducted and others organized by emigration societies. Much of the terrain was unsuitable for agriculture, but conditions in the British Isles were so bad during the first half of the nineteenth century that, whatever the hardships in Upper Canada, the attitude was common that settlers could hardly be worse off in the New Land.

In this book are the results of wide-ranging research on the region, its settlers, and their experiences. We see the Ballygibblins, who found the mere presence at a fair or election of Scots or lumbermen sufficient to induce a riot. Other groups, of course, were no better, relaxation from hardship and isolation bringing out crude and primitive emotions. Orangemen were described with critical vehemence by no less a Tory than Colonel James Fitzgibbon, when he came to Lanark to investigate conditions. "All the deeds of violence," he said, "have appeared in every instance to have been committed by Orangemen." And the Rev. William Bell, unsparing of himself yet over-strict as he sought to enforce his conception of Christian morality, wrote in his Journal that Orangemen "have not only disturbed the peace of Ireland but of every place where they have come, all over the world".

Replete with a wide coverage of manuscript sources in archival and private collections, Miss McGill's account includes as well contemporary travel books and diaries, local records and newspapers, and reminiscences of experiences to round out official reports and descriptions. John Mactaggart's *Three Years in Canada* (1829) and John M'Donald's vivid, if understandably pessimistic, *Narrative of a Voyage to Quebec and a Journey from thence to New Lanark in Upper Canada* (1822) are given the attention they deserve, and *The* McNab's vicious 18-year rule over his deluded and impoverished Scots is treated with similar fidelity.

Here you will find accounts of defamation of character, often a concomitant of early (and later) settlement, and of religion and education where bitter argument and recrimination seemed at times more important than Christian charity or the education of youth. Here too are described characteristic pioneer crimes of maiming cattle or beating up neighbours whose political views differed from yours. But you will also find accounts of the founding of community libraries like those at Ramsay and Watson's Corners, where the Scots—to whom we owe so much for their fervour for education—came on foot from far and near, bringing and borrowing boxfuls of classics like Gibbon's *Decline and Fall of the Roman Empire*, to say nothing of religious tracts and dissertations that few clergymen would find readable today, much less a spiritual force in the lives of hard-pressed and isolated settlers. It is hard to exaggerate the sordid and violent in pioneering, but most people were inherently decent; and in every locality there were the public-spirited and cultured, the highly intelligent and well-disposed, who set the pattern by their civilizing influence.

In these days of Centennial publications and government supported local histories I do not know of a better account of early settlement than *A Pioneer History of the County of Lanark*.

Toronto, February 1, 1968. Edwin C. Guillet

*CONTENTS*

# CHAPTER I

## EARLY ARRIVALS ON THE FRINGE OF THE RIDEAU

In 1800 Upper Canada northwest of the Ottawa and Rideau rivers was a dense forest inhabited only by Indians and wild animals—bears, deer, wolves, and smaller furbearers. No particular notice had been taken by the Upper Canada government of this great wooded land stretching northward over the Precambrian Shield. At this time the government was preoccupied with building up communities bordering the Lower Lakes and the St. Lawrence River where travelling was easier for incomers and where the border needed many hands for protection against threats from the American colonies to the south.

United Empire Loyalists were moving steadily into Canada following new and enticing land offers by the government. The head of each family could now claim 200 acres of land, plus 50 acres for each child under 21 years of age, and 200 acres for each son and daughter as they reached their 21st birthday. Special grants were given millwrights for building grist or saw mills, and many "Yankees" took advantage of these government offers to set up in business as capitalists.

To take care of the Loyalists, government surveyors were busy laying out townships inland from the St. Lawrence. In 1774 William Fortune had begun the survey of Montague Township, which was then part of Leeds County but now belongs to Lanark. This survey was completed by John Stegemann and by 1797 a census taken by Stegemann revealed that the township contained a handful of settlers—Daniel Nettleton, Samuel Heck, Joseph Barton, William Merrick, Stephen Burritt, Michel Landery, William Brown and William McRaye.*

William Merrick, of Welsh stock and a veteran of the American Revolution, arrived from Massachusetts in 1794. A millwright by

* Ontario Archives, Surveyor-General Reports, 1797.

trade he stayed some time in Elizabethtown (now Brockville), then, learning from Indians of a waterfall further north, he pushed on to the Rideau River. Finding the waterfall of sufficient power for milling operations, he built a log cabin on the north shore and before long had begun to build a grist mill. Here he brought his wife and two children. This was the beginning of the present village of Merrickville.

Following on his heels came Samuel McCrea, his wife Janet, and ten children from Ballston, N.Y. The McCreas spent some time with an elder son, James, at Prescott, then pushed on into the wilderness and located near the Merricks. As a United Empire Loyalist with many children, Samuel McCrea was entitled to 1200 acres of land and most of this was taken up in Montague.

McCrea had served as a private in Colonel Schoonover's Army near Albany, N.Y., and his health was already poor when he arrived in Canada. He died in 1806 at the age of 55. His sons and daughters married neighbours and occupied land near the Rideau River. John, the eldest was a carter during the early years and was hired to transport emigrants inland from Maitland along the St. Lawrence. He cut the first road from Montague Township to Perth. He was a powerful man and many tales were told in the early days about his feats of strength. Once he carried from Brockville on his back flour from one bushel of wheat, one broad axe, one set of drag teeth, one log chain. Once he drove to Montreal for salt and on the way home his horses fell through the ice on the river. He swam around his team and eventually was able to pull them out. On shore he discovered the remains of a fire left by campers. This saved his life.*

The Stafford family also settled in Montague at this time. The ancestral Staffords had come from England to Plymouth in 1626, but Samuel had no qualms about leaving the civilization of Saratoga Springs, N.Y., in 1794 for a backwoods cabin in the wilds of Montague Township. Perhaps he already anticipated the conflict about to break out between Canada and the 14 colonies. Stafford obtained employment as an agent to bring in new settlers and received considerable land for his services so that he and the McCreas eventually owned much of Montague and the adjoining township of Elmsley. Stafford worked with John Stegemann on the survey of Russell Township. The name of this township was changed to Elmsley in 1797.

By 1797 John Chester had opened a store in Merrick's Mills

* It is believed Joel McCrea, the Hollywood actor, is a descendant of John McCrea.

and Samuel Dow a blacksmith shop. Elmira Dow, his daughter, was the first teacher at Merrick's Mills. She later married Bradish Billings and moved to a point near Ottawa now called "Billings Bridge." In Wolford Township, south of the Rideau, there were already many settlers and the little settlement around Mr. Merrick's mills soon became a thriving village.

By 1802 the population of Montague numbered "90 souls" as the Dominion of Canada Atlas for 1880 called them. Among these were: "Henry and Richard Arnold, William Mars, Gideon Haskins, Leonard Hodgkins, Thomas Jarvis, Archibald Hill, Samuel Stafford and others."* Jesse McIntyre, a Baptist preacher, and his son Amasa arrived and Jesse opened a school for his neighbours' children north of Merrick's Mills. Samuel Heck, son of Wesleyan Methodist founder, Barbara Heck, had moved into Montague prior to 1800, but not until 1812 did the Methodists make any attempt to organize a following in this area. Then they arranged a camp-meeting at Kilmarnock, but the people had barely gathered when word came of war with the fourteen colonies and the Methodists disbanded and hastened home, many to prepare for army service. There was no other Protestant denomination in evidence in this part of Upper Canada until after the arrival of the Scottish and military settlers north of the Rideau in 1815-16.

Surveys of Elmsley and Burgess followed on that of Montague and the Loyalists took up land; but much of it they never occupied, particularly in Burgess which was rock-strewn and difficult to cultivate for agriculture. Much of the land lay waste for many years and eventually passed to speculators.

All of this settlement had been done on an individual basis and the affairs of Montague and adjacent townships were run by a few magistrates with no attempt at organization.

* *Illustrated Atlas of the Dominion of Canada, 1880.*

# CHAPTER II

## THE RIDEAU SETTLEMENT

By the end of the war with the Americans the large tract of land north of the Rideau was still largely unsurveyed and a virtual wilderness where a few squatters eked out a meagre living. By now, however, the British government had recognized that a loyal population must be established inland away from the St. Lawrence "front" as a second line of defence in any future threat.

In England Lord Bathurst, Secretary of State for the Colonies, was working on a plan of emigration to relieve some of the economic stress there. The industrial revolution of the century previous had continued to displace tradesmen and craftsmen throughout the British Isles. Now with the end of the war of 1812-14, Great Britain was overrun with discharged soldiers also seeking employment. Something had to be done quickly and emigration to North America seemed a solution.

Poverty such as existed in Great Britain during the first fifty years of the 19th Century is almost unbelievable today. In his book *The Great Migration* Edwin C. Guillet tells in vivid detail the conditions in the British Isles at that time and the perilous sailing-ship voyages to the land of promise, North America. Describing the plight of Scottish farmers, he relates how the members of a committee of investigation were invited into the hut of a starving man. Inside they found on one side of the fire a very old man "apparently dying" and on the other side a young man with a child on his knee, whose mother had recently died. Upstairs they found the husband of the dead woman ill in bed and, "turning down the rags which he was unable to remove himself," they discovered another man who would probably die before the end of the day.

This picture of starvation is but one horrifying example of a situation multiplied all over Scotland. Compared with this, nothing, including a wilderness across the sea, could be worse.

In Ireland absentee landlords were the villains, raising rents on their already impoverished tenants, leading to riots and rebellions. Living conditions in Ireland were worse than in England and Scotland. One reporter speaks of finding ten to twelve families living in one miserable dwelling "with scarcely a window remaining" and "not an article of furniture but the remains of an old oak table or a solitary chair. One iron pot sufficed for all cooking." People on the street were in rags, emaciated, hopeless, and despairing. "In Ireland," wrote the historian Macaulay, "there are ten degrees of poverty lower than any in England."

That poverty and starvation were accepted as part and parcel of the Irish peasant of this time is reflected in the attitude of sailing-ship owners; indeed it was used as an excuse by some to provide emigrant passengers with the worst accommodation and food. In this they were supported by officials in the United States and Canada, and at times with considerable logic. A. C. Buchanan, Chief Emigration Agent at Quebec, contended that giving unaccustomed food such as beef, biscuit, salt pork, and coffee to the Irish emigrant would only make him ill. R. J. Uniacke, Attorney-General of Nova Scotia, reporting on some 300 emigrants to Cape Breton, substantiated this view that the emigrants should bring their own food, saying that in this particular case each person took one pound of oatmeal for each day and a little molasses, butter, and a few eggs and remained healthy. He says the Irish would suffer from change of environment more than the Scots or English:

> The Irish emigrant before he comes out knows not what it is to lie on a bed; he has not been accustomed to a bed; if you put him in a bed and give him pork and flour you make the man sick; but when a man comes to Newfoundland he gets no more than his breadth and length upon the deck of the ship, and he has no provisions but a few herrings and he comes out a hearty man; and he has no doctor.*

There were three types of emigrant ships—those carrying cabin passengers only, those with both cabin and steerage accommodation, and those with only steerage. Conditions on the worst of these vessels of the time were terrible despite the various Passenger Acts passed to improve them. Later the Passenger Vessel Act of 1817 provided for food to be issued to passengers, but very often it was withheld until

* *The Great Migration*, by Edwin C. Guillet (New York, 1937), 2nd Edition, 1963, University of Toronto Press.

rotten and inedible, or sold only at prohibitive prices. At the time the Rideau settlement began, many ships were carrying timber to Great Britain from Lower Canada and returning to Canada empty, so they were glad to take passengers. This was the background for the settlement of the area now called Lanark County.

In England Lord Bathurst drew up a proclamation setting forth the government's intentions and chose John Campbell, Sr., Writer of the Signet, Edinburgh, to publish it in the Scottish newspapers. It first made its appearance in 1815, stating that persons desiring to emigrate to Canada would be conveyed free of charge. The government would also supply provisions on the voyage, and on arrival a grant of 100 acres would be allotted each family as well as to each male child on reaching age 21.

For the first six or eight months these immigrants would be allowed rations from government stores, and further aid might be granted in certain circumstances. Axes and other implements might be supplied at a fixed price "not exceeding half of the prime cost".

Families wishing to settle near each other, or those possessing joint stock or funds, could have lands allotted in the same neighbourhood. Land was to be set aside for a church and the maintenance of a clergyman and a schoolmaster. Persons desiring to emigrate under these terms must embark in April in government vessels in readiness at ports on the Clyde, but a deposit of £16, refundable after two years of settlement, had to be paid for each male over 16 and £2 for each wife.

Campbell reported in March that 500 had filed applications at Edinburgh and 200 at Glasgow. Enquiries poured into his office, and among various items settled by correspondence with Lord Bathurst was that children would be included but not single women unless sisters of single men. Widows were not encouraged to emigrate, with or without their families. Surgeons, clergymen, and schoolmasters were allowed to emigrate, but they were not particularly encouraged, other than being allotted the usual 100 acres of land. Churches and schools in the new land would have to be built by the settlers themselves, but £100 for clergymen and £50 for schoolmasters might be provided as salary.

On the 12th of March Lord Bathurst advised that the number of emigrants for the season would be limited to 2,000 of age 16 and up, with a proportion of children. The deposit of £16 proved a deterrent since many desiring to leave Scotland had no savings. The ports of

National Marine Museum, Greenock R. Salmon

THE *ANN* EMIGRANT SHIP

embarkation were set as Glasgow and Greenock. Up to the 25th of April deposits had been received from 62 men and 61 women, with 181 children. The Transport Board was slow in supplying suitable vessels and April passed, then May. The waiting emigrants were bitter because of loss of time and the expense of waiting while their supplies and money disappeared, and some demanded reimbursement from the government. Not until the middle of June did the transport vessels arrive. Campbell reported on the 23rd that the agent of the Transport Board had issued allowances to those persons in Glasgow and vicinity who had suffered from the delay. As several of the women were pregnant, a surgeon was allotted to each vessel.

Eventually, on the 10th of July, 1815, Campbell was able to send a letter to Sir Gordon Drummond, informing him that the emigrants would at once proceed to Quebec in four transports under the command of Lieutenant Champion of the Royal Navy; and on the 11th, 12th, and 14th July the *Dorothy*, the *Baltic Merchant*, and the *Atlas* sailed, carrying in all about 500 emigrants. The *Eliza* sailed from Greenock on the 3rd August with 122.

Although the Rev. William Bell, first clergyman for the new settlement along the Rideau, did not emigrate until 1817, his voyage aboard the *Rothiemurchus* is typical of what the poor emigrants suffered en route; Mr. Bell, his wife, and six children travelled steerage. The accommodation consisted of an aisle with double rows of berths made of rough planks. To each berth were assigned six adults. In the aisle they piled their belongings–food, utensils, and luggage. When seasickness struck, one can imagine the special horror to the sick amid the congestion. It is small wonder that, as one writer said, some cursed Columbus for ever having discovered America. In his MS "A History of the Christian Church in This Settlement", and in his guidebook *Hints to Emigrants*, Mr. Bell gives a graphic description of their first day at sea when berths had still not been allotted and confusion reigned among the passengers. He noticed that "the crying of the children, the swearing of the sailors, and the scolding of the women who had not got the beds they wanted" produced a most inharmonious effect, which "was heightened by the darkness of the night and the rolling of the ship".

> The morning was fine [he wrote] and the ebbing tide in a few hours carried us out of the river. During the day the wind, though light, continued favorably and we had, literally speaking, a pleasure sail. Every heart was light and every face wore a smile. Some were reading the books they had the precaution to take along with them; some conversing about their prospects in America, or the friends they

*Illustrated London News*

DANCING IN THE STEERAGE

> were leaving behind; and between decks a party of young people were dancing a good part of the day. . . . On the following morning I was awakened at an early hour by the violent motion of the ship and an unusual bustle on deck. On getting up I found that we were likely to have dancing enough against our will. A gale blew from the north-west. The sea roared and foamed around us, the passengers became sick, and everything began to wear a discouraging aspect. As we entered the Murray Firth things began to grow worse and worse. . . . Consternation and alarm were soon visible in every countenance; children were crying, and women wringing their hands wishing they had remained at home.

Passengers and crew totalled about one hundred and twenty aboard the *Rothiemurchus* and Mr. Bell had chosen space between the decks where there seemed to be plenty of room:

> Two tiers of beds were arranged along each side of the ship for she took no cargo; but went out for a load of timber. Each of these berths was six feet long, four feet wide, and three feet high and one was allotted for every two adults or three children. In the middle between the bed places was a space of about fifteen feet wide and sixty feet long. Part of the space was occupied by the more necessary part of our baggage such as chests and trunks, and the rest was put below. We were allowed two meals a day—breakfast and dinner. Those who wanted a third had to find it themselves. To this we had no objections had the provisions been good but we soon found that the salt beef and biscuit were not fit for hogs. For breakfast we had at first porridge with molasses and water, for dinner we had soup, beef, and biscuit. But as soon as we were at sea we found our situation every day getting worse and worse. Our porridge was sometimes so abominably dirty that it was impossible to taste it and sometimes it was shamefully burnt by the carelessness of the cook. The first three days we had good provisions but after that they were detestable. Brose of oatmeal was now served up for breakfast and nothing to it but water. For dinner we had beef, so old and ill preserved that it was black, stinking, rotten, and quite bitter to the taste. My family could not touch either it or the biscuit which was also rotten and full of vermin. It was said that both had been purchased the year before at a government sale of condemned stores.

The soup issued from time to time was "merely stinking water in which stinking beef had been boiled, which no dog would taste unless he were starving". On another occasion, during a storm, the only food served was "rotten Dutch cheese, as bitter as soot, and bread partly alive". "Many of our passengers," wrote Bell, "were seized with a dysentery in consequence of eating putrid fresh beef; I mean that some were fresh when we left Leith, five weeks ago. They were not allowed to taste it until it was unfit for use, and then they were made welcome to use it. Three or four seemed almost in a dying condition and were placed under the doctor's care." With respect to the water supply for the voyage, Mr. Bell says:

> Our water for some time past has been very bad. When it was drawn out of the casks it was no clearer than that of a dirty kennel after a heavy shower of rain; so that its appearance alone was sufficient to sicken one. But its dirty appearance was not its worst quality. It had such a rancid smell that to be in the same neighborhood was enough to turn one's stomach; judge then what its taste must have been. . . .

The passengers found their situation worse as the voyage proceeded, and on the 25th of April their unrest came to the point of mutiny.

> A list of provisions ordered by a late Act of Parliament [he wrote] was handed about among the passengers which included two pounds of flour and a half pound of butter per week for each person. Hitherto we had got none of these, and the abominable beef and biscuit had rendered the passengers perfectly furious. I endeavoured to pacify them by a promise of speaking to the Captain on the subject which I did without delay. He at first blustered a good deal and threatened to make our situation worse than before but the same afternoon he served out a week's provisions including both flour and water.

When the ship finally reached Quebec, Bell was still comparatively well but "Mrs. Bell and several of the children were reduced to the very brink of the grave by long sickness and the barbarous treatment they had received". They were fortunate to have shelter for six days before proceeding further, but many of the settlers continued without rest and found the succeeding tedious trip by boat and on foot to Upper Canada and the Perth settlement too arduous in their weakened state and died en route.

The first group of emigrants arrived at Quebec in mid-September, and the *Eliza* appeared in the St. Lawrence on the 27th September. Three possible locations were open to the newcomers—one in Glen-

WILLIAM BELL

MRS. WILLIAM BELL

garry, one along the Rideau River, and the third at the head of the Bay of Quinte.

Since it was already early Fall, Sir Gordon Drummond, the Administrator, decided they should not proceed to their locations until the following spring. Some unmarried men in the group proceeded to Kingston and were employed by the Engineer's department on the King's works. About 300 settlers were transported to Cornwall and lodged under poor conditions with provisions from the military storehouse. Thirty more families proceeded to Brockville and were accommodated in military barracks, adjoining huts which they rented, or at neighbouring farm homes where some of them secured employment. This latter group were considered to be the nucleus for a Rideau settlement where a depot was to be set up under the superintendence of Alexander McDonnell, staff-surgeon Thom, Deputy Assistant Commissary-General Grey, and Lieutenant McIvor, Assistant Deputy Superintendent.

Late in the Fall of 1815 a party of the Brockville arrivals set out for the nebulous spot north of the Rideau where it had been decided a depot would be set up and a community established. Surveyors were still at work on this area and it was almost necessary to blaze one's own trail through the forest once the Rideau was crossed. It was an impressive journey. On their return to Brockville, they drew up a petition asking instead for a location along Lake Ontario, preferably on the Bay of Quinte and gave it to their surgeon, Dr. Thom, to send to the Lieutenant-Governor of Upper Canada, Sir Francis Gore.* The Governor was adamant as regards the location of the settlers, and orders were issued for them to proceed to the Rideau as soon as feasible in the Spring.

Meanwhile John Holliday, who had accompanied the settlers as their schoolmaster, had refused to teach school during the winter unless paid an extra $2 for each settler's child. This, despite the fact that he had been offered a room and fuel by Captain Barnes at the Brockville Barracks and would receive his annual salary from the Imperial government. However, Barnes had gone ahead and authorized a schoolroom, ready for occupation should the settlers accept Holliday on his terms.

This was the beginning of John Holliday's long conflict with the government over his salary, a dispute partly due to his own irascible personality and partly to official stupidity. His troubles climaxed at a later period in our history.

Typical of government arrangements, some of their plans for settlement were still on the drawing board. Although they had set in motion an emigration scheme for opening up the Rideau area, they had not yet negotiated a treaty with the Indians, who still legally owned the whole area north of the Rideau River; and it was not until the 22nd February, 1816, that Captain Ferguson, Resident Agent of Indian Affairs at Kingston, received Lieutenant-Governor Gore's instructions in the following terms:

> It being the object of His Majesty's Government to make a purchase for four or five townships in the rear of those mentioned in the margin [Crosby, Burgess, Elmsley, Montague and Marlboro], you will immediately communicate the same by wampum to the Chiefs of the Chippewa and Missesáwguay Nations, owners of the said lands, and inform them previous to your making a provisional agreement with them, that the King, their great Father, will make an establishment on the land described to which I am confident no objection on their part will be made.†

* This petition was signed by: Francis Allen, Robert Gardner, Archibald Morrison, John Brash, John Allan, James Fraser, Robert Gibson, James Taylor, William Holderness, William W. Scott, John Kingston, John Flood, Otto Thid, John Millar, Thomas McLean, George Wilson, William Johnstone, William Old, Thomas Barber, Hugh McKay, Thomas Cuddie, William McGillivray, John Holliday, John Ferrier, Abraham Ferrier.

† Public Archives, Upper Canada Sundries, Q.320.

The instructions were accompanied by a plan showing in outline the land to be acquired by the survey of these new townships covering nearly 300,000 acres (Bathurst, Drummond, and Beckwith townships).

Alexander McDonnell, late deputy-paymaster, was appointed superintendent of both soldier and civilian settlement and Lieutenant Angus McDonnell of the Glengarry Light Infantry Fencibles to take charge of the settlers and receive applications. Through the winter the new superintendent had his own problems over surveys. Captain Reuben Sherwood, who was in charge of survey, reveals in his survey diaries that he was careless in his work and frequently absent when his surveyors required his advice and assistance. There were unaccountable and exasperating delays in getting the work done, causing discontent among the settlers. Even as late as the winter of 1815-16 groups of surveyors and their parties were proceeding through the Rideau wilderness trying to set up boundaries, and this continued in the Rideau lakes area until as late as 1817.* It was not until the 26th of March, 1816, that a road had been completed to "The Depot" where the government storehouse was to be.

During the survey of townships in winter, when chains were broken from dragging them through the snow and ice, they were frequently patched lacking a link or more, so that every four-acre block would lack upwards of four feet. Sherwood learned this when he returned to the survey party, but apparently was too indifferent to rectify it. In Beckwith, when the chain broke, willow links were put in. These stretched and the lots became irregular in size. Some lots which should have been 200 acres ran up to 225, while others would only contain 125 instead of 200. Since Sherwood was usually absent from location, the surveyors had to make their own arrangements in getting men to work for them. Sometimes they hired Indians but this was generally unsatisfactory, for the Indians had no sense of responsibility and might disappear overnight never to return. Some of the men who worked during the winter of 1815-16 were emigrants from the Brockville group but they were ill-equipped for continual camping out-of-doors enduring the severe cold and dampness of the Canadian winter, and many had to give up the work before they had scarcely begun.

On the 12th of March Superintendent McDonnell called together

* Surveyors employed in the area were: John Booth, J. B. Demers, William Fraser, Benjamin Ecuyere, R. B. Hay, Duncan McDonnell, and William Conger, some of whom left small, incomplete diaries of survey.

Public Archives of Canada

THE RIDEAU SETTLEMENT IN 1818

Dr. Thom, Reuben Sherwood, and Joseph Daverne—the proposed clerk of the military depot to be established—and one or two advisors. Sketches and plans were made for the actual settlement. McDonnell then went to Kingston to enlist the interest of Colonel Cockburn, Deputy Quartermaster General. On the 16th March Colonel Cockburn and Captain Otty, of the Navy, arrived at Brockville, and, together with Sherwood and Daverne, McDonnell set out for the Rideau Lake area. They travelled down the Lake to the "Carrying Place" (Oliver's Ferry) where they left their sleighs, and crossed the neck of land to a smaller inner lake which Colonel Cockburn named Otty Lake after the Captain. A creek connected Otty Lake with Pike Creek (the Pike was later changed to Tay, after the river in Scotland) and it was decided that the settlement should commence on the east bank of this creek, in Township No. 2, or Drummond as it was later called. Sherwood stated he would cut a road through before the first sleighs arrived. By the 26th March he had blazed a trail from Perth's "Depot" to a point on the Rideau Lake now known as Port Elmsley, a road which would later link the Perth settlement with the community of Merrickville.

McDonnell arranged to have a storehouse built within three weeks, 60 feet by 20 feet in size, on the present site of Perth. By the 28th of March 30 loads of provisions had arrived, a location had been cleared, and some timbers had been fitted to place the stores upon. McDonnell ordered a bridge to be built across Pike Creek, near the site of the government storehouse. Already some settlers had arrived with knapsacks and axes.

The first locations were taken up along the town line, later called the Scotch Line, which separated the townships of Bathurst and Burgess, with a small portion of North Elmsley bordering on Drummond. Along this line in April 1816 the following located: John Holliday, Lot A; Alexander McFarlane and James McDonald, Lot 1; William McGillivray and Alexander Cameron, Lot 2; John Brash and William Rutherford, Lot 3; John Millar and Robert Gardner, Lot 4; James Drysdale and John Allan, Lot 6; John Ferrier, Lot 7; Abraham Ferrier and Thomas Barber, Lot 8, all on the south side of the town line, in the township of Burgess. All of these first settlers received their patents in 1820, with the exception of Robert Gardner who appears to have left the settlement.

During the spring and summer of 1816 steady traffic proceeded along the route set by McDonnell and Cockburn. The incomers trav-

Archives of Ontario Thomas Burrowes

OLIVER'S FERRY, RIDEAU LAKE

elled by wagon north from Brockville some 26 miles to the Stone Mills at the eastern end of Upper Beverley Lake in the township of Bastard, then north to the Rideau Lake, 12 miles further, near the present village of Portland.

From here they were conveyed down the Rideau by a scow, owned by an old settler named Lindsay. From a bay above the mouth of the Pike Creek they travelled by ox-sled through the woods about a mile and a half to a point on the Pike above Pike Falls. Another scow took them up the Pike River to Perth.

Rapidly the northern half of the Scotch Line in Bathurst township was taken up by settlers. Here located: James Miller and John Simpson, Lot 26; William Spalding and John Hay, Lot 25; John Ferguson and John Flood, Lot 23; William Holderness, Lot 19; Alexander Kidd and James Fraser, Lot 18; George Wilson and William Johnston, Lot 16; Robert Gibson and Isaac Wilson, Lot 15; John McNee and John McLaren, Lot 14; John McLeod and James Bryce, Lot 13; Sam Pardie and Thomas Scott, Lot 12; George Lester and Thomas Barrie, Lot 11; John Richie, Sr. and Jr., Lot 10, all on the first concession of Bathurst. Most of these settlers received their patents in 1820.

In North Elmsley, at the other end of the Scotch Line, the following settled: Peter and William McPherson (father and son) on Lots 10 and 27; James Taylor and James McLaren, Lot 28; Alexander

Simpson and Hugh McKay, Lot 29, all in the 10th Concession. John Holliday, the schoolmaster, was to have his school on Lot 21, in the first Concession of Bathurst. This would serve the children of the Scotch Line settlers.

To each group of four families the government storehouse issued a grindstone and a cross-cut and whip-saw; each family received an adze, hand-saw, drawing knife, shell auger, two gimlets, door-lock and hinges, scythe and snath, rasping-hook, two hoes, hay fork, skillet and camp kettle, and a blanket for each member of the family.

Superintendent McDonnell found it increasingly difficult to get information from Sherwood so that he could plan the best locations for settlement as the settlers continued to pour in. From the Indians he learned much about the topography of the land and lakes around Perth. In a letter dated May 11, 1816, to Captain Fowler he complained of lack of money and of not receiving his barrack allowance, and noted that "the price of labour here is out of all reason in consequence of the difficulty of transporting provisions". He indicated that he would have to return to Brockville for a time because he had been "deprived of every comfort and labouring under every inconvenience, my bodily and mental strength cannot bear me up longer. . . . I cannot and do not depend on very much information which Captain Sherwood and Mr. Graves give me . . . am far from being satisfied with Captain Sherwood, having withheld . . . information, he may profit more than me".*

In another letter dated the 16th May, 1816, he remarks of Sherwood that he only returns "to Perth in his own interests". In this letter McDonnell asks for proper assistance to have the land surrounding Perth surveyed and located.

McDonnell also had complaints to relay to Captain Fowler about the tools being supplied the settlers. The type of axe being sent from the homeland, for instance, was like a large hatchet and quite useless in the forests of Canada. A pioneer writing about them says "the axes are light, thin, and flat and were long used in the settlement for cutting ice or splitting pumpkins, but never for cutting down trees". American implements, perfected over the hundreds of years they had been cutting down the forests of the continent, were the ideal tools for the new Canadians, and were occasionally available through the generosity of an itinerant "Yankee".

In June 1816 the military settlers arrived. These were discharged

* Perth Museum, Record Book of Orders.

soldiers from the Glengarry Light Infantry and the Canadian Fencibles. The latter was composed of Germans, Poles, Belgians, and Italians taken prisoner during the Napoleonic Wars and who had won their freedom by taking up arms under Major-General de Watteville, a Belgian, in the war against the Americans in 1812-14. The Glengarry veterans for the most part stayed with their locations, but many of the de Watteville Fencibles locating in the 6th, 7th, and 8th Concessions of Burgess later abandoned their locations and moved south of the border, or elsewhere in the Canadas.

*Superintendent's Office,*
*Perth, U C.* 17th April 1816

THE BEARER, Peter McPherson Ensign is Located to the S West half of Lot No. Twenty seven in the Tenth Concession of the Township of Elmsley County of Leeds — and District of Johnstown

THE CONDITION of this Location is such, That if the above named Peter McPherson is not residing upon, and improving the above described Lot, clearing and putting in crops at least four acres yearly, then this Title to be void and of no effect, and subject to be immediately re-granted.

N. B. After Location no exchange can take place, nor is this certificate of any value but to the original Grantee.

By Order,

[illegible]

*Superintending Settlers.*

Public Archives of Canada

LOCATION TICKET

Land was granted according to rank—Lieutenant-Colonel receiving 1200 acres; Major—1000 acres; Captain 800 acres; Subaltern—500 acres; Sergeant-Major and Quartermaster Sergeant—300 acres; Sergeant—200 acres; and Private—100 acres. Their location tickets were similar to those granted civilian settlers, and subject to the same conditions of three years' occupation and cultivation of the land before patents would be granted. Officers and men, however, were to receive provisions for themselves and their families from the government storehouse for the period of one year, while civilians were allowed only six months' supplies from their time of location. In May and

June the de Watteville men swarmed in and McDonnell wrote to Captain Fowler:

> I find myself placed in a most unpleasant predicament from the not having in my power to place the men from the Regiment de Watteville on their lands. All that has been surveyed in township No. 1 [Bathurst] has been located on the 13th inst.
>
> I called on Captain Sherwood and requested to know what lands had been surveyed in No. 2 [Drummond]. I enclose his answer and field sketch. He informed me that what he had surveyed was very wet, and I have since been informed from good authority, that such is the case and that it is unfit for location.
>
> Had the time which has been employed in the survey of this township been devoted to No. 1, the whole of de Watteville's might have been placed on their lands, and you will in consequence, on your arrival here, find yourself at a loss where to place the located men. I must apprise you that the spirit of enterprise which appeared to actuate the de Watteville's on their first arrival has evaporated in consequence of their not being placed on their lands, and that some have already quitted the settlement and others have notified their intention of following their example.*

The surveyor's posts were set only at one corner of a lot of 200 acres, much of which might be swamp. Consequently, without a guide the settler was unable to determine the outline of his land. When Captain Fowler arrived in June he proceeded to straighten matters out and succeeded in getting Sherwood to improve his technique. Surveys thereafter proceeded more quickly. Of the de Watteville regiment settling in Bathurst Township, most stayed on their land long enough to receive deeds.

The Glengarrys located principally in Drummond Township close to Perth. Among these were Ensign Gould, Lot 8; John Balderson (after whom the village of Balderson was named), Lot 1; Henry McDonald, Lot 11; Thomas McCaffrey, Lot 12, all on the 8th Concession. John Malloch, Lot 14; James McGarry, Lot 10; Donald Campbell, Lot 3; Peter McLaren, Lot 8, on the 7th Concession. John King, Lot 12 on the 4th Concession; Peter Campbell, Lot 4 on the 6th Concession; James McNice and T. Bright, Lot 10 on the 9th Concession.

Other civilian settlers arriving on 1816 ships selected locations in Drummond. Among these were: John Tatlock, an Irishman, Lot 14,

* Public Archives of Canada, Upper Canada Sundries, June 18, 1816.

Concession 3, for whom the village of Tatlock in the township of Darling was later named. Edward James and his wife, Jane Godin, also from Wexford, Ireland, with their family of seven located on the second line of Drummond—an area later known as "the James Settlement". Hugh Robertson and Donald Macdonald took adjacent lots in what is now called Drummond Centre. Hugh Robertson, a graduate of Stirling Academy in Scotland, had been bookkeeper and overseer on the Drummond Estate at Etalkallan, Scotland. He and his wife, Christine Macdonald, sailed aboard *The Lady of the Lake*, arriving in September. On the same boat came his sister, Janet, and her husband, Donald Campbell; a few weeks later his brother-in-law, Donald Macdonald, arrived. Hugh Robertson was known as a seer in the pioneer community. On the Donald Macdonald farm was a small fenced-in burying-ground for the early settlers, which was used up until the 1830s. Here were laid to rest Donald Macdonald, his daughter Isabel, Andrew Caswell, and several other pioneers. The Campbells—Donald, and his brother Duncan—located further along the 6th Concession on Lot 3, near the point later called Armstrong's Corners on the Lanark Road.

Around Mississippi Lake in Drummond Township, near Flintoff Bay, eight farms were taken up and occupied in the late fall of 1816 by Thomas and William Hunter (Lot 19, Concession 7); Christopher Flintoff (Lot 19, Concession 6); James Robinson (Lot 25, Concession 6); John McNaughton (Lot 24, Concession 6); Duncan McNaughton, Jr. (Lot 25, Concession 6). On a corner of the land owned by John and Duncan McNaughton, Sr., grew the later village Tennyson.*

Bathurst Township was largely occupied, or granted as part of land allotment to soldiers and officers of the Glengarry Infantry. Among these were Captain Watson; Captain Blair, Adjutant of the Regiment; Captain McKay; Sergeant Quigley; John Hoover; Magnus Flett; Benjamin Johnston; and two Trumans. From the 104th Regiment came Col. Andrew W. Playfair, locating on Lot 22 of the 12th concession of Bathurst where he established grist and saw mills and did a thriving business in later years. Captain Thomas Consitt, a navy officer, drew several lots and settled on half of Lot 21 on the Bathurst side of the Scotch Line.

Military settlers locating along the Scotch Line in North Elmsley in 1816 included: Captain James O'Brien and Lieut. Joshua Pelton, Lot

* For Ships' Lists of 1815-16 settlers, see Appendix, page 232.

23; Lieut. Alexander Fraser and John Campbell, Lot 22; John Smith, Lot 21 (he later left the settlement); and Louis Grenier, Lot 18. After these the earliest settlers were: Ewen Cameron, Archie and Duncan Gilchrist, John Robertson, Robert Heddleston, and Joseph Cosgrove. Abraham Parsall, a Loyalist, settled along the Tay River on Lot 20, Concession 4 of Bathurst and here erected grist and saw mills. Captain Joshua Adams who was one of the first to draw a town lot of one acre in Perth, in 1820 fell heir to the mills of Parsall who had died. Adams then moved from Perth and established further enterprises on the Tay, the result of which was the village of Adamsville (now Glen Tay).

Most of the Army officers located in Perth and became the first businessmen of the village. They also were the magistrates and secured the best government positions, when they were established. William Morris opened the first store in a log building shortly after the government storehouse was completed. John Adamson built Adamson Inn, the leading hotel for many years (c. 1816, still standing). Benjamin DeLisle opened another general store across the street from that of William Morris. Staff-Surgeon Thom in charge of medicine and health for the military settlement chose a location on the Tay within the boundaries of the townsite where there was a waterfall sufficient to

Sketch by the author

ADAMSON'S INN (THE RED HOUSE)
Located on Craig Street, it was built in 1816 and is still in use as a dwelling.

run a mill; here he began to build a grist mill. Sergeant Angus Cameron opened a tavern north of the village on the later road to Lanark. Others locating in the village were: Captain Holmes; Captain Leslie; Captain McMillan; Roderick Matheson (Paymaster of the Glengarrys); Lieutenant-Colonel Marshall; Surgeon-Major Reade; Lieutenant-Colonel Powell; Lieutenant-Colonel Josiah Taylor; Major Fowler; Major Greig; Captain Fitzmaurice; Captain Alexander Ferguson; Sergeants Manion, Ritchie, and Naughty; Henry Graham; William Hunter; Dr. James O'Hare; Captain Mason; John Ferguson, Jr.; and John Stewart, a former army teacher.

Colonel Cockburn reported to Sir John Sherbrooke, the Governor, in September 1816, that much was amiss in the Rideau settlement—the Superintendent's staff was inadequate, Staff-Surgeon Thom could not possibly handle all the medical problems of the community, and a hospital should be built; a barracks was required to house incoming settlers until their land could be cleared and dwellings built; a schoolhouse was needed; and proper burying ground should be laid out. Nothing was done about any of these situations for some time to come.

Lieutenant-Governor Francis Gore paid the new settlement a visit and sent further findings to Sherbrooke, recommending that additional rations be issued the settlers until they could support themselves, since winter was approaching and the Fall arrivals had scarcely cleared their land. Still not satisfied, Sherbrooke sent his Deputy Quartermaster General, Colonel Myers, to review the situation. He reported:

> This new settlement was commenced on the 18th April, 1816. The new village of Perth is situated on a small river, now called the Tay, formerly the Pike, which empties itself into the Rideau Lake about 5½ miles below; it is distant from Brockville by 42 miles, 21 of which is an old-fashioned and good road; the remainder is a road recently cut through the woods, and is good for the passage of wagons. Much praise is due to Captain Fowler for his exertions in opening this communication, by which a great saving in transportation has taken place.
>
> In the village there are twenty houses, and in the immediate vicinity there are 250 habitations, which will be in readiness for occupation before the winter. Amongst the settlers are about eighty head of cattle, and there are 800 bushels of fall wheat now in the ground. At present there are 840 men, 207 women, and 458 children, equal to 1,100 military rations of provisions per diem. The settlement is generally provisioned to the 24th of October; about fifty families

> of Scotch to the 24th of December, and provisions for the whole are at the depot till the 24th of January, next. The settlers recently gone up are not included in this statement. Their numbers, as far as I can form a judgment, will not exceed 200 rations per day. Of the number of settlers from the United States, and who had emigrated from home to that country, it is not possible to speak with any degree of certainty.
>
> I am of the opinion that none of the settlers of the Perth community, and in its immediate neighbourhood are in a state to provide for themselves during the coming winter; the earliest of them only commenced on clearing their land in April last. I would, therefore beg to recommend that rations of provisions be issued to them until next June. Further indulgence will, I think, be absolutely necessary. Those in the townships of Wolford, Kitley, Bastard, Montague and Oxford, being in the country tolerably well settled, and who have been a year or more on their lands the 24th of December next, may be struck off at that time; their numbers will be about equal to 150 rations per day.*

The year 1816 closed with Alexander McDonnell gladly relinquishing his position to Captain Fowler. McDonnell left the settlement to become Assistant Secretary of the Department of Indian Affairs in the more sophisticated atmosphere of York. Captain Fowler remained in charge of the Perth settlement until it was taken over by Joseph Daverne, the clerk of stores, in 1817.

* Public Archives of Canada, Upper Canada Sundries, Q.137.

## CHAPTER III

## CONDITIONS SURROUNDING THE FIRST SETTLERS

The topography, "the lay of the land," the conditions with which the pioneer had to struggle in the wilderness, deserve attention.

To begin with, as previously mentioned, surveys were carelessly done causing considerable dispute and trouble for the settlers later. Sometimes they had to have their land re-surveyed, for which they had to pay.

The land was generally divided up into townships of ten miles square, sub-divided into 12 concessions, and each of these divided into 27 lots, containing 200 acres except the last which contained 100 acres. This was the general plan although some townships had less than 12 concessions (Montague has ten).

In all the southeastern townships of Lanark County the concessions run east and west, while in the northwestern townships, the concessions run north and south. North and South Sherbrooke form a 60° pie-shaped triangle, the lower half of which has east-west concession lines, while the north half has north-south concession lines. The reason is not known why Burgess, Elmsley, Montague, Bathurst, Drummond, and Beckwith have east-west concession lines while Dalhousie, Lanark, Ramsay, Pakenham, Darling, and Lavant have northwest ones. It would not appear to have anything to do with natural boundary lines since Sherwood, the head surveyor, was, and has been since, severely criticized for not using natural boundaries as part of his plan. To find one's land boundaries alone in the conglomeration of swamp, marsh, and thick woods was a major project.

A post was placed in the ground to mark the limit or edge of each concession, both in front and rear. When an immigrant arrived he had to take a guide to find the location of his chosen lot. Generally two or three settlers went together and hired a guide who charged five or six shillings a day. Most settlers had a choice of two lots, and this meant, if three men travelled together, they had to inspect 600 acres. So exhausting was this three-day (or more) stint, due to the oppressive heat in the forest by day and the damp heavy dews at night, that men were often confined to bed with fever after such a journey.* At this time, Lanark County was a land of dense forests, as the same writer described it gloomily, "through which the sun never penetrated." Clearings for the settlers' houses were surrounded by trees so tall that the clearing, if small, never benefited by the sun's rays. In this new land were birds of all kinds—many now extinct—and beautiful flowers of great variety. Likewise a wealth of berry and forest fruit, lakes full of fish, and abundance everywhere, as is always found in fertile areas where the destructive hand of man has not yet reached. Wild life abounded, so that if a man were hardy and skilled, he could have food for the taking, but it required skill to survive until his farm yielded crops to purchase the staples—flour, butter, tea, sugar—and the et ceteras. In 1817 the census revealed that there was only one cow in all of Bathurst District, which then comprised all of the present counties of Lanark and Renfrew and part of Carleton north of the Rideau River. One is inclined to think the census takers, Sam Purdy and John Ferguson, both resident at Perth, did not venture very far afield in their survey, for Robert Gourlay, the pioneer journalist who interviewed Scotch Line settlers in 1818, reported 44 cows and 22 oxen among this small group of settlers alone!† There was plenty of game in the woods—bears, wolves, wolverines, wild cats, deer, partridge.

It was a well-watered area sustained by two extensive waterways. From the north-west, rising near the Trent Valley system, came the Mississippi River with its major tributary, the Clyde, and many lakes and small streams. The Mississippi flows the entire breadth of the County, draining the whole sector north of Perth and flowing northward through Pakenham Township, draining into the Ottawa River at Chats Lake. The Rideau waterway with its major tributaries the Tay and the Jock rivers, flows north-easterly along the base of the County towards the Ottawa River.

The dense forests comprised a great variety of trees. Most valuable of Canadian woods was the white pine, and to these the British

* John M'Donald, *Narrative of a Voyage to Quebec and Journey Thence to New Lanark in Upper Canada* (1822).

† Robert Gourlay, *Statistical Account of Upper Canada* (1822).

*Canadian Illustrated News*

LOGGING IN UPPER CANADA
Early woodcuts are effective illustrations.

government reserved rights when issuing grants to settlers. The Imperial government also reserved the right to all mines of gold or silver.

According to the Agricultural Commission of 1881, Bathurst Township had no swampy land that could not be cultivated, and "hardly any wet springy land".† Beckwith Township had heavy clay, sand, and gravel with some flat, rocky soil. Drummond Township had average to good soil. Montague, whose land had been granted and partially settled by Loyalists long before the Rideau and Perth military settlement, had generally poor soil—some of it worthless. Lanark Township had sandy loam. Darling had light soil, with much rock and swamp. Pine grew profusely. Ramsay had good soil—clay and sandy loam, and it eventually became the choice land agriculturally. South Sherbrooke had sandy loam. Pakenham had clay and sandy loam.

On May 31, 1819, at Kingston, a treaty had been signed "effected by Captain John Ferguson, Resident Agent of Indian Affairs, of Kingston, representing the Crown (King George III) of the First Part and the Chiefs or 'Principal Men of the Mississauga Nation' of the Second Part. . . . The price promised to be paid by the Crown was an annuity of £642.10s. provincial currency, in goods at the Montreal price".* This parcel of land included the eastern part of Renfrew

† Ontario Agricultural Commission Report, 1881, Appendix I.
* Ontario Historical Society, *Papers and Records*, Vol. 27, 1931.

County, the eastern part of Carleton, and all of Lanark except a southern fringe along the Rideau Lake and River.

The Indians still roamed the forests according to their rights, although dispossessed of their land. The Mississaugas were a subtribe of the Ojibways who spread east and west from the Trent River basin and occupied a large part of old Ontario. The river *Mississippi* (Mishi-sippi) received its name from the Ojibway word meaning large river.

During the survey of the new settlement, Indians were occasionally hired as chainbearers but there is little or no record of their success as labourers. They continued for the most part to live as their forbears, hunting and fishing and camping along the waterways. The Rev. William Bell described the first Indians he saw at the Perth depot in August of 1817, not long after his arrival:

> They came down the river [Tay] and pitched their tent upon the island in the middle of the village [Cockburn Island]. . . . They had deer, muskrat, and various kinds of fowl which they exposed for sale. . . . They had all black hair, brown complexions, and active well-formed bodies. All of them, even the children, had silver ornaments in their ears.*

Later he speaks of the sufferings of Indians taken ill and left behind by travelling parties. One incident concerned an old Indian woman, left sick by the riverside on one of the coldest days in winter. A young man from Perth, travelling the route, discovered her, borrowed a sleigh and brought her to a tavern kept by a widow who administered hot food and put her to bed. For the most part the Indians in the Rideau seemed a peaceable lot, content with their nomadic life, occasionally bringing woven baskets and pelts to sell in Perth.

The Rideau settlement abounded in wild fruits and berries—onions, plums, cherry and walnut trees, gooseberry and currant bushes, raspberries, strawberries, cranberries, beans, cresses, and several kinds of "wild tea". John M'Donald who came to Lanark in 1821, mentions substitutes for tea used by the pioneers. There was "velvet" tea made from a marsh plant whose leaves were green on one side and yellow on the other. There was "maiden hair" tea made from the fern. The inner bark of the maple brewed a sweet tea and one of the evergreens was used to make "wintergreen" tea.†

* Rev. William Bell's Journals, MS., Douglas Library, Queen's University.
† M'Donald, *Narrative*.

Andrew Bell, the Rev. William Bell's son, writing home to Scotland in 1819, describes their life in the new land and speaks of: "a kind of bush called *mouseweed*, the back of which makes as good cordage as hemp, . . . a kind of thing with roots like potatoes, but the size of a turkey bean". He mentions the method of clearing the land with oxen and the growth of crops of oats, wheat, potatoes, Indian corn, buckwheat, pumpkins, melons, cucumbers, and a great many kinds of French beans "besides all the kinds of things you grow at home". There was sugar from the maple tree, and the lakes abounded in fish. The Bells by then owned three cows. Bell had divided one of his town lots among four of his sons, and Andrew was then busy planting his quarter with potatoes and Indian corn.

Andrew speaks of the houses:

> The country houses are built of logs and covered with planks or bark of trees. The town houses are frames covered with planed boards, lapped over one another to send off the rain and covered with pieces of wood about the size of slats. These are called shingles. Some houses are painted white, some yellow, some red. Provisions are cheap and wages high. . . . Tell my grandmother that we were never in better health, nor happier than we are now.

The Bells, however, were privileged in owning considerable land. It was not the same story for settlers outside the village of Perth.

Mosquitoes ("They torment us both day and night continually", said John M'Donald) were a major annoyance for the first settlers. Mr. Bell frequently mentions them in his Journals—apparently they were his constant companions on missionary travels through the townships during the spring and summer months for as long as land remained uncleared.

Cranberry marshes were numerous but infested with snakes, and the settlers often hired Indians to gather cranberries for them since they knew how to deal with the serpents. Between Rideau Lake and Lake Ontario was an 18-mile long cranberry marsh which John Mactaggart, a Scottish engineer engaged in building the Rideau Canal in the 1820's, depicts vividly. This lake was covered with extensive flats of cranberry bushes, having foot long tangled roots so that the bushes floated on top of the water. "If a person jumps out of the canoe onto the cranberry flats, these sink slowly with him and he shortly discovers he has gone down to his middle."*

* John Mactaggart, *Three Years in Canada* (1829).

Mactaggart believed the fetid water of the lake harboured malaria and ague, as many of the labourers and mechanics working on the canal were laid up and some died after contact with the marsh. He mentions a hot bath the Indians used for combatting these diseases. They built a bath of rude stone and sand beside a lake or river and in it made a fire, keeping it burning until the stones and sand were very hot. They then carried the patient to the bath and poured water over the hot stones. The water flew hissing on to the body. Then they wrapped the patient in a buffalo skin and a deep sweat followed.

One of the greatest difficulties faced by the settlers was the lack of roads—trails being cut through the forest oftimes so rough as to be only suitable for travel on foot.

In 1818 another military depot was set up at Richmond and in due course a government road (if such it might be called) built through to link it with the Perth depot. But the first settlers into Beckwith had none of this luxury and blazed their own trail through the bush.

Archives of Ontario Thomas Burrowes

CRANBERRY LAKE AND ITS FLOATING BOGS

# CHAPTER IV

## THE BECKWITH SETTLEMENT

Following on the Perth settlement of 1816-17 came emigration into Beckwith Township, whose survey had been completed in 1816. Here Booth and Sherwood had surveyed the land in strips—one concession at a time. When they reached the end of the first concession they found they had 50 acres left over, so distances between concession lines are today scarcely ever equal.

As in other parts of eastern Upper Canada, fertile land lay side by side with swamps or rocky pasture land. Meandering through the township is the Jock River (called Jacques in the early days, probably by some itinerant Frenchman of an earlier period) which splits the area known as The Derry with impenetrable marshes. So today one finds in Beckwith concession lines that dwindle away into dead ends of marsh.

Along the banks of the Jock beaver hay and timber grew in abundance. A difficult section of land to drain down through the years, it nevertheless provided an economic alternative to farming in later periods, its timber being turned into fence logs, railway ties, telegraph and hop poles, shingle wood, cordwood, and fence posts. Limestone outcrops, gravel ridges, and rich fields of loam today lie side by side in Beckwith.

The township, named in honour of Sir Sidney Beckwith, Quartermaster General in Canada in 1812, had, despite much waste land and swamp, the distinction of being almostly completely settled within six years after the first influx of pioneers in 1816.

A few individual settlers from the 1816-17 sailing ventured from the Perth depot into Beckwith. Among these were several Irishmen—Arthur McAulay, Constantine O'Neill, and the McDonnell brothers. The remainder were Scots. Many of the pioneers were illiterate and did not know how their names were spelled, so that in Ships Lists,

Land Returns of the Superintendent, and the present Patents Office there is considerable discrepancy in the spelling of names. The most familiar spelling has been given here.

Locating near the Mississippi Lake and Drummond Township were: Alex. McDonald (Lot 4) on the 8th Concession; Donald McLellan and Archibald McDonnell (Lot 3), Duncan McNaughton, Sr. and Constantine O'Neill (Lot 4), John McDonnell, Jr. (Lot 6) all on the 7th Concession; and Alex. McKenzie (Lot 4) and Arthur McAulay (Lot 8) on the 6th Concession.

Other incomers at the same time were Stephen Redmond (Lot 10), Phineas Lowe (Lot 8), and James Whiting (Lot 2) on the 3rd Concession; Duncan McKercher (Lot 15), Austin Allen (Lot 9), George Perry (Lot 8) on the 2nd Concession; and Josiah Moss (Lot 13) on the 1st Concession.

Stephen Redmond and Josiah Moss were the first to whom town lots were granted when the village of Franktown was laid out in 1821. Both received their patents for 25 acres in the village in 1824. Phineas Lowe was a discharged private from the 6th Foot Regiment and 27 years of age when he settled in Beckwith. Born near the parish of Roxton, near Oldham, Lancashire, England, he had been a weaver by trade. He received the deed for his land in 1821. Thomas Wickham who located on Lot 9 of the 2nd Concession was also close to the later village of Franktown where he owned and operated one of the first inns.

In September 1816 Colonel Cockburn had written to Governor Sherbrooke advising him of Perth's dimensions and suggesting that a similar village be set up between Townships Three (Beckwith) and Four (Goulbourn—now in Carleton County) and a road cut through connecting with Perth.

By 1817, however, the cost of colonizing along the Rideau waterway had mounted rapidly and the British government was trying to curtail its expenses. No depot similar to the government storehouse of provisions and supplies at Perth had yet been set up by 1818 and settlers—soldiers or civilians—who wished to move into those townships had to struggle over forest trails 20 miles or more towards the Ottawa River, carrying their rations and implements from the storehouse at Perth. There was as yet no road inland from the Ottawa River, nor any organized method of transport along the Ottawa from Montreal.

By the summer of 1818 the 99th Foot Regiment was disbanded

and some 400 soldiers and officers were to receive lands in the new townships. Colonel Cockburn again wrote to Sir John Sherbrooke urging him to establish a new military depot, centrally located between Perth and the Ottawa River, for the use of these men and further settlers. At this time the Duke of Richmond was proceeding to Canada to take over his duties as Governor-General from Sir John Sherbrooke. A site for the new depot, indicated by Cockburn and situated on the River Jock, was chosen and named Richmond in honour of the new Governor-General.

While plans were going ahead for the new military depot, a party of 300 Scottish farmers under the direction of John Robertson of Breadalbane, Scotland, arrived from Perthshire desiring to settle in Beckwith. These independent immigrants had made their own arrangements for emigration with the Earl of Bathurst. They paid their own passage to Quebec and were conveyed to their land at the expense of the government.

They came from Montreal by way of the Ottawa River to Point Nepean where they pitched their tents. No road had yet been cut through the woods when they arrived late in June so they left their families camped on the banks of the Ottawa and set out to blaze a trail. Several disasters occurred for the families left at Point Nepean. Some lost their baggage through fire and several died of sickness and the intense heat. Eventually the trail was completed and the first families trudged through the woods carrying their belongings.

Most of these settlers came from Loch Earn and Loch Tay and other points in parishes such as Comrie, Dull, Balquhidder, Fortingall, Killen, and Kenmore. A few were from points as far south as Blair Drummond and Dunblane, and as far north as Blair Atholl. They sailed on three ships, the *Jane*, *Sophia*, and the brig *Curlew*, in early spring. The Andersons, Carmichaels, Clarks, Comries, Crams, Dewars, Drummonds, Fergusons, McArthurs, McCallums, McEwans, McDiarmids, McFarlanes, McGregors, McLarens were families well represented. There were also Robertsons, Scotts, Stewarts, Kings, and Kennedys.

The mid-eastern section of Beckwith known as The Derry ("place of oak"), so-called after a similar spot in Scotland, was largely settled by the 1818 immigrants. Others took up land in an area near the township of Montague, known as The Cuckoo's Nest. The Derry lies between the 5th and 6th Concessions of Beckwith. Originally the whole area was hardwood bush. On three sides it is surrounded by swamp or marsh, cutting it off from the surrounding settlement. To the south, and to a lesser degree on the north, it is open to the neighbouring community. Duncan McDiarmid, heading a small group, brought his party to a halt in a maple grove in this area. Here they camped until they could file their claims for nearby lots. Duncan McDiarmid and Robert Ferguson located on Lot 22, Robert Ferguson also took 100 acres on Lot 23, Duncan Ferguson taking the other 100 acres. James Ferguson located on the 6th Concession on Lot 24, and John Ferguson on the 4th Concession, Lot 23.

Another Derry settler was Colin McLaren who emigrated at the same time, and located first at Chatham, a small village west of Hull. Here he did business as a shoemaker until reports from old friends in Beckwith induced him to go homesteading there in 1820 on Lot 21 of the 5th Concession. Finlay McEwan, another 1818 emigrant, after viewing the wild animal infested forest at Nepean Point decided to leave his family at Hull. Here he built a small house for his wife and six children and set out for Beckwith with his son, John, then only 12 years old. After selecting his 100 acres on Lot 23 of the 7th Concession, McEwan set about building a house and moved his family from Hull the following spring. McEwan was noted in the community as an accomplished violinist. Five generations of McEwans were to continue on the old homestead. John selected adjoining land on the 8th Concession when he came of age.

Next to the McEwan farm on the same Lot 23 located Malcolm Dewar. Separated from them by the Clergy Reserve lot 24 were the adjacent farms of Archibald and Peter Dewar, and across the 8th Line road were the farms of Robert and John Kennedy. On the latter farm one of the early pioneer cemeteries still stands beside the town-line road. Here were buried Scotts, McLarens, McEwans, McDiarmids, Fergusons, and Stewarts. Across from it is the more recent Dewar cemetery where later generations of Derry people were laid to rest.

The Dewars came from the parish of Comrie and were hereditary guardians of the *Quigrich* or staff of St. Fillan, a monk of the 8th Century to whom various wells and churches are dedicated in Scotland, where the traditions of St. Fillan held an important place. St. Fillan traditionally left five relics, committing each to the care or custody of a separate clan. The *Quigrich* was entrusted to the Clan MacNab and to Malise Dewar of this clan in 1428. To Canada in 1818 came the head of the Saint's crozier with Archibald Dewar. Its

PIONEERS OF BECKWITH
Left to right: Duncan Cram and wife, Alex. Dewar and wife, Robert Kennedy and wife.

powers were legendary. Pioneers came long distances with vessels of water to have the staff immersed therein, believing that in this way miraculous powers of healing were imparted to the water. The head of the crozier was of silver plate with a smaller crozier head of bronze enclosed in it. Later the crozier was returned to the National Museum of Antiquaries in Scotland by Archibald Dewar's son. Of all of St. Fillan's relics, only the *Quigrich* and a bell remain today.

The story goes that another 7th Concession settler, James McArthur, parted from a friend of his, John Anderson, in Montreal. McArthur proceeded to Beckwith by way of the Ottawa River and Anderson went via Perth. Both arrived on the 7th Concession of Beckwith and lived there for two years without knowing that the other was anywhere near.

One of the incoming settlers, Duncan McNabb, was a weaver and an ardent Baptist. He preached as well as farmed, holding Baptist prayer meetings in his home. On a Saturday, he would leave his loom and walk barefoot through the swamps and bush trails preaching in settlements along the way, travelling as far as Bathurst Township on his missionary circuit. When the Rev. William Bell travelled through Beckwith he invariably stayed with McNabb and his family, and usually held a service of worship for the neighbours in the McNabb home. In 1833 Duncan McNabb moved to North Elmsley and organized a church there for Baptists.

It was customary in the 19th Century for large Scottish families to repeat Christian names within the same family and this led to much confusion. At one time there were nine Sandy Stewarts living in Beckwith, each with a different qualification. These were: The Widow's Sandy, Soldier Sandy, Big Sandy, Sandy's Sandy, Merchant Sandy (Alexander at Black's Corners), Shoemaker Sandy (at Franktown), Sandy F., Sandy-on-the-Hill (near Ashton), and Blacksmith Sandy. The Stewarts were the first of the families of this emigration to leave Beckwith. They moved west in 1887. Alexander Stewart from Blair Atholl was the last survivor of the Perthshire pioneers of 1818. He died in 1892 in his 100th year. Mr. Stewart lived at Black's Corners for 75 years as a farmer and merchant. He was noted for his proficiency in manufacturing shingles and could cut with his hand knife as many as 3000 a day. During the early years, like many settlers, he manufactured and sold potash. He was a Reformer and a Presbyterian and active in the building of the first church in Beckwith. He was buried in the old Kennedy cemetery.

While the Perthshire settlers had battled their way through the woods from the Ottawa River to the land of their choice, the discharged soldiers of the 99th Regiment were still waiting at Lachine for the opening up of a road and the establishment of a military depot at Richmond. The first of these arrived in August and by late November Colonel Cockburn could report to the Duke of Richmond that "a very good road" had been built from the bay below the Chaudière Falls at Ottawa and the village now known as Richmond. This road followed much the same route as the Richmond Road does today. By November 400 heads of families had already located in the vicinity of Richmond, "several houses are building in the village, and seven or eight half-pay officers have fixed upon it as their future place of residence".*

Cockburn had also linked the depots of Perth and Richmond with a bush road. Beginning at Richmond, this road followed the 4th Concession lines of Goulbourn and Beckwith as far west as the centre of Beckwith (now the highway linking Franktown and Richmond). From here it ran south to the third line, followed it for a time (the road to Gillies Corners) until it turned obliquely southwest to the second line of Drummond which it followed through to Perth. In reporting to the Duke about this road, Cockburn said:

It is on this road, and as nearly as circumstances will admit, in

* Public Archives of Canada, Q.152, p. 6.

Archives of Ontario Thomas Burrowes

RICHMOND ON THE RIVER JOCK IN 1830

> the centre of the township of Beckwith, that a provision store is to be built.
>
> The road will be sufficiently opened in the course of a month to admit of the sleighs passing over it during the winter, and I would earnestly recommend that an expenditure of 3 or 400 pounds, exclusive of two or three months' rations and rum, might be allowed for the payment and subsistence of about 80 men to be employed in making it passable for waggons during the summer.
>
> A reference to the accompanying plan will show that when this road is opened and a provision store built in Beckwith, each of the new townships will be equally eligible for a settlement, and thus a very large proportion of land will be anxiously sought after, which the settlers hitherto have been averse to being placed on.*

The provision store referred to here formed the foundation for the village of Franktown, which Colonel Cockburn possibly expected to grow into a large centre. It did in fact flourish as a trading centre during the 1850's, but deteriorated with the building of the railway which by-passed it, and thereafter diminished in size and prosperity. Franktown was called after Colonel Cockburn whose Christian name was Francis.

Following the Perthshire emigration, came a wave of settlers from

* Public Archives of Canada, Q.152, p. 6.

Ireland. Of these Patrick Madrigan on Lot 17 of the 5th Concession, was the only Roman Catholic to settle in The Derry. The farm next to a Clergy Reserve lot remained in the Madrigan family until the 1880's when they moved to Dakota.

Anglican Irishmen settling in The Derry were the Kidds, the Leeches, and the Garlands. Of these the Kidd name only is known to the present generation. Andrew Kidd came from Coon (Wexford, Ireland) with his wife and children. His eldest son John also emigrated and took up land on the 6th Concession, Lot 21, near the McDiarmid and Ferguson farms. John Kidd's wife had died at sea or upon landing in Canada, and he placed his baby son Andrew with a foster mother in Quebec City until he could claim him two years later. Andrew Kidd, Sr., moved to Montague township. In 1819 John Garland and family, neighbours of the Kidds in Ireland, settled on Lot 20, the next farm to John Kidd. A few years later John Kidd married Margaret Garland, the young couple walking to Perth for the ceremony.

Within three or four years every farm bordering on the 6th Concession line had been claimed by either settler or squatter. Some located permanently, but names such as Ward, Thomas and Edward Leech, James and John Lucas, Richard and Nancy Edwards, Nicholas and James Garland, Leslie, Holbrook, and Kennedy mean little to residents of Beckwith today. Yet all were resident of The Derry in the 1820's. At Franktown cemetery are buried the Irish settlers of the Derry, almost all of whom were Anglicans. The earliest inscribed tombstone there reads "John Upton, 1823".

William May who settled on Lot 7 of the 5th Concession came from Ottawa with his wife and four children on foot in 1819. He carried his bed on his back and on top of this the youngest child. Only the "blaze" and some "string pieces" in wet places guided them along the bush trail. Around them in the woods lurked wolf, lynx, and bear. On his homestead in Beckwith stood an oak which was a sapling when Mr. May carved "1819" upon it.*

The Kerfoots emigrated from Coolcullen, County Kilkenny, Ireland. George Kerfoot, an aged widower, came with his children, grandchildren, and two great grandchildren in 1819, landing at Nepean's Point—a family party of eleven. While camped there, the great-grandfather died. His son William, a stonemason, proceeded with his three sons George, Thomas, and Samuel to Beckwith township. William Sr.

* John May, "Bush Life in the Ottawa Valley Eighty Years Ago", Ontario Historical Society *Papers and Records*, Vol. 12.

located on the 4th Concession on Lot 25 which he shared with his son Samuel, near the present village of Prospect. In 1824 he donated a corner of his farm and helped to build thereon the Prospect Methodist Church, a small log building, across the road from the present stone United Church. In this Methodist cemetery are buried many Irish pioneers who settled on the third and fourth concessions of Beckwith and Goulbourn. The earliest inscribed date is "Hugh Conn, January 1830, age 39," who had settled on Lot 24 of the 4th Concession and received his patent in 1828.

William Kerfoot died in 1862 and was buried in the same cemetery on his own property, where his wife, Elizabeth, who lived to be 93, was also buried. William's son George settled with his wife and two small children on Lot 15 of the 2nd Concession in The Cuckoo's Nest. Thomas Kerfoot located on Lot 15 on the 1st Concession.

William Kerfoot, endeavouring to seek wives for all his sons, made preparations and invited to Canada a very stylish lady from the old land, Eliza Phillips. He informed his son Thomas that this lady would be his wife. Thomas, however, had other intentions, and before his prospective wife arrived in Canada he married Ann Tomlinson, the daughter of another pioneer, William Tomlinson. When Eliza Phillips arrived William commanded son Samuel to step into the gap. And he did!* Samuel's wife was henceforth known by all the Kerfoots as "The Lady". They lived in the house built by William on the old homestead, a large frame building with a two-tier veranda running the full length of the house and decorated with "gingerbread".

A sister of William, Ann Kerfoot, emigrated with her husband, Jacob Smith, and son Joseph, locating across the road from the George Kerfoot homestead on Lot 15 of the 3rd Concession.

The village of Franktown was laid out on Lots 11, 12 and 13 of the 3rd Concession and a number of Irish settlers located there, occupying 25-acre lots and engaging in business or trades. Patrick Nowlan and Thomas Wickham built inns about the same time. Nowlan's was the favourite stopping-place for all visiting dignitaries. Charles McCarthy, Owen McCarthy, Andrew Houghton, John Conboy, George Nesbitt, and John Nesbitt were among the first to whom patents were granted at Franktown. Both Nowlan and Wickham are listed among Licensed Innkeepers for the years 1820-21.†

Archibald Gillies on the 1st Concession also built a hotel on his

* J. M. Morris, *A Kerfoot History*.

† *Upper Canada Assembly Journals 1818-21*, edited by Alexander Fraser.

property in 1820 and ran it as a licensed inn until the 1850's. Its location on the government road to Perth was known as Gillies Corners.

Edmond Morphy, after whom Morphy's Falls was called, emigrated with his sons, William, John, and James from Tipperary County, Ireland, locating on Lots 14 and 15 of the 12th Concession along the Mississippi River. Here they built a house on the south bank of the river. Near them located another Irish family—the Willises. Henry Willis sailed on the ship *Eolus* in 1819 with Thomas Pearce, James Wall, and William Jones who also located in Beckwith. James McNeely, from Antrim, Ireland, also settled near Morphy's Falls with his family of two sons and four daughters. David and Alexander Snedden came to Beckwith from Scotland about the same time, locating on Lot 26 of the 11th Concession, and later moving to Ramsay Township.

In 1820 the three sons of Edmond Morphy built houses on the Morphy property. The same year one Coleman purchased waterpower along one-half of the Morphy farm, intending to build a mill thereon. The agreement was that Coleman should grind a bushel of wheat in the mill within 6 months. Unable to fulfill his obligations Coleman sold his interest to Hugh Bolton who established the first grist mill between Perth and the Ottawa River. The same year George Bailey, Sr., settled on the outskirts of Morphy's Falls on Lot 15, Concession 12, not far from the Bolton mill. Here he established a saw mill. This site was called Bailey's Mills, and eventually Arklan, and included a large island in the Mississippi River.

Other 1820 settlers were Donald McDonald, Robert Hampton, David Moffatt, John Griffith, and Sam Jones. Many settled close to Morphy's Falls which was to become the only town in the township. The same year William Cooper opened a blacksmith shop and Robert Barnet a cooperage and by 1821 Alexander Morris had started a tannery, potash factory, store, and "groggery", more respectably known as a "hotel". It was in Morris' "groggery" that the famous Ballygibblin riot took place in 1824 involving the Scots and Irish from both Ramsay and Beckwith townships. Captain Thomas Glendinning, who occupied all of Glen Isle at this time, was one of the king-pins in this riot.

Though the Irish immigrants might get along without religious guidance, the Scots were not inclined to be satisfied without their own ordained leader. In March 1819 a group of the Perthshire immigrants walked to Perth to consult the Rev. William Bell as to how they should go about obtaining a minister, and in April Bell made his first visit to the new settlement leaving his horse at Franktown and walking to a Mrs. Ferguson's "shantie" five miles into the interior where he preached and baptised two children. It was three years, however, before a minister was obtained for Beckwith.

The subsequent pastor secured for the Beckwith settlement was the Rev. George Buchanan. One of his daughters in later years described their life in Beckwith in a biography entitled *The Pioneer Pastor*. The hardships endured were common to most of the pioneers of Lanark County:

> Cutting grain with the old-fashioned sickle and scythe on ground [with] stumps dotted thickly, was slow laborious work. A cumbrous plough, hard to pull and harder to guide, a V-shaped harrow, alike heavy and unwieldy, a clumsy sled, in keeping with the plough and harrow, home-made rakes weighty as iron and sure to blister the hands of the users, forked-stick pitch fork, first cousins of the awkward rakes, and gnarled flails certain to raise lumps on the heads of unskilled threshers, with two or three scythes and sickles represented the average agricultural equipment. . . . Not a horse, chimney, stove or even a chair could be found in Beckwith. Two arm chairs constructed for father and mother by Donald Kennedy, a wood-worker, were the first in the township.
>
> Women bore their full share of the burden. . . . All spring and summer they worked in the fields early and late, burning brush, logging, planting, and reaping. Much of the cooking, washing, and mending was done before dawn or after dark, while the men slept peacefully. At noon they prepared dinner, ate a bite hastily and hurried back to drudge until the sun went down. They then got supper, put the youngsters to bed, patched, darned, and did a multitude of chores. . . . Sabbath was the one oasis in the desert, the one breathing spell in the week. . . . When obliged to help outdoors, young mothers took their babies with them . . . to the field and laid them in sap troughs while they worked nearby. . . .
>
> Autumn brought little relief except to vary the style of work. The women carded wool with hand-cards and spun it on small wheels for stocking yarn and weaver's loom. Knitting was an endless task by the light of the hearth fire or the feeble flicker of a tallow-dip, and everybody wore homespun.*

* Campbell, *The Pioneer Pastor* (1900).

# CHAPTER V

## THE MILITARY DEPOT AT PERTH

The Perth settlement had two classes of citizens—the Scottish civilians who, whatever their background, were committed to settling on the land and farming; and the discharged soldiers of whom the commissioned and non-commissioned officers were on half-pay. These latter received their monthly stipend from the Imperial government and were the only persons with cash in the early community. These formed the élite of the settlement during the early years and long after military rule had ceased.

Some of these we have already mentioned. Others include: Colonel Josiah Taylor who occupied part of Cockburn Island and also Lot 1 on the north side of Craig Street. Here, near the corner of Wilson Street, he built a residence in 1817. Colonel Taylor was the first Postmaster. Mail was carried from Brockville first on foot, later by horseback, and eventually by stage-coach. Colonel Taylor later added a store to his enterprises.

Along with the general stores of William Morris and Benjamin Delisle, there was Captain John Watson's built on his land (Lot 5) on the south side of Craig Street. He was a first Justice of the Peace and also the first Treasurer of Bathurst when it was established in 1823 as a separate District. These general stores stocked all sorts of merchandise—food, clothing, medicine, tools, and liquors shared the shelves.

Upon the scene in 1817 arrived one of the most colourful figures of pioneer days in Lanark County. This was the Rev. William Bell, first resident minister for the Rideau settlement, who crossed the Atlantic with his wife and family in the spring of 1817 and whose experiences we have already mentioned. Mr. Bell was a man of strong character and fixed opinion—a dour Scot with a wry sense of humour, a rigid Presbyterian of the old school. He soon aired his views on the new settlement which he found full of evils—moral, social, and physical. As a missionary he had a busy life from the time of his arrival, for the military men who had spent much of their lives in the army were indisposed to moral disciplines.

Mr. Bell arrived in June, travelling from Mrs. Talman's Inn near Brockville through "a narrow avenue cut in the forest" encountering snakes and mosquitoes in profusion. He recorded: "My cranium was so covered with bumps, a phrenologist would have been at no loss to discover the bump of anything he pleased.*

At Perth, Bell found two large buildings—one the Storehouse (60 x 20 feet), holding all government supplies for the settlers, the other a large house, diagonally opposite, belonging to Captain Fowler. This was the intersection of the future Harvey and Gore streets. There were some thirty other buildings, with tents and huts surrounding them. Dr. Thom's new saw mill was nearing completion.

Mr. Bell presented his papers to Captain Fowler and was granted an acre building lot in the village and 25 acres just outside. In addition, the British government was to pay him £100 a year as resident clergyman.

He dined with Captain Fowler and temporarily took up residence in the Adamson Inn on Craig Street. His first duty was to visit the settlers along the Scotch Line, and that accomplished he set about to find a house which he might rent for his family, who had not yet arrived from Brockville.

He held his first Sabbath worship on June 29, 1817, in a large upper room of Adamson's Inn—a room unfurnished and unfinished and reached by a ladder. About thirty people including government agents, magistrates, and half-pay officers were present. Mr. Bell preached to them at 11 a.m. and again at 2:00 p.m. It was a test of endurance for his polite congregation since there were no benches and they had to stand throughout. Regardless of the inconveniences, news of the church service brought an even larger attendance the next Sunday and Bell took advantage of this opportunity to organize a church meeting for the following Wednesday when trustees might be selected to arrange to have a church built; he also opened the first Sunday School with five children present.

The village needed a school. Things were not going well between

* Quotations from Mr. Bell throughout this chapter are taken from his MS. Journals.

John Holliday, the schoolmaster on the Scotch Line, and the authorities in Perth. When Mr. Bell arrived the officials were withholding Holliday's pay for "insubordination". Also his school was actually too far from Perth for the smaller children to walk the distance twice a day. The village officials welcomed Bell's proposal to open a school within the village and promised to pay him the annual salary of £50. John Adamson had a small log house which he offered to rent as a temporary schoolhouse, and while Sam Purdy and Captain Hunter were making the necessary repairs to it, Bell opened school in his newly rented home. He had 18 pupils including his own children.

Church services were to continue at the Adamson Inn until a proper church could be built. The schoolhouse was to be used for church meetings. At the second church meeting Bell observed with regret that some came barefooted and very poorly clad. "The pov-

Sketch by the author

HOME OF FIRST SCHOOL TEACHER, JOHN HOLLIDAY
On the Scotch Line, near Perth, it was built in 1826 and is still standing.

erty of the people [he noted] prevented anything being done at this meeting beyond appointing a committee to manage the affairs of the congregation." At this time "the rations of the settlers from the government store being stopped, and many of them not having yet raised enough from their own land to support them, they were all in a state of commotion, and many of them left the settlement". Potato seed and the three bushels of Fall wheat provided each settler by the government had been planted the previous year, but the potato crop had been destroyed by frost and rust had damaged the wheat. The year 1817 was a year of privation and hardship. Some families lived for weeks on wild leeks from the woods. Eventually an application was made to the government for an additional half-ration per head from the government storehouse and the famine was averted. Thereafter the crops improved year by year.

In August, Bell wrote to Captain Noah Freer who had gone to Montreal to be Assistant Military Secretary at Quebec, asking for money to build a schoolhouse. Freer was still interested in the military settlement and collected money by subscription from his friends but not enough to build in 1817, and he suggested in a letter to Bell that construction plans be put off until the following year.

The first township meeting was held in 1817 and Sam Purdy and John Ferguson selected to conduct an assessment, the first in the new settlement. The assessment showed among other things only one cow in the entire district, probably belonging to Mr. Bell who noted in his 1817 Journals that "Mr Purdy having gone to the Rideau settlement to purchase a cow for us returned with a cow and calf but there was no pasture for the poor beast and we found it difficult to keep her in milk". Bell's 25-acre park lot was on the outskirts of Perth and every morning he and his eldest sons, William, John, and Robert, rose at 4 a.m. and worked there until breakfast. In this way they managed to grow their own food and the rest of Bell's day was free for his missionary duties.

In June 1817 Robert Gourlay, pioneer journalist and investigator, had arrived at Perth on a survey he was then making of Upper Canada. He later sent a report on the Perth settlement to a number of newspapers, as well as to Lord Bathurst in England. In 1822 he had these and further findings on Upper Canada published in London. Gourlay tabled statistics concerning a number of the Scotch Line settlers, his report revealing the size of dwelling erected, acreage cleared, crops grown, and number of animals owned by 1818.* His report indicated that there were 44 cows and 22 oxen among this small group of settlers alone. The mystery of the "one cow" discovered by the assessors of 1817 is further confounded by a letter from Colonel Myers to Sir John Sherbrooke, dated October 1816, in which he reports: "Amongst the settlers there are about 80 head of cattle and there are 800 bushels of Fall wheat now in the ground".† It is possible that many cattle were lost during the winter. Bell commented that the settlers from Scotland,

* See Appendix, page 230.

† Public Archives of Canada, Q.137.

being unaccustomed to looking after animals, did not make necessary preparations for winter by laying in a supply of fodder and grain, with the result that many animals died of starvation.

By the Fall of 1817 Bell had already set out on a missionary circuit he was to continue almost until his death in the 1850s, travelling through the townships conducting services in homes wherever a few families could be gathered together. At the same time many social problems in the new settlement were demanding his attention. Shortly after his arrival at Perth, couples came to him wishing to be married.

In Upper Canada at this time the Church of England was the only Protestant church officially recognized. The Marriage Act permitted a Presbyterian or Baptist marriage ceremony only if one of the parties had been a member of the minister's congregation for at least six months, and if the clergyman had acquired a special license. Other denominations, such as the Methodists, could not sanction marriage at all. As there was no Anglican clergyman in the new settlement at Perth an official marriage was almost impossible to obtain, and it is natural to suppose that many unions were formed that had no validity.

John Mactaggart, a civil engineer working with Colonel By on the Rideau Canal in 1826, recalls in his *Three Years in Canada* coming across one of these unions. He and his engineers were wandering through the woods in winter and discovered a snug cabin where lived a man, his spouse, three children, some handsome grey cats, and "a very respectable looking dog". Mactaggart enjoyed the hospitality of the squatter and his family and "over a glass and a pipe" learned his story. His name was Peter Armstrong and he had paid his passage to Canada in 1812 or 1813. He had gone into the bush and whittled himself a hut (which his pet deer was now living in). He worked at clearing his land, in later years making a journey to Perth twice a year to buy his "wee needfuls" and had finally acquired a horse and sleigh. By the end of five years he had cleared 400 acres of land. On one of his visits to Perth in 1818 he met a Scotch lass who had been a byre-woman on the same Laird's estate in Scotland where he had been a herd-lad. In his own words, "she came awa'" with him to the woods and there they lived as man and wife and brought up their children. They were both Christians, of a very high character, said Mactaggart, and read their Bible on Sunday and lived a simple, happy, honest life. The author remarked he had met many others in like situation but most were "Yankees" and "they did not read any Bibles nor sing hamely sangs like Armstrong and his Tibby".

This kind of situation was one of the earliest to arouse Bell's ire against the Anglicans and set him on a course to extend the rights of the Presbyterians. In this he had a strong and influential supporter, the merchant William Morris who was later to head the Presbyterian cause in Upper Canada. A Roman Catholic ex-army chaplain, Rev. Abbé Peter la Motte who had been with the de Wattevilles, was granted land around Adam's Lake in 1817, but instead of staying with the French-speaking discharged soldiers he moved into Perth and set up a small Catholic school. There were few Roman Catholics in Perth at this time, however, so that although he had authority to perform a marriage service, few couples desired to embrace the Roman Catholic faith on the sole grounds of a legal marriage.

Mr. Bell took action in October to secure the necessary license. He went to Brockville to appear at the Court of Quarter Sessions but upon arrival was told he had not given the Clerk sufficient notice and would have to renew his application and wait another three months before his license could be registered. Back he went to Perth, on horseback part of the way, and the remaining miles on foot through the forest—a tedious two-day journey. In January 1818 he again went to Brockville accompanied by seven of his congregation and Mr. Smart of the capital. The certificate cost him $2.00.

In December 1817 a Methodist minister from the Rideau circuit, one Brown, arrived to look the military settlement over. He held his services in Joshua Adam's house. Mr. Bell wryly commented in his Journals that he was told by one present that "in his prayer, he [Brown] fervently gave God thanks that through his agency the gospel had at length had been brought to the settlement".

The fervour of the Methodists evidently found a responsive note in Joshua Adams who supported them faithfully after this initial visit; his son Ava later became a Methodist preacher, and his eldest daughter Beulah married the Methodist circuit-rider John Carroll. Alex Richey, writing to the Perth *Courier* in 1911, recalled the Adams family with affection:

> The first time I remember the Adams was when I went to school in 1833. . . . They were all very kind to me, just a new boy from Lanark Village. The Captain boarded most of his men, and he had a number of them too, in the sawmill, flour mill, oat mill, carding and fulling mill; men working on the farm and teamsters hauling lumber to town. The oldest son was a Methodist minister, Rev. Ava Adams, who afterwards had mills in the Fall River. Asa and Bernard the

> next two oldest sons, went in in 1844. The oldest daughter, Beulah, married Rev. John Carroll. Elizabeth married Henry Moorehouse, a useful citizen of your good town for many years, Lucinda married a son of Barbara Heck. The youngest daughter married Rev. Armstrong. Daniel and Franklyn worked in one of the mills and Joshua became a lawyer in Perth.
>
> The Captain and his wife were the living embodiment of charity and goodwill. There were a number of Indians about the headwaters of the Tay River at that time. They went down to the Lake of Two Mountains every spring to sell their furs. In the fall they returned to their various hunting grounds. They passed our place with seven or eight canoes one fall, loaded with their families and goods, a Union Jack at the bow and stern of each canoe. . . . When the Indians got as far as the Captain's he was on the watch for them for they most always had a white child picked up in some way or given to them by some unfortunate mother. The Captain saved several and brought them up to be cared for as one of the family. The Captain, I believe, was of the same family that gave two presidents to the United States, John Adams, second president, and John Quincy Adams, his son, sixth president. The Captain died about 1856 or 1857. He was one of nature's noble men.

Mr. Bell drew criticism from some quarters for his rigid principles concerning baptism. When requested to baptise a child, he first "examined" the parents and if they did not conduct home worship daily, nor attend church, he refused baptism; and there were other conditions to which parents must conform. In a frontier society this was a rather drastic stand to take, especially when Jesus had said "Suffer little children . . . to come unto me." Since Bell was the only Protestant minister resident, the settlers either had to conform to his requirements or else have their children baptised Roman Catholic by the Rev. Abbé la Motte.

An early incident points up Bell's attitude. In December 1817, on a Sunday afternoon, he had a visit from a man and woman with a sick child they wished baptised. It was such a cold day that he had preached to his congregation in the Adamson kitchen rather than in the "loft". In the afternoon a couple appeared at his door saying they were the god-parents of the child they brought with them, the parents being ill at the home. They had been afraid the child would die without baptism and so had risked the extreme cold. Bell explained the "nature of baptism" to them and refused to baptise the child without the parents' presence. The man became very angry and declared that the Roman

Catholic priest would baptise the child. Off they went returning later to inform Bell that Abbé la Motte had baptised the baby for 50¢ and no questions asked. "The whole service had been conducted in the French language", Bell recorded in his Journal, "and they understood not a word of it".

In a February notation the same winter he says: "Dr. Thom made a furious attack upon me for not baptizing the children of all as they come to hand—good, bad, and indifferent, when I explained the mistake under which he seemed to labour".

Mr. Bell and Dr. Thom seem to have been natural enemies. With his saw mill and grist mill enterprises, Dr. Thom had little time left for serving the community as a physician. Bell complained that "Dr. Thom received a salary from the government for attending the sick yet he often treated them with the greatest brutality". Bell also learned from his friend, Archibald Morrison of Elmsley Township, that Dr. Thom and Daverne, the Clerk of the storehouse, were regarded as the "tyrants" of the settlement.

Daverne was also working against Mr. Bell. In March 1818 a Roman Catholic teacher, one Murdock, arrived in Perth and opened a school, but Bell lost only one pupil to him. Like padré La Motte, the authorities had intended that Murdock serve the Roman Catholic interests in Burgess Township. Instead, with the assistance of Daverne and Dr. Thom, he established himself in Perth. Meanwhile at Montreal, Captain Freer had collected sufficient funds for building Bell's schoolhouse and sent the money to Daverne. Daverne had the building erected but then put Murdock in charge. Mr. Bell complained to Colonel Cockburn and Daverne was compelled to hand the key over to the pastor.

Daverne hatched another plot. He drew up a petition requesting an Episcopalian minister for Perth and circulated it in the village and neighbourhood, impudently asking Mr. Bell to add his signature to the others. Bell relates: "I declined on the ground that it contained a gross falsehood, namely that the settlers were destitute of religious instruction and baptism of their children. On the subject I wrote a letter to the Duke of Richmond."

Reports were also reaching the Duke of Richmond, the new Governor-General, from other sources, full of complaints about Superintendent Daverne. The upshot of this was the Duke's fateful visit in June 1819, when he died from the bite of a rabid fox.

Early in 1818 the Presbyterians were busy building a church. By this time Mr. Bell had acquired for £30 a house built by George Graham and William Stacey. Another social problem was then engaging his attention—"profanation of the Sabbath".

As merchants of the village acquired horses, carriages, and sleighs, it became the pleasure of the élite to drive about the village on Sunday afternoons. It was a remarkably tame and peaceful kind of recreation, but to the Scots Presbyterian of those days any activity on Sunday was sinful.

In January 1818 Bell collected some of his elders and went on a house-to-house campaign to try to arouse more respect for the Sabbath. All those interviewed agreed to coöperate except Captain Francis LeLievre who said he liked to have a little amusement on Sunday.

About this time Bell wrote to Archdeacon Strachan at York (now Toronto) airing his grievances. Strachan's reply seems mild and tolerant in contrast to Bell's parochial views. He indicated he had tried to get a bill passed in the Upper Canada legislature covering the Lord's Day but there had been objections because the laws could not be applied in the same way in Canada as in England where the Poor Law administered funds collected from fines for breaking the Sabbath. Strachan rather rebuked Bell not to be so severe with "sinners", advising:

> Our population must be won over rather by mild persuasion than severity. Our object is reformation, and punishments tend, in general, rather to harden than reform.
>
> In all matters of indifference, we must be yielding and condescending and reserve our firmness and resolution when principles are attached. In this way your success will be much greater than by assuming severe, stiff, formal carriage. Even in your address from the pulpit, affectionate invitations and encouragement should predominate because your audience are not so deficient in understanding as in practice.*

Strachan cited his own experience of twenty years in Canada including the time he served as Army chaplain during the war. Of the Methodists, he considered they did more good than harm as they kept people aware of religion and challenged the Presbyterians and Anglicans to equal them. He ended on a friendly note:

* Wm. Bell's MS. Book of Letters, Douglas Library, Kingston.

> I shall be happy at all times in giving you any information and assistance in your labours for though differing a little in form and manner, I trust we are both Christians and running the race of immortality.

On the 21st of June 1819 the Duke of Richmond, accompanied by his two sons, three daughters, and attendants, set out from Quebec City aboard a steamer to visit the new military settlements at Richmond and Perth. Colonel Cockburn, one of the party, hurried on ahead from Sorel where the Duke's party remained for some days. It was his intention to investigate the activities of Daverne at Perth before the Duke arrived. When he reached Perth he appointed Joshua Adams, Dr. Thom, Captains McMillan and Taylor, and Mr. Bell to form a Court of Inquiry.

It was soon discovered that Daverne had embezzled the government stores to a large amount. He had also sworn the correctness of his returns but apparently the large book in his office used for taking an oath had been a French Dictionary—not a Bible! The Court was held on a Saturday night and adjourned until Monday morning when Bell recorded "crowds of settlers came from the country to complain of Mr. Daverne's conduct to them". Daverne, however, had made his escape over the weekend, taking with him all the money he could lay his hands on. Major James H. Powell was appointed Secretary and Superintendent in his place, and the incident was apparently forgotten by the government. Powell, an Irishman who had served with the 103rd Regiment in the campaign of 1813, was one of the disbanded military men who had settled in Perth.

Colonel Cockburn hurried on to Prescott to meet the Vice-Regal party. One of the Duke's servants had purchased a pet fox in whom the Duke had shown an interest. The fox was tied to a tent by the servant and left in the scorching sun which probably irritated it so that when the Duke approached to pet the animal, it bit him severely through the thumb. Next morning the Duke felt an uneasy sensation in his shoulder but it was forgotten in a flurry of duties and social events. The party continued southwestward and the Duke visited York and the Niagara settlements. On the return journey in August 1819 he arrived at Kingston and proceeded to Perth—a tiresome journey, partly on foot, partly by boat, and partly on horseback.

Elaborate preparations were in full swing at Perth for the honour conferred on the settlement. Mr. Bell had been asked to prepare an address to Sir Peregrine Maitland, the Duke's son-in-law, the Lieutenant-Governor of Upper Canada. The Duke arrived on the 21st of August and stayed at the Adamson Inn.*

The following day the Duke walked for several miles along the Scotch Line between Elmsley and Bathurst to note improvements. On his return to the village he was greeted by the inhabitants *in toto* and the Rev. William Bell presented his address, expressing gratitude to the Imperial government for its attention to the needs of the Perth Military Settlement and wishing health and safety to the Duke and his party. A gala dinner was held afterwards at which 30 to 40 gentlemen were present.

With the exception of Lord Dalhousie's visit the following year, Perth was rarely to entertain so distinguished a visitor. Colonel Powell, Captain Thomas Consitt of the Navy, and Captain Alston were among those who entertained the Duke's party lavishly, and wine flowed freely.

During his visit His Grace complained of feeling unwell but set out on the 24th of August for Richmond, having to travel on foot a rough bush trail because of the swamps and rivers in the way. The weather was hot and droves of mosquitoes harassed the travellers as they proceeded. Eventually they reached Richmond and lodged in the Masonic Arms Inn where the Duke gave a dinner to the chief men of the new settlement. At the dinner the Duke appeared restless. Later Dr. Collis, a half-pay army doctor of the village, tried bleeding and throat gargle.

Next morning they set out for Bytown (now Ottawa) but they had gone but a short distance by canoe when the Duke begged to be put ashore and rushed headlong into the woods and was found prostrate in some hay in a little barn. They carried him to a shanty and sent for Dr. Collis to come from Richmond and Dr. Reade from Perth, but the Duke was dead long before their arrival. It was a tragic ending to the Duke of Richmond's short reign as Governor-General of Upper and Lower Canada.

The year 1819 ended with the arrival of an Anglican clergyman upon the scene at Perth. In October 1819 the Rev. Michael Harris, an M.A. of Trinity College, Dublin, reached Perth and for the next thirty-seven years worked side by side with Mr. Bell, ministering to

* It was apparently on this occasion that he said to Mrs. Adamson: "Paint your house red, Mrs. Adamson, and you will never have to paint it again." They did paint it red and called it "The Red House". The paint withstood the weather for forty years.

the spiritual needs of the community. Both clergymen, though others came and went, carried on in their respective fields at Perth as long as health permitted.

Unfortunately the two religious men got off to a bad start. In 1818 Mr. Bell had run into trouble with the Scotch Line people over his right to maintain a school in Perth only four or five miles distant from that of John Holliday. Now, however, when Mr. Harris arrived, with the government's sanction, the Episcopalian indicated his intention to take over Bell's schoolhouse and schoolteaching in Perth. Again Mr. Bell appealed to Colonel Cockburn. Cockburn consulted Captain Freer but he denied having anything to do with the original construction of the schoolhouse, not wishing to jeopardize his position with government authorities. A letter from Cockburn settled the dispute and placed the schoolhouse in Mr. Harris' hands.

Another wave of immigration in 1820 brought the Lanark Society settlers. Colonel Marshall, until then resident in Perth (Lot 1, south side of Brock Street), moved to the newly-surveyed location of a government storehouse in the wilds north of Perth and undertook to superintend the Lanark settlement. With him went Captain Alex. Ferguson to build a grist mill on the Clyde for the use of the immigrants.

When the first election took place in May 1820, Marshall, although

Douglas Library, Kingston

HON. WILLIAM MORRIS
First Member of Parliament, 1820

nominated as a candidate, was much too busy to involve himself in politics and declined to stand. William Morris already well established as a Perth merchant, with affluent and influential brothers—storekeepers at Brockville—was the most likely candidate to achieve attention in the legislature. Benjamin DeLisle was his opponent but was no match for Morris and soon conceded the election.

At this time the Lanark Society settlers were passing through Perth in large numbers on their way to the new townships. In August 1820 Mr. Bell recorded that "the stables and barns are full of them".

About this time John Adamson of the Red House lost his wife to a man named Forrest. This unhappy innkeeper had many domestic troubles to judge from the notations which Mr. Bell made from time to time in his Journals. The Adamson Inn was the main stopping-place in Perth. The upstairs was interesting. When a ballroom was required for some function, one of the partitions which was hinged to the ceiling could be lifted and fastened to the ceiling by an iron hook, making one room of the upper floor. The red paint applied after the Duke of Richmond's visit was damaged by fire in the 1860s. Donald Fraser, a grandson of Adamson, remarked of the fire that one of the "ludicrous scenes was R. T. Livingstone and Sam Revans struggling with a barrel of flour on the stairs; they were met by a full head of water from the branch pipe at close range. . . . They were rescued, the flour was not, but they could never wear their suits after."* At that time the inn belonged to Donald Fraser's father, William, who had married Adamson's daughter. The Red House was used for public gatherings, Masonic meetings, political rallies. It was customary on election day for the successful candidate and his party to adjourn to the Red House to celebrate victory. In addition to running the inn, Adamson performed other duties in the settlement. One of his road-building contracts was a particularly difficult mile of the Long Swamp on the Kingston road to Ottawa. William Fraser married Catherine Adamson in 1835 and took over the inn in 1841. According to Mr. Bell, the unhappy Adamson died of the favourite beverage of the settlement, a fate that seems to have overtaken many of the former military officers who formed the first settlement.

A Registry Office was opened for Lanark and Renfrew counties in 1820 and Colonel Alex McMillan was appointed first Registrar. On the urging of Mr. Morris, Colonel McMillan stood for office in several elections but was unsuccessful. In 1841 he was appointed the

* *Perth Courier*, June 30. 1905.

first Warden of Bathurst District and in 1842 became Registrar of Carleton County whose capital seat was then Bytown.

Alcohol, taverns, distilleries, and drunkenness provided another area of pioneer life which engaged Mr. Bell's attention. The early settlement had almost as many taverns as houses. Captain Henry Graham, an Irishman who had fought in the Peninsula War with Wellington, drew 600 acres of land and opened a distillery on Gore Street in 1818. Later he sold out to J. A. McLaren who by 1877 was manufacturing Scotch whiskey said to be "one of the most perfect in the Dominion". Captain Graham owned all of Lot 2 on Herriott Street and later built the Graham Block in 1830. This was replaced by the Code Block in later years.

In the *Upper Canada Assembly Journals* for 1820-21, Graham's distillery was the only one listed for the Perth settlement, and that year he paid taxes on fifty-four gallons of whiskey. Graham was one of the prominent local citizens appointed to the Senate at the time of Confederation.

In 1820-21 the only licensed innkeepers from the Perth Military settlement were: Joshua Adams, Angus Cameron, Wellesley Ritchie, John Adamson, John Balderson, Joseph Legary, and William Blair. Balderson and Legary had inns north of Perth on the way to Lanark. William Blair settled on Lot 23 of the 3rd Concession of Bathurst at the north end of the village. Here he kept his inn. It is said that the first brick made in Perth was fabricated by Blair who had learned the art in Scotland. It was triangular in shape and a sample now resides in the Perth Museum. Blair died in 1821.

Liquor licenses were also issued in 1820-21 to Ezekial Rose in Montague Township; Patrick Nowlan and Thomas Wickham at Franktown; Daniel Shipman of Shipman's Mills; John Oliver of Oliver's Ferry; James Hall at Lanark Village; and Ebenezer Wilson in North Sherbrooke. Shopkeepers also sold liquor at this time, and those licensed in the 1821 records included William Morris & Company, Benjamin DeLisle, John Watson, Roderick Matheson, and Patrick Nowlan.

The Rev. William Bell refused to baptise the children of "drunkards, Sabbath breakers, and neglectors of religious duties". When recording proceedings of the Courts of Quarter Session he invariably mentioned that one or other of the magistrates was "drunk". Whether this meant the man was incoherent or merely that he had been drinking is not always clear. In any case the effects of the early products of

Upper Canadian distilleries were much more potent than the whiskey of today.

When John Mactaggart visited Perth in the late 1820's he sampled "a whiskey made after the Glenlivet mode by Mr. Ferguson [John Ferguson] of Foster Street called *Craigdarroch of Perth.* The flavour is very good: it is by far the most excellent spirit distilled in this country. . . . A distillery is a thing quite indispensable so that *raw grain* whiskey may be produced at a couple of shillings per gallon, the flavour of which is qualified by frosty potatoes and yellow pumpkins. Such *aqua* is extremely delicious, and those who know what *Glenlivet* is may, perhaps, touch it with a long stick confining their nostrils at the same time. . . . I am happy to find by a late Act, passed by the Provincial government of Upper Canada that potato whiskey will be almost put an end to, for this is the absolute poison of Upper Canada—the laudanum that sends thousands of settlers to their eternal rest every season . . . a distillation made of frosty potatoes, hemlock, pumpkins, and black mouldy rye".*

It is supposed that some of the Rev. William Bell's early "enemies" who died from drink were victims of this potato whiskey. Whatever they drank it was cheap and plentiful. Bell relates in his Journal that a neighbour of his used to send his child to a grocery store before breakfast with a tea kettle to collect a quart of whiskey to last the day! He also had a neighbour, an Irish bootmaker, who drank heavily. On some of his drunken bouts he would do strange things. Once Mr. Bell saw him standing on his doorstep with a Bible in hand preaching "with a degree of animation and eloquence I never could equal".

One of the early brewers was William Lock who formed a partnership with William Wordie. Later they sold their establishment to Spalding & Stewart in 1841. Their "Mountain Dew" was another popular whiskey. Their distillery stood at the corner of Gore and Harvey streets.

The first jail in Perth was built in 1821 on the south side of the river. Sergeant William Matheson, a Loyalist, was the first jailer. The first coroner was Thomas Sproule who emigrated from Ireland to Richmond in 1820. By 1829 Mr. Matheson had become coroner and James Young jailer.

The first court house was built in 1821. There was no resident lawyer in Perth, however, until 1823 when James Boulton arrived

* John Mactaggart, *Three Years in Canada* (1829).

from Toronto. Lawyers at Brockville and Kingston served the settlement.

The disbanded officers at Perth served as magistrates at the Courts of Quarter Session where all cases were tried and expenditures approved for the district. These magistrates included: William Morris, Benjamin DeLisle, Anthony Leslie, Christopher Bell, Alexander McMillan, Josias Taylor, John Alston, Roderick Matheson, John F. Elliott, and John Watson.

John Elliott had been granted 300 acres of land in Bathurst Township (Concession 11, Lot 22) between Fallbrook and Playfair Mills. Christopher James Bell (not a relative of the Rev. William Bell) had been a lieutenant in the Royal Navy and lost his leg during the war of 1812 in an attack on Plattsburgh. He farmed near Perth and later bought up land on the Bonnechère River where he built a saw mill near its mouth. For a time he was engaged in lumbering during the 1830s but was unfamiliar with the business and had to give up for financial reasons. He died in 1836. All the other magistrates resided in Perth except Captain Alston, who lived first on the Scotch Line and later in Beckwith Township.

One of the most prominent magistrates was Roderick Matheson. Like Morris and DeLisle he kept a general store. A native of Rothshire, Scotland, Matheson had come to Canada at the age of 12 with an elder brother, receiving his education in Lower Canada. During the War of 1812 he fought at Lundy's Lane, Fort Erie, and Niagara. He had been a drummer at the start of the war and worked his way up to be Paymaster of the Glengarry Fencibles. In later years he was sometimes the target of practical jokes concerning his humble beginnings as a drummer-boy.

Matheson lived first on the corner of Drummond and Herriott streets and later, in 1840, built an imposing stone residence on the south side of Gore Street near Foster (now the building housing the Perth Museum). The early drawing-room was hung with squares of rare and very ancient hand-painted Chinese wallpaper, a specimen of which can be seen in the Museum. Mr. Matheson built the structure which later contained Shaw's store, and here he had his store. Shaw & McKerracher bought him out in later years.

When the Rev. William Bell arrived at Perth, Matheson was a bachelor and a close friend of Colonel McMillan. With William Fraser they formed a faction of Bell's congregation often in opposition to his proposals regarding church affairs. According to the Bell Journals, Matheson and McMillan began the agitation for a Presbyterian minister from the Established Church of Scotland (Bell belonged to the Secession Church). It was they who finally circulated a petition among his parishioners, later sent to the Presbytery, asking for a pastor. Despite disagreements Bell's son John went to work in Matheson's store in 1824, apprenticing there for three years, and in his Journals Bell conceded he was well treated by his employer.

Matheson married Mary Robertson of Brockville in 1823. The *Cyclopedia of Canadian Biography* states that Mr. Matheson, a staunch Conservative, was appointed a life member of the Legislative Council in 1847, although there is no record of his ever having sat in the Assembly. At Confederation he was appointed to the Senate.

Captain Anthony Leslie, another magistrate, was appointed agent for the Commercial Bank in the 1830s. There was little currency in the early days and most business was carried on by barter. The half-pay officers were issued "specie".

According to the *Perth Courier* Roderick Matheson conducted the first banking business in Perth under the City Bank, but business was slow and the branch soon closed. When the Commercial Bank opened an office Leslie was appointed the agent. He lived at the west end of Wilson Street, almost in the country. He had a small square frame house surrounded by an old-fashioned garden. His office was a stone building adjoining his house. A huge bell (now in the Perth Museum) was attached to the roof and provided with a rope which hung down from a table. He had few customers but when one did arrive he had to ring the bell and Leslie would stroll in from his garden or field. If he was close enough to observe who his customer was and decided the man had no money to bank he would go on with his gardening. Sometimes conversation was passed but no money. Despite his casual way of doing business, Captain Leslie continued to hold the agency for 22 years when, in 1857, James Bell, the Rev. William Bell's son, succeeded him as manager.

The military settlement seems not to have had much choice in doctors. Dr. Thom was too busy with his commercial affairs to attend the sick. Another discharged Army medical man, Dr. James O'Hare, was located on Lot 4, Craig Street, next door to Adamson's Inn. He appears periodically in the Rev. William Bell's Journal but seems to have been somewhat temperamental and explosive, an ardent Methodist and fond of the prevailing beverage of the settlement. Whether he carried on a medical practice to any extent is not known. He died of cholera during the epidemic of 1832.

Home remedies were much used in the settlement. Bell who had little use for doctors at any time, cured his colds, coughs, fevers, and accidents by home-made poultice and herbal mixtures, for which there were plenty of medicinal plants available in the woods.

Another Army surgeon, Dr. George Hume Reade, carried on a medical practice until 1821. Reade had been an apothecary in the army and apparently did a booming business in drugs. In the early days Bell and he often had words over the subject of public and private health. During the 1832 cholera epidemic Reade tried to prevent local merchants from supplying the very expensive drug quinine since he considered he should have a monopoly of all drugs. Both William Morris and the Bell brothers, then in business, were selling the valuable medicine at a much lower price. Dr. Reade was Health Inspector at this time. He was one of the early coroners, a Justice of the Peace, and in 1823 Clerk of the Peace. He built a brick house and adjoining frame house on Drummond Street near Brock for use as home and office. He had retired from the British army in 1813 and was at the time of the Perth settlement on half-pay. In the late 1830s Dr. Reade apparently moved from Perth to Quebec City.

Dr. Thom built his residence on Harvey Street in 1821. This was later owned by his son-in-law, a civil engineer, C. H. Gamsby, and the property was eventually called Gamsby's Farm. Thom remained official army doctor of the Perth military settlement until military rule ceased in 1822. He was chairman of the Court of Quarter Sessions and one of the early magistrates. His bush and the portion of the Tay River running through his farm formed a favourite haunt of schoolboys in the early days. It seems the very best fish were caught on his premises, the conquest no doubt being particularly enticing because he had a cross dog and a crosser hired man! A very deep and quiet spot adjacent to the slide and dam near his mills yielded an "inexhaustible" supply of fish to the boys who dared to approach it.

In 1821 a civilian doctor arrived in Perth whose interests and abilities were not only an asset to the community during his lifetime but contributed a valuable legacy to future generations. James Wilson, M.D., was a graduate of Edinburgh University with an interest in science and especially geology. He was one of the pioneer amateur mineralogists and geologists of Canada and before he had been long at Perth was rock-hunting in the district. His investigations eventually led him to the discovery of two new minerals, later called *Wilsonite* (in his honour) and *Perthite*. Dr. Wilson became a personal friend of Sir William Logan, founder and first director of the Geological Survey of Canada. The bulk of his interesting mineral collection occupies a good portion of the Perth Museum. Dr. Wilson provided the community with much-needed professional medical service and earned an affectionate title "the wee doctor" from his Scottish compatriots.

Several of the Rev. William Bell's friends died early in 1822. Captain Oliver, the hospitable innkeeper at Oliver's Ferry, whose wife had passed away the previous year, shot himself. Captain Fowler died in April. Bell was called to the inn kept by Angus Cameron where his church elder "seemed to be dying". Bell made out his will and attested his signature. In May Mr. Cameron died. Cameron had been a member of the Masonic Lodge and although Bell had oftimes conducted worship services for the local fraternity, he seems to have been ill-prepared for "the fopperies of free masonry employed on the occasion".

Malcolm Cameron left the community two years later to work in Montreal. Mrs. Cameron moved to Perth and carried on as proprietor there with the assistance of another son, John, who later left the community to study medicine. A daughter, Christena, married Henry Glass of Lanark Village in 1821. Later Mr. Glass left Lanark and moved to Perth where he formed a partnership in general merchandise with Malcolm Cameron.

The Buchanans arrived from Edinburgh to take up residence in Beckwith, and in September 1822 Dr. George Buchanan accompanied by his two eldest daughters paid Perth a visit, bringing letters to Mr. Bell from Scotland. The young Buchanan girls, Helen and Elizabeth, having looked the village over and finding it more agreeable to their social background than life in the backwoods of Beckwith, were not long in returning. In May 1823 they rented a house from Mrs. LeLievre and opened a school for young ladies. They had five students.

Robert Bell went to Brockville in 1823 to the *Recorder* office of Mr. Buell to learn the art of printing. Early the same summer William Bell began an apprenticeship in William Morris' general store, working for his room, board, and washing. Andrew Bell left for Glasgow University to study for the ministry. The next year John Bell apprenticed to Roderick Matheson, his indenture to be for three years.

In 1822 the military reign in Perth came to an end. The position of Superintendent was abolished and Major Powell was appointed the first Sheriff of the new District of Bathurst, a position he held until 1831 when he died on a trip home to Ireland.*

In 1823 Perth became the judicial seat for the new District which included all of what is now Lanark County, Renfrew County, and part of what is now Carleton County. Bytown was non-existent until the Rideau Canal was built in 1826 and Perth was to be the largest centre in the whole vast area stretching to the Ottawa River and northward into the wilderness, for many years. It was already a thriving centre and would now add lawyers to its list of professional men. Since all court cases must be tried here for the District there was a steady stream of traffic to and from the town. The change in governing the settlement would not make much difference for some years to come since the military men of the town held most of the new offices by appointment.

* His eldest son, John A. Powell, who had been in business at Pakenham Mills, became Sheriff in his stead and continued until 1841 when succeeded by Andrew Dickson of Pakenham.

COLONEL JOSIAH TAYLOR'S HOUSE, PERTH
Probably built in the late 1820s. He later added a store.
This building is still used as store and dwelling.

# CHAPTER VI

## SETTLEMENT THROUGH THE LANARK SOCIETIES

Perhaps the hardest hit by the depression following the Napoleonic Wars were the Glasgow weavers. Their wages in 1803 were 25 shillings a week but by 1819 had fallen to 5½ shillings and people were forced to pawn their belongings in order to meet costs of food and shelter.

Lord Hamilton, representative for Lanarkshire in the British House of Commons, brought their plight before Parliament and on the 21st of December 1819 presented a petition signed by fourteen parishes in the Presbytery of Hamilton, Lanarkshire, showing that the labourers' wages could not sustain their families. On the 1st of June 1820, John Maxwell, M.P. for Renfrewshire, presented a similar petition from the mechanics of Paisley asking assistance in emigrating, preferably to Canada.

Meanwhile in Scotland several societies had been formed to urge the British government to action. They raised money by subscription in Glasgow and Barony Parish and collected almost 1200 people desiring to emigrate. Each of these were to receive £1 which was to be paid to the ships' owners as part of their passage money.

Lord Bathurst, Secretary of War and the Colonies, wrote to Sir Peregrine Maitland, Lieutenant-Governor of Upper Canada, advising him that approximately 1200 settlers would proceed shortly to Quebec, and that these settlers wished to be located in the vicinity of Perth and the Rideau, since they had had favourable reports from friends or neighbours already located there. The British government would assist them with an advance in money to be repaid within two years' time.

The settlers for the 1820 emigration were promptly furnished with ships. For this despatch of settlers, John Graham headed twelve families from the Glasgow Emigration Society; William Gordon had charge of nine families from the Abercrombie Friendly Emigration

Society; William Granger had charge of 39 families from the Anderson Rutherglen Society; Thomas Scott's charge numbered "170 souls" from the Lesmahagow Society; John McLachlan headed 139 men, women and children from three societies—Trans-Atlantic, Bridgetown, Abercrombie and Winslow. Almost 1200 emigrants set sail in June 1820 aboard the *Commerce* and the *Prompt*.*

Shortly afterward, £500 was raised in London to send out the remaining members of the societies who, for lack of funds, had been unable to pay for their passage. These were chosen by ballot and arrangements made with the owners of the ship *Brock* to transport 100 passengers.† John McLachlan sailed with some of his party aboard the *Brock* but the heads of the other societies sailed in the first two ships.

Meanwhile Lord Dalhousie, now Governor-General, had arranged for the emigrants to be located in the newly surveyed townships of Lanark and Dalhousie. Captain Sherwood and his assistants had almost completed surveys of North and South Sherbrooke, Ramsay, and Huntley.

By August Colonel William Marshall from Perth had been established at the new location as secretary and superintendent of the Lanark Society settlers, and a hut had been built upon the bank of the river Clyde in Lanark Township as his temporary storehouse and registry office. James Shaw from Perth was to be clerk of the Lanark Depot at 5 shillings a day, and John A. Murdock, former Roman Catholic teacher at Perth, was to issue stores at 3s.6d. a day. Captain Alex Ferguson from Perth had taken up land on Lot 1 of the 2nd Concession where he was going to build a grist mill. A rough road had been hacked out of the forest connecting Perth with the new settlement—a distance of 12 miles with the Mississippi River intervening. At this point on the Lanark Road, Malcolm Cameron, son of innkeeper Angus Cameron, ferried the settlers across the Mississippi.

For the new settlers' comfort, the government had been most generous, advancing money for surveys, provisions, and road improvements as well as cash loans. Lord Dalhousie, moreover, arrived to make a personal inspection of the new location, his visit coinciding with the arrival of the first emigrants. In a letter to his friend, Judge Stewart of Halifax, he later commented:

* See Appendix, page 238, for list.

† See Appendix, page 238, for list.

> In two days after I saw the first of them, with a Captain Marshall as Superintendent and a surveyor attached to him, set forward into the woods to occupy their lots. Several townships had been surveyed last year in preparation for settlers, and every man is obliged to sit down on the lot assigned to him. I never saw people in more joyous spirit, or more elated in their prospect. . . . It is an expensive job to Government, but it will do much good in more ways than one.*

Colonel Marshall was a kindly, sympathetic and diligent man who made every effort to organize his colony and prepare them for the Canadian winter ahead. He lost no time in getting the men located on their lots so that they could start clearing their land and building homes. The settlers spread out from the central depot at Lanark through the townships of Lanark and Dalhousie.

The first log house erected on the village site was that of David Bower who had come aboard the ship *Commerce.* James Hall, Peter McLaren, Captain Matthew Leech and William Gordon, head of the Abercombie Society settlers, were the next to build log houses. John A. Murdock, the Issuer of Stores, recalled the original settlement years later in reminiscences which he gave to the Almonte *Gazette*:

> Before the mills were erected settlers had scattered in the woods and proceeded to put up shanties. This was in the summer of 1820. The walls of the rude lodges were of logs, the roofs were made of basswood troughs, and the spaces between the logs were stuffed with moss or plastered with clay. The lower portion of the chimneys was built of stone; the upper part was of pieces of split cedar, something like lathe, and plastered on the inside with clay. The fire was composed of several logs. . . . An iron bar was extended near the fire . . . served to support the pots used for cooking. Baking was done in metal ovens that each held a loaf of bread and in these flat pots meat could also be roasted. Hot coals were placed under the oven, and hot coals covered the lid. Sheltered by the almost unbroken forests from every storm and with plenty of excellent firewood close by, these shanties were by no means uncomfortable as the fire was not permitted to go out during the cold season, and afforded the only light available during the long winter nights when the wolves were howling in the woods. . . . A large log house was erected on the west bank of the river where the village of Lanark now is and the rude structure formed the centre of the settlement. A few blankets and some axes and implements of a worthless character were provided [by the government]. Fortunately a num-

* Public Archives of Canada, Q.155.

ber of United Empire Loyalists had occupied land among the Scotch settlers and noticing the fine falls on the rivers and the abundance of pine timber that existed, the United Empire Loyalists proceeded to erect mills which formed centres that afterward became Almonte, Carleton Place, Lanark and Fallbrook. . . . The United Empire Loyalists taught the Scotch settlers the proper kind of axes to use, and how to fell the trees to advantage with the tops as much together as possible in order to avoid the necessity of piling the brush. . . . An experienced hunter named Church had wandered into the new settlement bringing with him an excellent American rifle and the good-natured old Loyalist shot scores of deer which he distributed in a most liberal manner.*

Courtesy Mrs. John McGill, Sr.

OUTDOOR BAKE OVENS

By December 1820 Colonel Marshall writing to Robert Lamond could report that a government storehouse and dwelling had been built for himself and "three respectable merchant stores and a dozen houses" in the village.† Henry Glass and John Hall both opened stores, but it is not known to whom the third belonged. By the next year Alexander Ferguson had opened a store in his house and had completed the grist mill.

Most of Lanark Township close to the depot was soon taken up.

* Almonte *Gazette*, 1897.

† Robert Lamond, *Narrative of the Rise and Progress of Emigration . . . to the New Settlements in Upper Canada* (1821).

Some emigrants located as far north as the present site of Hopetown. Robert Cannon and John Robertson selected land on the second concession that later became part of that village. Robert Cannon kept a cooperage and a tavern in pioneer days and was later Postmaster at Hopetown.

Robert Affleck, a weaver, brought his wife and nine children to settle near the site of the present village of Galbraith, twenty-six miles from Perth. His son Robert married Mary Borrowman, daughter of another 1820 settler. Mary Borrowman lived on their farm near Middleville until 1916 when she died at the age of 103. Longevity was not usual among the pioneers, but some who survived the first years of hardship lived to a remarkable age.

James Campbell who emigrated independent of government assistance purchased land in the centre of the township, some of which he later sold to become part of the village of Middleville. His wife, Jean Whyte, whom he had left behind in Scotland, came out in the spring of 1822 with their three children. Campbell had been a manufacturer in the old country and was not trained for farming. Like many other settlers from an urban environment, he and his wife endured great hardships.

A number of Irish settlers arrived about this time to settle in Lanark Township. The Braidens, Boyds, Bertrams, Forsyths, Flemings, Francises, Foleys, Grahams, Hopkins, Hammonds, Iretons, Maloneys, and McMannises took up land along the Mississippi River north of the present village of Ferguson's Falls. The Boyds' location was later called Boyd Settlement. Seven enterprising Irish bachelors also took up land about the same time near here. They had made a pact before leaving Ireland that they would stick together come hell or high water, and where all could not get work together none would remain. These were John Quinn, Patrick Quinn, Terrance Doyle, James Power, John Cullen, James Carberry, and William Scanlon. Six were from Waterford County and one from County Limerick. When they arrived at Perth, Colonel Powell the superintendent gave them employment clearing 10 acres of land for cropping the following autumn. When Powell learned of their pact he secured a block of land for them in Lanark Township consisting of lots four and five on the 9th concession and part of lot four on the 10th. Here they built one house and all lived together, taking turns at cooking and carrying provisions from Perth fourteen miles away. Thus they worked together until each had enough funds to build on his lot. Their hospitality to incomers was proverbial and anyone could be assured of help in settling, advice on crops to plant, tools to use, and other pioneer lore. John Quinn married Catharine Phelan from Ireland. It is said he walked all the way to Montreal to meet his bride at the boat. Patrick Quinn married Catharine's sister Mary. Charles Hollinger, the well-known auctioneer and drover from Lanark, was a descendant of these Quinns.

Some of the 1820 settlers pushed through the bush as far as Ramsay Township, most of them settling near the Lanark Township line in the Union Hall area—the Sutherlands, Stevensons, Wilsons, Robertsons, Nicholsons, McArtons, Bains, Taylors, Kemps, Bowlands, Gemmills, and Dunlops from Ireland and Scotland. Most of these men had been cabinet-makers, weavers, or tradesmen and found it very difficult to make a living as pioneer farmers.

Possibly the first settlers in the township of Dalhousie were four families from the Trans-Atlantic Bridgetown Society who arrived on board the ship *Brock* in the late summer of 1820. These were James Blair, John McNangle, Neil Campbell, and John McLelland who took up land along the first concession near the Lanark depot. En route to their locations under the guidance of one Ravelin, who had been a chainman on the survey of the township, they came across the wigwam of James Braiden, one of the settlers from the *Commerce*. He was the first white man they had seen since leaving Perth, and they chose their locations near him.

John McLelland, a native of Cambuslang, Scotland, brought his wife and four children with him. Mrs. McLelland later recalled those early days:

> I walked on foot through the thick bushes, crossing two rivers on rafts, and carrying one child in my arms and a stone of meal on my back. . . . My heart is in the land yet. It was drawn by another Glasgow man at the office in Perth in 1820 but when he saw it, he came back and renounced it. My gude man liked it as well as any he had seen and took me to it and the children. . . . Oh! it was a faithful piece of land. When we had cleared it all, save what was reserved for firewood, we maintained eleven sons and two daughters, and now one daughter has fourteen children. We put most of them to learn trades and saved something for bye. . . . I had my dining-room and parlour, and lovely garden and orchard, and the beautiful fields always so faithful in their crops, no matter what we put in them.

When the husband left for Oswego to work for the summer of 1823, leaving his wife and four children to fend for themselves, Mrs. McLelland recalled how her son aged nine helped her plant potatoes:

> I took heart and with the boy began to dig between the stumps and plant potatoes. When the fall of the year came and we had gathered them in, how many do you think we had? No less than 350 bushels of potatoes, and thirty bushels of corn raised by myself and my little boy.*

After these first four Dalhousie settlers, others arrived travelling by wagon from Perth to the Clyde. One of these families was that of John McNicol from Argyllshire, who was married to Flora Munroe, a first cousin of James Monroe who became fifth president of the United States. The McNicols, members of a clan of ancient Gaelic origin, arrived in Canada with a family of eight—seven boys and one girl. They found when they drew lots for location that their farm adjoined that of Robert Urquhart, a neighbour from Scotland. The McNicols located on Lot 11 of the first concession of Dalhousie while the Urquharts were on Lot 11 of the first concession of Lanark. A descendant of the McNicol family, Donald, relates in a family history that during the early days most of the Scots spoke nothing but Gaelic, and even a hundred years later the Scottish vernacular was still in evidence. He said that the Scottish women brought with them great hanks of wool yarn with which they passed the hours on board ship knitting socks, mittens, and stockings. They also brought with them bolts of cloth and fashioned coats, pants and waistcoats for the men, providing a diversion on the tedious voyage and a supply of warm clothing for the subzero winter ahead in Upper Canada. As anticipated, once located in "the bush", the women were too busy with other duties to have time left for sewing.

McNicol reports that forty families, comprising 300 persons, settled about the same time in the adjoining townships of Lanark and Dalhousie. Most of these Scots brought with them a supply of books, carefully chosen for inherent values, and these formed the basis of the Dalhousie Library later formed at Watson's Corners.† Such books as: Blackstone's Commentaries on the Laws of England; History of Scotland; English Grammar; The British Constitution; Macaulay's and

* *Perth Courier*, March 15, 1861, reprint of Letters originally in the Montreal *Gazette*.

† See Andrew Haydon, *Pioneer Sketches in the District of Bathurst* (1925).

Carlyle's Essays; these were the sort of fare they chose. They gave little room to novels.*

Passengers of the *Prompt* remained in Perth until the end of September 1820 when the government paid an instalment of one-third of their bonus money. Then they set out for Lanark Village, over the almost impassable road, crossing the Mississippi River on scows. A group of these also drew lots in Dalhousie and settled a short distance from the later village of Watson's Corners. These were James Martin, William Miller, Charles Bailey, James Watson (after whom Watson's Corners was named), George Brown, Thomas Easton, George Easton, Peter Shields, James Donald, John Duncan, Andrew Park, James Park, John Todd, William Jack, Thomas Scott, Robert Forest. George Richmond, the school teacher sent out with the Society, was tragically killed during the winter by a falling tree. James Watson built a kind of storehouse near the present Corners to hold supplies for the incoming settlers.

William Miller who settled near the Parks and the Hoods on Lot 14 of the second concession, was full of praise and thanksgiving for his new land. Of Perth he says, in writing to his father in October 1820:

> It is only four years since Perth was a wilderness of wood. There are four churches in it . . . six or eight large stores where you can get anything, as you and I could in Glasgow, but cast metal is very dear and crockery ware. . . . I have ten acres of meadow hay. . . . I am just getting off Monday to build my house; it is a most nice lot of ground. If I had been here two months earlier, I would have had a cow this winter; if I have time, I will cut the hay and get a cow. . . . Let my brothers, Robert, James and Andrew know that I wish them to come here as I think this is the country to live in. Let Robert . . . know there are farms to buy here every day. You will get them from 15 to 20 acres cleared and a good house for 25 pounds or 30 pounds in Perth till I have my house up and provisions for them. . . . Thanks be to God for being so fortunate as I am.†

Thomas Scott who had charge of the Lesmahagow Society emigrants settled with his wife and seven children on the fourth concession. Later, under his leadership, a St. Andrew's Society was formed during the early years and the St. Andrew's hall built at Watson's Corners. Alex. Watt who located at the further end of the

* Donald M. McNicol, MS., "A History of Dalhousie Folks" (1934).
† Robert Lamond, *Narrative*.

second concession near the rocky ridges of Lavant Township and the community later known as Lammermoor, recorded his progress in a letter to a friend in Glasgow, dated October 10, 1820:

> All of our society were settled in the course of a few days. There are twenty of us settled in the first line or road between the second and third concession. I am on the 25th lot, east side of the second concession of Dalhousie, one and a half miles from the Clyde, which runs through our township and joins the Mississippi at the township of New Lanark. . . . I am well pleased with my land. It is nearly covered with sugar maple. I suppose I have 4,000 sugar trees and a great deal of beech and ash, and a few cedars. I saw twenty fir. I have a small swamp for grass and a fine beaver meadow. I could keep a cow on it. . . . I have got very good neighbours and I have long wished to have you beside me. There are three lots on the north side of mine not yet taken up; but to tell you the truth I do not know what kind of ground they are, for I have not seen them, but the ground beside which I saw are very good.*

At the close of December 1820, Colonel Marshall sent a report to the Glasgow Committee showing remarkable progress in the three months since the first settlers had arrived at the Lanark Depot. The village site by December included twenty farm lots subdivided into town and park lots, the latter containing 25 acres each. Lots of 10 acres each were reserved for mechanics. He advised the Glasgow people to send their next settlers earlier—"they ought to be here by July"—and that they should come well equipped with clothing so that whatever money they had could be kept for other vital necessities.

Through the winter the Home government agents were at work organizing the next emigration of Lanark Society settlers. The societies had been advised to see that girls emigrating should be taught to knit coarse woollen stockings and to spin wool and linen yarn for family use. Boys were to be taught how to make fishing nets and tackle for lakes and rivers. Government terms of emigration were similar to that of the previous year, with an emphasis on a good supply of food. Each emigrant must supply for his own use and have on board on the day of sailing, 18 lbs. of Irish mess beef; 42 lbs. biscuits; 132 lbs. oatmeal; 6 lbs. butter; 3 lbs. molasses. This food had to last a possible 84 days' journey to Quebec and perhaps a few days in Greenock prior to sailing.

* Lamond's *Narrative*.

By March 1821, arrangements had been made with Q. & J. Leitch of Greenock for a supply of ships to carry 1,800 emigrants. These were to have comforts not known to earlier passengers such as: good water and a regular daily supply of it, measured out in small casks for each person; satisfactory cooking facilities on board ship; a surgeon and medicines; provision for public worship, and accommodation for women who might be overtaken in childbirth.

In April and May 1821, 1,883 emigrants sailed from Greenock on board four vessels—the *George Canning*, *Earl of Buckinghamshire*, *Commerce* and *David of London.*

Meanwhile at Lanark, in January the Presbyterian committee met again and proceeded to ground allotted for the school where they cut logs sufficient "to raise the school house". For some unknown reason, nothing further was done about the school until June when a "building bee" was organized. By July it had been erected.

Listed on board the *David of London* were five families of Gilmours, three Bairds, two Parks, two McIlquhams, four Whittons, as well as Robert Carswell, James Leitch, William Gourlay, James Bryson, several McDonalds, John Findlay, James Dick, James Bowes, and James Gillies.

James Gillies had been a small holder in Scotland and also belonged to the craft and guild of weavers who at the end of the 18th Century and beginning of the 19th Century wove in their own homes for large firms in Glasgow, Stirling, and other centres. At 55 years of age, he left his homeland with his wife Janet (then 45) and five children ranging from age one to 21. He paid his own way to Canada and settled on Lot 10, Concession 5 of Lanark Township which even today is only reached by narrow roads through pasture land and wooded slopes which drop away to a nearby marshy pond still known as Gillies Lake. Through the manufacture of potash laboriously produced the Gillies bought the necessities. It was James Gillies' son, John, who later went into the saw mill and lumbering business on the Clyde, eventually extending his interests to Carleton Place, Braeside, and Renfrew.

John M'Donald who sailed aboard the *David of London* kept a diary which was later published under the title *Narrative of a Voyage to Quebec and Journey Thence to New Lanark in Upper Canada* (1823). M'Donald speaks of the terrible conditions on board ship during the five weeks' journey across the ocean. Fierce storms assailed them, the worst being at Quebec the night of their arrival. When they arrived in Montreal their clothing was drenched by rain and their food was waterlogged. There was no accommodation and for days they had to continue

> night and day in wet clothes. Sometimes we got access to farm-houses, and sometimes not. Some got into barns, but the most part of them lodged out in the fields for five nights—120 miles from Lachine to Prescott. In the morning my nightcap, blankets and mat were so soaked with dew they might have been wrung. At Prescott we began to feel the effects of our rough journey. Many were afflicted with the bloody flux. Some took fevers and many died of a few days' illness. Here we were three weeks. The great numbers caused delay. Two families were left orphans—one by the name of Dick with nine or ten children, whose father was drowned while bathing at Lachine.

When they arrived at Prescott they found half of the *Earl of Buckinghamshire* passengers and all of those of the ship *Commerce* there—a total of 1000 people and "it took a long time to carry their baggage along a road of 74 miles to New Lanark".

It was James Dick of Bathgate, Scotland, who had been drowned at Lachine. His wife and 11 children ranging in age from three to twenty-one years continued on to Lanark where they located on Lot 13 of the 9th Concession of Lanark Township. The shock of the voyage and the death of her husband affected the health of Mrs. Dick and late in 1821 she passed away leaving the children orphans. John, the eldest, remained on the homestead and married Mary Gemmill, daughter of another immigrant. Robert who had been only eight years of age on arrival in Canada, began to work in the bush with an axe and by the age of 14 was doing a man's work. He had to quit school but studied by candlelight at night and taught himself Latin and higher mathematics. Eventually he went to the United States. He was later known as inventor of a method of using gummed labels to address newspapers, an invention he patented about 1857, called the "Dick Mailer". He moved to Chicago and with the money acquired from his invention, became an independent evangelist, preaching in Chicago saloons.

Despite their early handicaps, all the Dick children achieved an education. Four of the boys became Baptist ministers. Margaret, the eldest daughter, married Robert Stead, and their grandson, Robert J. C. Stead, became a well-known novelist in the early 1900s.

John M'Donald's diary portrayed a gloomy picture of New Lanark in 1821—torrential rains, dense forests which kept the settlers' clearings in perpetual shade and prevented prevailing winds from blowing away the corrupted atmosphere, and the eternal "musquitoes which torment us by day and night continually".

> We saw a number of squirrels running about our beds and we were frequently deprived of sleep for the unwholesome intrusion of oxen and cows, which, straying from their owners, came close to our tents and we were much terrified lest they should have pulled our tabernacles about our ears. The swine would come to our very heads and take away anything they could find, running away with it in their mouths, so that we were obliged to pursue them in order to recover it. . . . Many of those who arrived first got the best lots, as they had the first choice, and if not pleased with it when viewed, Colonel Marshall still indulged them with more tickets for other lots till they were satisfied. They are all furnished with tickets for such townships as they choose to settle in, namely, Lanark, Dalhousie, Sherbrooke, and Ramsay. Those who came first tried very naturally to obtain the most eligible situations. On this account inferior or worse lots are left to those who follow.

His diary paints a cheerless and forbidding picture regardless of what topic he deals with. "It is dull travelling through the woods; nature seems as if dead; there are no signs of animal life. All these circumstances throw a damp and gloom over the mind of the traveller." He was indeed a dour Scot. There were a number of McDonalds who settled throughout the county, and possibly a John McDonald who located on the eighth concession of Dalhousie, near the present McDonald's Corners, was the diarist.

Also on board the *David of London* was James Bowes from Glamis, Scotland. Bowes was a designer by trade and had worked with a printing industry as engraver and blockcutter. He was a cousin of one of the present Queen Mother's ancestors. His wife had been Margaret Monteith, daughter of Lord Thomas and Lady Catherine Monteith of Inverary Castle, Argyllshire, who had left her family to elope with the lowly tradesman. The Bowes family spent the winter in Lanark Township with James Patterson who located on Lot 22 of the sixth concession of Ramsay Township, then took up their own land the following spring adjacent to the Patterson farm—Lot 21. James Bowes, Jr., took part of Lot 20 across the Clayton road from his father. Another son, John, married Jane Dick and settled on the west half of Lot 23 of the seventh concession in Ramsay. Robert, another son, married Mary Black, daughter of pioneer Walter Black, who arrived in Ramsay about the same time as the Bowes family and took up Lot 21 of the seventh concession.

Aboard the *Earl of Buckinghamshire* came William Caldwell, James McIlraith, Andrew Lang, John Leckie, and many others. William Caldwell was doing well in the Paisley shawl trade following the Napoleonic war when financial disaster struck. With others in like circumstances, he left for Canada and a new life. He found land to his liking, Lot 24 on the second concession of Lanark Township near the town line of Darling. On the next lot, (No. 25) located James McIlraith.* Here in a rocky, hummocked sector of Lanark Township, the Caldwells and McIlraiths hewed out homes and cultivated the soil, such as it was. The area later was known as "Brightside". William Caldwell's sons early learned the art of logging on the Clyde River. Alexander became one of the lumbering "barons" in the 1850s. James McIlraith's descendants also contributed to the national life. George McIlraith, the Member of Parliament for Ottawa West, is a direct descendant, as is Evan J. McIlraith of Evanston, Illinois, who invented the stop-light system used in regulating city traffic. Boyd Caldwell, a brother of Alexander, established woollen mills and also engaged in lumbering. The Caldwell enterprises sustained Lanark Village for many years after 1850 and the name Caldwell still means much to people of Lanark though over a century has passed since the mills and rivers boomed.

John Leckie and his family settled on the west half of Lot 9 on the eighth concession of Dalhousie, close to Lake Dalhousie and the Mississippi River. Leckie knew nothing about farming but set about with his sons to learn. They cleared the land turning the great trees into potash to earn a little cash. Eventually the cultivated soil yielded crops. Twelve children were born to the Leckies. In a history of this family the narrator tells of the courtship of Alice Leckie and William Houston, son of a Ramsay immigrant. On the occasion of the subsequent marriage, "Wully and Alie", as they are affectionately called in the narrative, walked to Perth, some 14 miles, for the wedding ceremony and then walked to their new home in Ramsay, a distance of over 30 miles.

Many of the 1821 Lanark Society settlers found the best land of Lanark and Dalhousie townships had already been taken up by the emigrants of the preceding year, and so they moved on into the Sher-

* The McIlraith homestead now occupies a place in Upper Canada Village.

brookes and Ramsay. Reuben Sherwood had completed his survey of North and South Sherbrooke about 1820. The base of both of these townships was principally granite with rocky hills and ridges, swamps and rivers, typical of the Laurentian shield. There were small strips of fertile soil scattered over this doubtful terrain and as the Ontario Agriculture Commission Report summed it up in 1881, it was "best adapted to stock raising".

One of the military ex-officers at Perth, John F. Elliott, seems to have been the first to draw land in North Sherbrooke as part of his military grant—200 acres on Lot 13 of the first concession. He was an absentee landowner, however, and the first actual settlers seem to have been Duncan Ferguson and John Williams who occupied Lot 7 of the 4th concession, near Oso Township boundary line.

Next came the Lanark Society settlers of 1821. Members of the Lesmahagow Society were probably the first to occupy land. Along the first concession were: Alexander Campbell (Lot 1); William Christelaw (Lot 5); George Eaton (Lot 6); Archibald McEwen and John Warnock (Lot 7); John Porter (Lot 8); James Nesbit and Josias Davies (Lot 10); Duncan and Archibald McDougall (Lot 11); Ebenezer Wilson and Dan Ritchie (Lot 12). On the second concession: Robert Young and Geo. Gilroy (Lot 4); John Smith and Archibald Campbell (Lot 6); Hugh Currie, Sr. and Duncan Campbell, Sr. (Lot 7); Andrew McAlpine and Robert Sym (Lot 9); Arthur Stocks, Jr. and Sr. (Lot 11); Robert Twaddell and James Twaddell (Lot 12); Anthony McBride and James Easson (Lot 13); James and William Gilmour (Lot 4). The first settlers along the third concession were: Richard and James MacConnell (Lot 3); Hugh McLean (Lot 5); John Currie and Don McLean (Lot 6); Wm. Bryce, Jr. and Sr. (Lot 7 and Lot 8); Robert Smith, Jr. and Sr. (Lot 10); David Wylie (Lot 11); Wm. Dunlop and Andrew Edwards (Lot 12); James Smith (Lot 13). Along the fourth concession were: Robert Love (Lot 4); John Currie and Hugh Currie, Jr. (Lot 6); George Harrower and Walter Sym (Lot 9); James Dunlop (Lot 13). Along the fifth concession located: John McColl (Lot 5) and Henry Thompson (Lot 6).

Some of these left their land and the township before receiving deeds. The Upper Canada Land Report in 1836 noted that only the following had completed their settlement obligations and were eligible to receive deeds: James and William Gilmour, David Wylie, Arthur Stocks, Jr. and Sr., Anthony McBride, James Nesbit, Ebenezer Wilson,

James and Robert Twaddell, James Easson, Robert Bain, Robert Smith, Jr.

One of these, Ebenezer Wilson, according to one report, was not a Lanark Society member, but belonged to a group sent out from Britain known as the *Radical* settlers. He sailed aboard the ship *Buchan* and took up land near Dalhousie Lake. Mr. Wilson was well-educated and had superintended a mill in Britain but undertook to learn farming in Upper Canada and cleared the land with the help of his eldest son John, then a boy of 12. John Wilson later became a lawyer and was the victor of the famous duel fought in Perth. His father had some knowledge of medicine when he arrived in Canada, and during the early days when long distances separated the pioneers from a doctor Mr. Wilson prescribed remedies for disease, settlers coming many miles for advice. He was a respected citizen of the new settlement and presently served as a magistrate at Perth's courts of quarter session. He kept a licensed inn for awhile and was one of the first Directors of the County of Lanark Agricultural Society, organized in 1836.

South Sherbrooke, a much larger township than North Sherbrooke, cut up with lakes and swamp, received its first occupants in 1821. North of Fagan's Lake on the 10th concession located John Milliken (Lot 20) and James Parker (Lot 19); on the north shore of Fagan's Lake settled George Taylor (Lot 21, 9th concession); and further along the 9th concession were George White (Lot 19) and Charles White (Lot 20). Along the 11th concession were: Henry Tatlock and Wm. Tatlock, Jr. (Lot 14), Patrick Codley and Thomas Codley (Lot 16); John Codley and Ed. Comer (Lot 17). Sam and William Tatlock (Lot 14) located on the 12th concession. Near Christie's Lake settled Michael Carrier (Con. 4, Lot 19). On the third concession were Louis Rendt (Lot 10) and Joseph Corbeija (Lot 13); on the second concession Hugh Scott at the south side of Christie's Lake (Lot 18), James Laidley (Lot 6) and James Dobie (part of Lot 7). Along the first concession were: James Dermot (Lot 14), Sam McClelland (Lot 13), John O'Brien, Jr. and Sr. (Lot 11), Thos. and Geo. Farrell (Lot 10). The Deacons, Codleys, and O'Briens were Irish, and a number of other Irish families arrived between 1824 and 1831. Among these were Robert FitzSimmons and George Perkins who located on Lot 20 of the 6th Concession, and John Buchanan (Con. 9, Lot 13). John Buchanan was shoe repairer for his neighbours, as well as a farmer.

Settlers in the Sherbrookes were relatively close to Perth, the hub of the whole new district. Despite the lack of roads they could still reach the depot without too great difficulty. North of Dalhousie and Lanark townships, another two townships had been surveyed and these were more barren and rocky than any of the others. It is surprising, consequently, to find that as early as 1820 any immigrant should venture to take up land there. Nevertheless a few of the 1820 Lanark Society settlers selected land in Darling, where already Billa Flint, a wealthy merchant and land speculator of Brockville, owned 700 acres. William McIntyre, who arrived aboard the *Prompt*, located on Lot 1 of the 11th concession, near the township line dividing Darling and Lanark townships. Aboard the *Commerce* came Peter Barr who took up lot 6 of the sixth concession. Daniel Pretty, a later arrival, took 100 acres of the same lot. James Watt located on lot 2 of the eighth concession; Thomas Watt and Isaac Cole on lot 4 of the sixth concession.

Lanark Society arrivals of 1821 also located in Darling. John and William Whitton were on lot 1 of the 10th concession along the Indian River, next to William McIntyre. They later sold a mill site to William Hall to build a saw mill on the river bank, which later grew into Hall's Mills. John McDermot located on lot 2 of the tenth concession, and Andrew Hill on lot 13 of the second concession, relinquishing this land in 1837 for lot 4 of the tenth concession. Andrew Hill operated the first licensed inn in Darling (1825). William Craig, a cooper, located on the west half of lot 3 on the second concession.

Lavant, adjoining the township of Darling, was even more desolate, a large part of it covered by swamp. As late as 1842 the entire population of this township had reached only forty. There was an abundance of white pine which prospered its tenants during the lumbering boom in the 1850s but to the pioneers it offered nothing but toil and deprivation. Nevertheless settlers came in hopefully. Possibly Michael Brouse who occupied all 200 acres of lot 4 on the eighth concession, and Adam Davey who took up all 200 acres of lot 7 on the 7th concession, were the first settlers. John Robertson, an 1821 arrival on the *David of London*, selected 140 acres of lot 5 on the eighth concession bordering the lake named after him. He also took 100 acres of lot 6 on the seventh concession. On the seventh concession Peter Barr acquired 50 acres of land on lot 5. Later John and Archibald Browning and George Molyneux each took up 50 acres of the same lot and a small village and postal station named Lavant took shape. John Browning also occupied all 120 acres of lot 6 on the eighth concession at the north side of Robertson Lake, and Archibald Browning took 100 acres of lot 6 in the eleventh concession. The Brownings later purchased other land throughout Lavant. Residents in the more settled districts referred to the township as "the wilds of Lavant", and in the early years it was certainly well supplied with wild life, for Archibald Browning reported killing 82 wolves and 63 bears within a few years of settlement.

Mineral wealth was alleged to abound in land near his holdings, and later he did discover copper and developed his finding into a mine. This was leased in 1872 to the Canada Mining Company for 80 years. According to the 1880 Atlas, it was of a high quality, assaying 45% pure copper and the supply was believed at that time to be inexhaustible. Like other mines in Lanark County it has long since been abandoned and overgrown with shrub and brush. The mineral wealth of the county has yet to be developed and utilized.

A traveller to the backwoods of Lanark in 1827 related his experiences in a Montreal newspaper showing that the Scots he visited had improved on their lot in the auld land and were, for the most part, content with the new. (It is believed the family he particularly mentions in his report was that of Robert Affleck on the 9th concession of Lanark Township.)

> R.A.K., in whose house I now was, had been a weaver in Lanark from his boyhood till the end of June 1820, when with a wife and, I believe, eight children, he set out with several other families from the same place to the township of the same name in Upper Canada. . . . Among all the people I did not hear one express the slightest regret that he had left Scotland or a desire to return permanently; but there was no forgetfulness or indifference to their native land.
>
> It is generally understood that the settlers in Upper Canada find considerable difficulty in procuring clothes, which cost much higher than at home. . . . I took particular notice of the way in which they were in general dressed. . . . The clothes of the males (present) were all made of Gallashiels cloth which would cost in Glasgow about 6s. a yard narrow. Their garments were all whole and very few of them had been mended. They resembled those still worn by very comfortable farmers in Scotland, and which at no distant date were the usual covering of all below the higher ranks. The females had gowns and frocks of cotton print. All these clothes can be had in Brockville, Perth, or even in Lanark, in exchange for grain. Every person I saw was not so well clothed as members of this family; yet upon the whole the settlers generally are as well put on

> as tradesmen at home in better times than the present, and in every other respect they are incomparably more comfortable. . . . When it became dark, a couple of mould candles were placed upon the table. They were of their own making, and burned quite as well as those you would buy in Glasgow.
>
> The people assembled on this occasion had each a year's provisions in their houses and barns with something over, and every year their stock is increasing. R.A.K. has now got fifty acres of land cleared. He has a yoke of oxen, three cows, two or three calves and several pigs. He has no sheep. There are very few of these in the township, but it is the intention of several of the settlers to set speedily about the rearing of these useful animals, after which they expect to make the greater part of their own clothes.*

The writer goes on to describe his journey back to Perth and remarks that he described the conditions of several families because he wanted to destroy the myth that "it is preposterous to place weavers and other tradesmen in the woods to become farmers—an objection to which the details I have given of the state of R.A.K. and G.R. form a sufficient answer. Let it not be forgot, however, that the present comfortable situation of the settlers is the fruit of long and incessant toil, and let none who are unwilling to perform the same come to Canada."†

Some years later a government inspector sent to investigate conditions among the Lanark Society settlers reported:

> The Bathurst District in Upper Canada is, taken altogether, a very inferior tract of country. There is, however, a vein of good land consisting of the townships of Fitzroy, eastern part of Ramsay, Drummond, and part of Bathurst . . . The western part of Ramsay, Lanark, Dalhousie, the northern part of Bathurst, Sherbrooke, Lavant, etc. is little else than a continued succession of rocky knolls or ridges with scraps of good land between . . . it appears a matter of surprise how the people managed to obtain a livelihood here.‡

His report brought about a remission of government claims for repayment of advances at the time of emigration. Most of the Lanark Society settlers were not to know prosperity until the lumbering era arrived, beginning with scattered saw mills in the 1830s and gathering momentum in the 1840s and 1850s.

* Dominion Archives, Q.345, p. 219.
† *Ibid.*
‡ Dominion Archives, Q.385, p. 3—Rankin's Report.

# CHAPTER VII

## SETTLEMENT IN RAMSAY TOWNSHIP

It is believed that the first settlers in Ramsay Township were Thomas Smart and Robert Wilkie who, in 1819, built shacks along the west bank of the Mississippi River about two miles southeast of present-day Almonte. They took up land on Lot 12 of the 9th concession. James Smart also located about this time on Lot 11 and Archibald Wilkie on Lot 19, northwest of Almonte.

Several other men came in about the same time—Thomas Lowry, Archibald Muir, John Million, Edward McManus, James Metcalf, Neil McKillop, and Andrew Rae. Thomas Lowry settled along the 9th line obliquely opposite the farm of Archibald Wilkie on Lot 18 and Neil McKillop on Lot 17 of the 8th concession. Archibald Muir located across the Mississippi River from Wilkie on Lot 19 of the 10th concession. John Million, Ed. McManus, James Metcalf, and Andrew Rae took up 100 acres each along the 9th line between the centres later called Almonte and Carleton Place on lots 12 and 13 of the 8th concession.

The same year David Shepherd, a United Empire Loyalist, constructed a saw mill on his 200-acre lot where Almonte now stands. His grant from the government was conditional upon his erecting a grist mill and having it in operation within a limited time. The mill was destroyed by fire in 1820 and the concession passed to a "Yankee" from Brockville named Boyce. Daniel Shipman, another Loyalist, married to Boyce's daughter, Prudence, proceeded to Ramsay and rebuilt the saw mill in 1821. Living in a log hut nearby, his family still in Brockville, Shipman with the help of a few settlers, added a grist mill in 1822. In the early years the location was called Shepherd's Mills, later changed to Shipman's Mills.

A few Lanark Society settlers of 1820 located along the first concession of Ramsay at Clayton Lake and in the Union Hall area. Several pushed further on into Ramsay which was reputed to have some of the finest land in the new settlement. John Graham, head of the Glasgow Emigration Society, who came aboard the *Commerce* in 1820, located on Lot 17 of the 10th concession at the northwest corner of Shepherd's Mills. Another was John Neilson, Sr., who with his wife Agnes came from Paisley, Scotland, to settle with their young family on the 12th concession of Ramsay on Lot 6.

In 1821 another group of emigrants arrived from the British Isles. Along the 9th line where highway 29 now runs, the following took up 100 acres each—John Donaghue, Thomas and Robert Mansell, William Lummox, Catin Willis, and William Hawkins. On the first, second, and third concessions of Ramsay were Thomas Forster, Alex. Leary, James Smith, Fred DeLisle, Patrick McDermot, Arthur Nugent, George Blackburn, Stephen Young, Charles Sterne, William Chapman, John McKerecher. Along the sixth line settled John and Donald McLean, Joseph Hewitt and John Dobson.

Late in the summer of 1821, the Lanark Society sponsored settlers began arriving in Ramsay. The experience of a few will serve to represent those of all.

John Gemmill from the parish of Dunlop, Ayrshire, Scotland, came to New Lanark with his wife and son, John A. Gemmill. Mrs. Gemmill died while the family was still at the Lanark depot. Mr. Gemmill took up land in Ramsay—the west half of lot 15 on the ninth concession, later known as "the Gemmill property" and today part of the town of Almonte. Here he built a shanty and opened the first store in Ramsay.

Arthur Lang, another of the Lanark Society settlers, also located near Shipman's Mills on the east bank of the Mississippi River (Con. 10, Lot 14). Lang sailed with his wife and six children aboard the *Earl of Buckinghamshire* on April 28, 1821. He kept a diary of the turbulent crossing and the voyage to New Lanark. They arrived at Lachine on June 20, where they were "huddled in cold, damp reeky barracks", and then began the tedious journey up the St. Lawrence, the men rowing the heavy sweeps of the cumbersome Durham boats. Ten days later they reached Prescott where they found the emigrants from the *Commerce*. From here they proceeded in wagons and on foot to Brockville and thence to Perth and Lanark Village. Women and children remained in thatched huts while the men located on their land, made small clearings, and erected log shanties.

> I set out for Ramsay settlement [Lang wrote on July 19th] to pick out 100 acres and after six days hard labour travelling through swamps and untrodden paths through woods, I had to return without land and now I have to do the same thing over again. Canada abounds in rocks and stones in the townships of Lanark and Dalhousie . . . you have no idea of cedar swamps but conceive Paisley moss for instance, all over-grown with large trees, some fresh and green, others half-rotten and a great deal rotten from top to bottom, almost as many lying in all directions as are standing, with not a living creature to be heard or seen except a bird or two, and the owl screaming in your ears at night.

On November 1st he wrote:

> I received the second instalment of money paid in sterling—if you had seen the foolishness of some who were willing to spend and be merry and the sad countenance of others who had lost the most of their families and of course had little to receive, I am sure you would have looked with contempt on the one, and your very heartstrings ached for the other. . . . Mankind are indeed a strange class of animals. . . . I have seen more inhumanity to man than I ever expected to see.

On November 7th Lang was finally able to bring his family to Ramsay, and heavy snow and a frozen river soon showed them how different the New Land was from the Old. He was one of the first—probably the first—school teacher in the township, opening a school in his home. His son John was later in the saw mill business at Almonte.

Other settlers, not wishing to leave their families behind at New Lanark, devised a method of transport by water. Among these were John Steele, Walter Black, John Downey, Thomas and James Craig, John Smith, William Moir, William Hart, and William Paul. They improvised scows of logs and rough timbers and proceeded from New Lanark down the Mississippi River to Ramsay Township, past Ferguson's Falls, through the rapids at Innisville, down the 10-mile expansion of the Mississippi at Morphy's Falls, past Appletree Falls (now Appleton) to Shipman's Mills in Ramsay. The story is told that when the party stopped at an island in Mississippi Lake to replenish their strength by food, a huge Indian appeared and strode ominously toward their camp. Apprehensive, the party froze except for John Steele, always equal to any occasion. He seized a loaf of bread and thrust it toward the Indian as a token of friendship. The offering was not accepted but the Indian departed peacefully for another part of the island. When the party reached Shipman's Mills they erected rough wigwams for their families until they could locate their allotments of land and clear portions for dwellings.

John Steele married Mary Johnstone and located on Lot 22 of the 7th concession. The land is still owned by the Steele family descendants.

Walter Black, a wheelwright of Dumfrieshire, Scotland, settled on Lot 21 of the 7th concession. Annals of the Black family include a story of whole grain being boiled to make an unsavoury but necessary food. Even this failed eventually, and at one time starvation was near. Mrs. Black stole from her cabin during early morning while her four children slept and, guided by instinct and sense of location, made her way to Snedden's grist mill, four miles away, where she obtained some cornmeal and returned to prepare a sumptuous breakfast before her children awoke. James Black, a son, recalling the early days, said the first flour in this small settlement was carried from Morphy's Falls by four Bowes brothers who had taken two bushels of wheat each, following a surveyor's blazed trail down the 7th line of Ramsay.

Courtesy Major and Mrs. Leys

MILL OF KINTAIL

Built in 1830 by pioneer John Baird, restored by sculptor Tait McKenzie, now a historical museum.

Along the west side of the 8th line in the neighbourhood of Bennies Corners, settled Walter Gardner, William Anderson, and Walter Bain. On the east side located James Bennie and Robert Carswell. Bennie's land was later situated at a crossroads point which became the village of Bennies Corners.

Walter Gardner and his wife, Mary Lindsay, with a son Walter and daughter-in-law, Cecilia Brown, settled on Lot 26 of the 7th concession. During the early days the Gardners walked 12 miles to Morphy's Falls every Sunday to church. Mr. Gardner once walked to Brockville with a block of cherry wood from his farm to have it made into a roller for a cheese press.*

Further along the 8th line located William Moir, James Johnston, Patrick Slattery, Thomas Buchanan, John Downie, James and Thomas Pollock, James More, Thomas Craig. Near the crossroads corner later known as "The Tannery" James Mitchell, Sr. and Jr., John and James Gilmour, Hugh Cherry, John Buchanan, James Kattans, James Nicholson, Allan and Hugh Gilmour took up land. As Ramsay grew in population the main line for traffic from Pakenham Township to Morphy's Falls was along this eighth line of Ramsay. Logs were laid across it corduroy-fashion wherever it was swampy, and at one time it extended through Wolf's Grove all the way to Perth. Today it is only a dirt road and a concession line.

Behind the land of James Bennie the Toshacks settled on the ninth concession. John Toshack wrote a friend in Glasgow, describing early hardships:

> I gladly embrace the opportunity of writing you by Mrs. Graham who has lost her husband† and is returning to Scotland. Our family are all well now. By the mercies of God, they are recovered. We had four of them in the fever since we came here—Margaret, Andrew, Helen, and Aeneas. Many have died since arriving in Canada, some of the fever, some of the flux, and others from the effects of fatigue. . . . William, John, and James Bennie, and I have got each 100 acres together in a square. It is most beautiful land and resembles Dalmarnock haughs, and according to what I have seen

* This relic is now among other historical artifacts at the Mill of Kintail near Almonte. The mill built in 1830 by pioneer John Baird became the summer home of Tait McKenzie, sculptor, native son of Ramsay. For some years it has been owned and operated as a museum by Major and Mrs. J. F. Leys, and includes casts and replicas of some of Tait McKenzie's best-known works.

† John Graham, head of the Glasgow Emigration Society settlers of 1820. He had located near Shipman's Mills on Lot 17, Concession 10 of Ramsay.

> on other land, it will produce abundantly all of which is necessary to support a family; but the land is by no means generally good. There is much rock and swamp in many lots. . . . We have built two flat boats of fir boards . . . I have got a house 22 x 16 feet which will do to begin with. Our land abounds with beautiful wood—elm, maple, birch, beech, pine, bass; the latter is somewhat like your saugh.

John Toshack goes on to give instructions to prospective settlers on how to find their way through dense woods. "Examine the trees", he wrote as a result of his own experience.

> The north side of large trees is covered with moss; the branches are longest on the south and south-east sides; these will serve as a compass. Birch trees are the compass for Indians, their strongest branches pointing eastward. Should you come to some river or brook, its course will lead to some settlement.

He also had something to say about plants and their uses:

> *Colt's foot*, called by Americans "snake root", has a leaf formed like the foot of a colt; it is of deep green colour, the roots run horizontally and are of the thickness of a tobacco pipe. They taste like lemon peel. By gathering of that root to eat, a person might exist for some time. It is taken as tea, to remove violent colds, when a little sweetened.

James Snedden took up 100 acres of land near to the Toshacks running from present No. 29 highway to the village now called Blakenay. His cousins, Alexander and David, had emigrated from Cambuslang, near Glasgow, Scotland, in 1819, locating in Beckwith Township near Ashton. In 1822 Alexander and his son came to Shipman's Mills and walked along a blazed trail (now the 9th line of Ramsay) until they reached a rapid on the Mississippi River which promised sufficient power for milling enterprises. Alexander, Jr., handed over his Beckwith property to his father and took an option on the mill site where Blakenay village later grew. By 1826 he had built a grist mill and gone into the lumbering business, making square timber from leases in the Renfrew area. Because of the abundance of pine the hamlet which grew up was named Norway Pine Falls. Here in 1830 a saw mill was added to Alex Snedden's business activities. James Snedden, Jr., sold his farm to Alexander and leased timber limits around Fort Coulonge and Bryson where he carried on a profitable timber business.

David Snedden returned to Scotland in 1823 on business and died of cholera. He was buried at sea. His sons, James, John, and William settled around Bennies Corners along the eighth line of Ramsay. The Snedden enterprises drew others to Norway Pine Falls and a community grew up called Snedden's Mills until 1850 when the name became Rosebank, and later Blakenay.

Snedden's Inn on the ninth line had a high reputation for hospitality among travellers in the early days. One traveller commenting on facilities in the Ottawa Valley queried: "Who in this portion of Victoria's domain has not heard of Snedden's as a stopping place? Ask any teamster on the upper Ottawa and he will satisfy you as to its capabilities of rendering the traveller oblivious to the comforts of his home."

Also along the ninth line of Ramsay, on the east side, settled David Leckie and William Lindsay. On the west side were James Rae from Ireland and John Toshack, Sr. In 1825, James Rae was joined by a brother, Hugh W., who was a cobbler. Later he went to Western Ontario, returning to Almonte after a time and opening a shoe store and general shopping mart. Across the Mississippi River from the Raes was William McEwen on the northeast half of Lot 25, a 100 acres later constituting the village of Rosebank.

Opposite the present Clayton county road, on the ninth line, settled William Lindsay from Wisha, Lanarkshire, with his wife and family. The Lindsays were about the only Lowland Clan to form themselves into a society. William, Jr., born in 1821, was one of the early school teachers in Ramsay. John, a stone mason, settled with his wife, Elizabeth Leitch, in the township of Pakenham.

Along the ninth line between Shipman's Mills and Appletree Falls located the Matthew McFarlanes, Sr. and Jr., and Thomas Patterson; while across the river along the 10th line located James Leitch, Arthur Lang, Peter McGregor, John Smith, James King, James Bryson, James Orr, Richard Dulmage, William and Robert Baird.

James Bryson from Paisley and James King took Lot 11 of the 10th concession. George Bryson, a son of James, was one of the first Lanark County pioneers to go into the lumbering trade in 1836 and later, with his brother Robert, engaged in lumbering at Fort Coulonge and along the Black River in the province of Quebec. George Bryson represented Pontiac County in that province and was called to the Legislative Assembly of Quebec in 1867. The village of Bryson was named after him.

Courtesy Mrs. Edna Rose

PIONEER HOME OF JOHN LINDSAY

His home on the 9th line of Pakenham was built by himself and is still standing.

Sketch by the author

ALEXANDER SNEDDEN

He emigrated to Beckwith in 1819 and moved to Ramsay in 1822.

During the lumbering era George Bryson and Simon Dunn established shanties throughout Ramsay and built the slide at Shipman's Mills. There was talk of running the slide in canoes to save portage but all flunked out except Robert Bryson who with Dunn ventured the risky trip in a large pine log canoe. The canoe and crew shot down the steep incline at a rapid clip and all went well until they came to a 14-foot drop from the end of the slide into the bay below. The canoe split in two and the men were thrown into the rapids below but were rescued by onlookers. Later aprons were built to the slide to make it navigable for canoe travel. The slide concession rights passed later to the Mississippi Lumber Company, then largely owned by the Gilmours of Lower Canada.

Near Appletree Falls located James Gemmill, Sr., from Paisley, on lot 5 of the 11th concession, and on lot 3 settled John Fummerton.

The seventh line of Ramsay contained William Cobb, John Bowes, Walter Black, John Steel, Lachlan McLean, Neil McQuarry, Robert McLaren, James Bowes, Jr., John McPherson, John Gillan, James Stewart, John More, and James Patterson. Lachlan McLean from Old Kirkpatrick, New Glasgow, was possibly the first poet Ramsay Township produced. His "The Dalshooie Feast" was widely known in his day.

James Patterson was one of the earliest tailors in Ramsay, having to travel to Brockville to obtain thread during pioneer days. It was said he sometimes had to use the bark of the "mousewood" tree as a substitute. The bark of this tree was also used for bag strings.

Along the sixth line between Shipman's Mills and Morphy's Falls settled James Yule, Sr., and his wife Barbara Collins, with their nine children, from Lanarkshire, Scotland. On the same lot settled Alexander Yuill. A daughter, Euphemia, married Andrew Paul whose lime-kiln was one of the earliest in the township. Many of the stone structures built at Almonte depended upon the Paul kiln for limestone. Lime was shipped as far as Merrickville from the "Mount Blow" kiln, as it was called, and old account books list buyers from Innisville, North Gower, Franktown, Smiths Falls, Prospect, Ashton, Huntley, Richmond, and other outlying points. The kiln was built of black iron stone on the site of a steep hill. It was barrel-shaped with an arched entrance, lined with fire brick and the front covered with dressed stone. Gum woods such as hemlock, tamarack, pine, spruce, and cedar were used for firing. The manufacturing season began generally in mid-February and ran to mid-December. There were 12 or 14 such kilns in operation on the Paul farm by 1866 and the greatest production year was 1885 when they sold 9000 bushels. John Paul & Sons were awarded a bronze medal at the Colonial and Indian Exhibition in London in 1886 for their sample of lime.

In the late summer of 1822 a McDonald family arrived in Ramsay, after several attempts to find suitable land elsewhere. John McDonald and his wife, Ishbel MacLaine, with their three sons, Donald, Lauchlin and Neil, and daughters, Sarah, Mary, Flora and Bell, had emigrated from Oban, near the Isle of Mull, in 1821. John McDonald was an independent emigrant, paying his own passage aboard the *Duchess of Richmond*. After five weeks they landed at Quebec, and sailed up to Pointe Fortune along the Ottawa; but not finding land to suit them they returned to Montreal and took a Durham boat to Prescott. Meeting friends there, they were persuaded to continue to Perth. Unsatisfied with the lots offered them they rented a farm in Drummond Township, near Mississippi Lake, twelve miles from Perth, from Duncan McNaughton, doing statute labour and paying taxes as rent. After a hard winter's work, they had cleared about 12 acres and set to work to plant it with corn, potatoes, wheat, and oats.

In the late summer of 1822 Neil and Lauchlin ventured into Ramsay to survey the situation, and decided on land along the 10th concession about halfway between Shipman's Mills and Norway Pine

Falls. They took up 400 acres of land on lots 22, 24, and 25, and also 19 of the 11th concession. The boys cleared an acre of land on lot 22 and built a shanty. That winter Neil and his sister Flora worked on the new farm. The parents, Lauchlin, and Donald remained on the rented land in Drummond Township. Ague was prevalent and the McDonalds were stricken with it. All recovered except Donald who died from after-affects of fever. Lauchlin died within a fortnight of his brother and the bodies of both were brought 22 miles to Ramsay on the shoulders of friends and interred in a family burying plot on lot 22.

In May 1824 the rest of the McDonald family moved to Ramsay bringing three cows and two pigs. They cleared the land and planted potatoes and wheat, logging the remainder of the clearing and burning great oaks and many fine pine trees.

Next to John McDonald's farm located Alexander McPhail and his wife Catherine on Lot 20. This property is still in the McPhail family. Alex McPhail had come from Argyllshire in 1822. On the back 100 acres of his property located Thomas McLaren, facing the 11th line of Ramsay. Archibald Muir and Archibald Colquhoun shared lot 19. Mr. Colquhoun's dwelling was situated near the 11th line.

The next large influx of settlers to the new district north of the Rideau was that planned and executed by Peter Robinson for the relief of intolerable conditions in Ireland. Many of these also located in Ramsay Township, although much of Ramsay had already been eagerly taken up by the Scottish emigrants.

Most of Robinson's settlers had endured greater poverty than the Scots; they were nearly all Roman Catholic while the Scots were Protestant. In none of the other townships was there such equal distribution of Scots and Irish, and the result was a lively social and political community during the pioneer days.

# CHAPTER VIII

## PETER ROBINSON'S IRISH EMIGRANTS

Political and economic stresses in Ireland following the close of the Napoleonic wars reached a climax in 1821 when the potato crop, main staple for the island, failed. Hundreds of men were idle; the poor were obliged to steal in order to eat; jails were overflowing.

The United Kingdom considered emigration as a possible solution and in 1823 put a scheme for Ireland's overpopulation into action. The Honourable Peter Robinson was entrusted with its superintendence. He had already served as Commissioner of Crown Lands and in succeeding years was to play a large part in settling emigrants successfully in Upper Canada.

Terms and requirements for this emigration scheme differed from those of the Scottish emigrants. The government would pay passage to Canada and conveyance to locations free of charge. Provisions and medical assistance were provided on board ship. Upon arrival in Canada every male over 18 years and under 45 years received a location ticket or order for 70 acres of land. An additional tract of 30 acres adjoining was set aside for each location and could be purchased at the end of 10 years at a nominal sum. Each tract of 70 acres was subject to an annual "Quit Rent" payment to the Crown of 2 pence per acre, to be paid twice yearly. Upon completion of settlement duties patents might be obtained, the settler paying for the expense of preparing them, which presumably would not exceed £2 10 s. on each patent.

This was a selective immigration and not all applicants were accepted. Attention was paid to habits, industry, temperance, and good character, and all successful applicants had to be endorsed by someone who knew their circumstances well. Many came from the estates of the landed gentry and had had experience in small farming. Single men were accepted but no one over 45 years of age.

By the 21st of May the Navy Board had provided troop ships *Hebe* and *Stakesby* for conveyance of some 568 men, women, and children from the Cove of Cork to Quebec. Both ships sailed on July 8th. The *Hebe* arrived at Quebec the end of August, the *Stakesby* on September 2nd. Provisions supplied passengers for the voyage were generous—beef, pork, oatmeal, cocoa, cheese, butter, biscuit, and beverage. Surgeons Dickson and Hamilton from the Royal Navy accompanied the emigrants as far as Fort Wellington. During the crossing four children died aboard the *Hebe* and one woman and four children on the *Stakesby*.

All certificates of passage were produced and given up at Prescott to the office of the Land Board, as a means of identification. Locations were made out, and the emigrant could then be forwarded and placed on his land.

In his report on this first emigration Robinson remarked that his Irish settlers arrived at a time when the country was free of mosquitoes and flies; that they were encamped among settlers of two or three years duration and could see around them the result of pioneering, perseverance, and thrift. He concluded that this would encourage them. He also notes that during his three months in the forest with them there was neither constable nor magistrate closer than 20 miles and that the Irish emigrants obeyed him in everything and were grateful for their removal from Ireland and other blessings.

Of this emigration only 10 were Protestants, the remainder Roman Catholic. Some had been mechanics in Ireland, blacksmiths or tradesmen who perhaps had cultivated an acre or less—a potato garden; others had been weavers or small farmers. Most could read and write and calculate their rations. They were industrious but had been through distressing periods of unemployment.

Robinson set out from Prescott by wagon for the Mississippi River, a distance of 60 miles. Arriving at Shipman's Mills he arranged for a temporary establishment there for his incoming settlers, and a government storehouse or depot to be built for provisions and tools. At Perth a Land Board under Major Powell was set up.

Almost all of Robinson's settlers located in Ramsay and Pakenham. Along the east side of the Mississippi River in Ramsay, Garnet Nagle took up land near the 10th line in the vicinity of Norway Pine Falls. Gerald Nagle settled across the Mississippi almost opposite Garnet's property. Thomas Stevenson and his son Walter also located on the 10th line, as did William Leahie. Along the 11th line were

William Barry and sons, Richard and James, and John Ruby. Between Shipman's Mills and Morphy's Falls were Dennis Galvin, William Hickey, Thomas O'Brien, Morris Bristnahan, John Curran, Garnet Dulmage, James Flynn, Francis Jessop, John Leahie, Jerome Mullane, Robert Armstrong, Patrick Ryan, John Benson, Robert D. Smithinch, John Thomson, Morris Buckley, John Young, Matthew Tierney, and the Teskeys on the 10th, 11th, and 12th concessions.

The others were scattered throughout the township: James and William Brown, Edmond and John Barry, Pat and Tim Buckley, John Coghlin, Florence Carey, Michael Corkery, Michael Donegan, John Dilohary, George Dooley, Patrick Dahill, William Drake, Patrick Donaghue, Patrick Foley, James Rea, William Gubbins, Patrick Haley, Michael McGaran, Thomas Hennissy, John Kinney, Chris Kelly, Patrick Lynch, John Mara, Bartholomew Murphy, Charles McCarty, Thomas Madden, Michael Reilly, John and Timothy O'Brien, Martin and Dan Ryan, Sam Regan, Bryan Ruby, Patrick Rourke, Cornelius Ryan, James Roche, Jr., Tim Sheehan, Timothy Rahilly, Denis Sweany, John Phelan, Richard Wynn, David Ward, Timothy Quinn, James Sullivan, Michael Regan. Of these thirty-four left their land without fulfilling settlement duties and receiving their patents.

John Teskey, Sr., with his wife and eight children, had come from Rathkeale in Limerick to take up land on lot 7 of the 11th concession of Ramsay, his land adjoining that of his son, John Jr.; and his son Robert located on lot 8. Across the concession line from the Teskeys was John Benson (lot 7, concession 10). Other neighbours were Scotsmen, Duncan McGregor and Alex Duncan on lot 6, 11th concession. Joseph Teskey, the eldest son of John, located near Appletree Falls on lot 4 of the 10th concession. Joseph was 24 years of age and with his brothers Robert (22) and John (20) built a small saw and grist mill at the falls. For the next 30 years the hamlet which grew up there was known as *Teskeyville.* By the mid 1850s the village contained Joseph Teskey's grist mill, Robert Teskey's saw mill and Albert Teskey's general store and post office. The old Teskey home on the east side of the river is still standing and in good condition, one of the best remaining models of architecture of that period. The mills were later sold to the Brown Company who resold them to Thomas Boyd Caldwell of Lanark. The Teskey family were one of the few Protestant Irish families to emigrate under Peter Robinson's plan. Another Protestant was Patrick Lynch who located on lot 8 of the 3rd con-

Sketch by the author

TESKEY HOME, APPLETON
Erected about 1830.

cession. He died in 1876 and was buried at the Anglican Cemetery just outside Carleton Place.

Robinson assisted his settlers in putting up log shanties on each lot and getting them settled for their first winter in 1823. A storehouse had been erected at Shipman's Mills to hold rations, medicines, and tools, and each family was provided with a cow. Major Powell's report in the Crown Land Papers indicates that each family also received two bolts of cotton serge and flannel, and leather for repairing their shoes or mocassins. Robinson remarks that the Irishmen were quite unaccustomed to the use of an axe and had to be assisted in getting dwellings erected.

Pakenham Township already had a few settlers before Peter Robinson's arrived, although survey of the township was not completed until 1822 or 1823.

A son of Lanark Society settler William Lindsay, Alexander Lindsay, had located with his wife on lot 2, concession 8 along the 9th line of Pakenham in 1821. John Lindsay, a brother emigrated at the same time and took up the east half of lot 4, concession 8, which he purchased from Jonas Jones, a magistrate and large landowner of Brockville. John Lindsay built a fine stone house, still standing and in good condition and typical of the better houses of the period. Thomas Bowes, whose parents had settled in Ramsay, also took up land in Pakenham, by permission of the Land Board, next to John Lindsay on lot 4, concession 8. He married Janet Dick, daughter of another emigrant of 1821.

Early in the summer of 1823 James Harvey came from Brockville, travelling by water along the Mississippi to the "Little Falls" where Pakenham Village was later to grow. Here, in partnership with John Powell, son of J. H. Powell of the Bathurst District Land Board at Perth, he cleared land, erected a shanty, and saw mill and potash works. Another settler, Hume, came about the same time to set up a store near the mill, stocking it with general basic merchandise. Their stock came over bush trails from Brockville via Perth or from Montreal up the Ottawa River to Fitzroy Harbour. The partners later added a grist mill to their enterprises.

In 1823 Irish settlers from the *Hebe* and *Stakesby* arrived. These included: John Ahern, Thomas Boyle, Denis Clahan, Timothy Clahan, Annever Cusick, Dennis Daley, John Dohorthy, Morris Fitzgerald, John French, Busted Green, George Green, John Green, Sr., John Green, Jr., Thomas Green, William Green, Michael Gregg, William Gregg, George Hanniver, Timothy Kennedy, William Lahie, Michael Lynch, Henry Mahony, James Mantle, Cornelius Roche, James Sayward, Denis Shanahan, Patrick Slattery, John Sullivan, Patrick Sullivan.*

John Mantle, father of James Mantle, was assigned land in Huntley Township, but later moved into Pakenham Township. According to some records James Sayward was issued land in Lanark Township, and earned his living as a shoemaker in Perth, but apparently he returned to his land near Pakenham for he was granted a deed in 1836.

Cornelius Roche, credited with occupying lot 10 of the 9th concession near Pakenham Village, appears to have shortly moved to Shipman's Mills in Ramsay where he set up a blacksmith shop. It was almost demolished during the Ballygibblin riots there. Robinson's report for 1826 indicates that Roche had by then departed for Montreal where he again took up his trade as blacksmith.

* Locations of these settlers are given in detail in *Pakenham 1823-1860* by Verna Ross McGiffin (Mississippi Publishers, Pakenham, 1963).

A few of Peter Robinson's 1823 settlers located in other townships: Jeremiah Abbot (lot 9, concession 12), John Roche (lot 16, concession 9), and Robert Shea (lot 15, concession 11) in Lanark Township. In Darling, Edmond Barry, Sr., took up lot 1 of concession 3, and Timothy O'Brien, lot 4 of concession 2. Michael Nagle settled in Bathurst Township on lot 19 of the 5th concession, and Beckwith Township acquired David Dooland (lot 23, concession 12), Edmond Dooland (lot 24, concession 12) and Timothy Mann (lot 23, concession 12).

Peter Robinson remained at Shipman's Mills for three months, then departed leaving Thomas Bain as clerk of stores at the supply depot. On December 6th Robinson went to York and then sailed for England. Bains later hired one of the emigrants, Leahie, as assistant.

With Robinson's departure some of the restraint was removed from the settlement and scenes of drunkenness and disturbance occurred at Shipman's Mills. An Orange Lodge was organized in 1824 at Perth and this did nothing to improve feelings between Irish and Scotch. Mr. Shipman himself was a strong Orangeman which did not enhance his position amid the newcomers.

The Scottish settlers looked upon the immigrant Irish with some jealousy, for not only had their way been paid to the new land by the government, but a more liberal supply of rations and other necessities had been given to them. Also the Irish were coming to a land partially settled and had neighbours to assist in clearing and cultivating the land. The hardships the first pioneers had endured had greatly diminished with clearance of land and establishment of forest trails. It seemed unfair that the government should be more generous toward the later emigrants.

Morphy's Falls at this time was already a village and a Protestant stronghold. On April 23rd, 1824, according to the rule and practice of the time, settlers in Ramsay, Beckwith, Goulbourn, and Huntley were called out to a general muster parade; and the newcomers from Ireland were also included in this call. The day coincided with the birthday of King George IV. The parade was held on the north side of the river, close to the groggery of Alexander Morris at Morphy's Falls. Local militia Captains Thomas Glendinning, William Moore, Duncan Fisher, and Dr. George Nesbit, all of Beckwith Township, and Lieutenant-Colonel Ulysses Fitzmaurice of Drummond Township were in charge.

Nothing might have occurred if Captain Glendinning of the 4th

Carleton Militia had not ordered the drinking of the King's health in the tavern afterward. The Scottish settlers first flocked into the tavern. Meanwhile the Irish "Ballygibblins", as they called themselves, led by Bart Murphy, had formed their own division outside and went in to drink, too. Rioting and skirmishes followed. Glendinning and Fitzmaurice had already left the inn to dine at the home of William Loucks in the village. Dr. Nesbit, a Franktown physician, collected them and all three went to investigate. John Nowlan of Franktown, in a later statement, reported he saw an Irish settler (not one of Robinson's nor a Catholic) seize Glendinning by the collar and call him a scoundrel, adding that he ought to encourage peaceful behaviour among the settlers rather than quarrelling and fighting, and although Glendinning was a tall man and the settler a short one, that he would gladly fight him.

Fitzmaurice intervened in this fracas but he also admonished Glendinning for encouraging battle. The Irish shortly retreated across the river, for there were only about six Ballygibblins to 20 Scots. Peace was temporarily restored, Nowlan ferrying the Ballygibblins across the river by canoe. The Irish, however, later returned with reinforcements, broke down the door of the groggery, and were fired on by John Fummerton from inside, two of the Irish being wounded.

Alexander Morris, the proprietor, departed for Perth that very evening. The next day, April 24th, about 20 Ramsay Irish crossed the river to Morphy's Falls and waited for Glendinning outside William Louck's store. Some of the settlers went inside searching for Glendinning, found him upstairs, and knocked him down with a club. Having satisfied their anger, they departed. The next day was Sunday, a day of truce, but on Monday a larger party of Ramsay settlers, possibly 100, marched to Morphy's Falls behind a leader carrying a large green flag for Ireland; all were armed with either guns or bludgeons. They crossed the river to Glen Isle and stormed up to Glendinning's house, allegedly to invite him to fight a duel with one of their party named Sullivan.

When they forced their way into the house they found only his wife and daughter, for Glendinning was hiding in a secret alcove behind a sliding panel in his living room. The Ballygibblins then proceeded to Morphy's Falls and ransacked Morris' tavern. Apparently another skirmish took place on the 7th line of Ramsay just outside Morphy's Falls.*

* Glendinning's house is still standing and in use as a dwelling on Glen Isle.

News of the riots had reached Perth by this time and Sheriff Powell, although ill, appointed a deputy who collected volunteers to send to Ramsay, arming them with equipment from the government storehouse. Three magistrates, William Marshall, Dr. Thom, and Henry Graham, accompanied this formidable force to Ramsay. They arrived at Shipman's Mills on the following Sunday when the Irish Catholics had assembled for Mass by the river.

It is not known who the Deputy Sheriff was, but a later government investigator called him a "poor choice" to lead any peacemaking force since he was a rabid Orangeman and a man of "overbearing and insolent conduct", whose father, it had been said, was murdered by Catholics in Ireland.*

Toronto Public Library

THE HONOURABLE
PETER ROBINSON

In any case the Deputy Sheriff ignored the advice of his magistrates and sent part of his party directly to the government storehouse, and the remainder to the blacksmith shop of Irish settler Cornelius Roche, where some of the Ballygibblins were accustomed to congregating. Someone inside the blacksmith shop fired upon the approaching armed party, wounding a constable. The Deputy's men returned fire, killing one Irishman and wounding two others inside.

* See Montreal *Herald*, September 8, 1824.

When the rest of the Deputy's men arrived at the depot armed the remaining Irish fled to the river. Ten Irishmen were arrested and carried off to the Perth jail. Fines were imposed for assault and for rioting. No mention was made at Perth that the Deputy's men had torn the roof from the blacksmith shop of Cornelius Roche and wrecked the building for no good reason.

The Irishmen were tried before Perth magistrates and fines of £10 imposed on John Coghlin, John French, Bart Murphy, and Patrick Sullivan, plus a sentence of two months' imprisonment. Those convicted were incapable of paying fines, and their releases were authorized before the end of the terms of imprisonment. Murphy and French left the settlement and drowned accidentally a year later at Kingston.

The Lieutenant-Governor ordered an investigation, which was conducted by Colonel James Fitzgibbon, Assistant Adjutant General of Militia. Fitzgibbon, himself an Irishman from the south of Ireland whose father had been scholarly but poor, had considerable sympathy for the trials of his fellow countrymen in the new land. In his report Fitzgibbon said:

> . . . for the cruel conduct of the men who attacked Roche's house, in beating and wounding people they found there, I can find no apology whatever. . . . Throughout the inquiry of all that happened on that day, I watched carefully to see if any English or Scotchman of the deputy sheriff's party had committed any violence upon the new settlers, and it is with great satisfaction I report to you that not a single instance of such has happened throughout the whole enquiry. All the deeds of violence have appeared in every instance to have been committed by Orangemen.*

Mr. Shipman of Shipman's Mills was much afraid for his life and the safety of his mills following this incident, for it was well known that he was an Orangeman. The Rev. William Bell, commenting on Orangemen, remarked: "[They] have not only disturbed the peace of Ireland but of every place where they have come, all over the world", and he had little sympathy with their militancy in the new settlement.†

In the trials following, Justice Campbell, presiding over the court at Perth, indicated his expectation that henceforth settlers for whom much had been done should be loyal and law-abiding, and that peace officers should not exceed or abuse their powers.

* See Haydon, *Pioneer Sketches in the District of Bathurst.*
† Bell, Journals.

Courtesy Kenneth W. Johnson

ORANGE PARADE, MILL STREET, ALMONTE

Glendinning and John Fummerton, charged with malicious shooting, were acquitted. Glendinning, an Englishman about 28 years of age, had been a lieutenant in the 60th Foot Regiment and had retired on half-pay from the Army, and settled in Beckwith in 1821, where he was granted a large part of Glen Isle in the Mississippi River near Morphy's Falls. Here he had built a limestone and field-stone house in 1823. He had married a high-born Englishwoman named Jane Hill, who died, apparently of a broken heart in the lonely wilderness, in 1842. She and their daughter Amelia are buried somewhere in the field behind the barn.* Glendinning later moved to Chatham.

A few more Irish Catholic settlers came out on the Peterborough emigration of Peter Robinson in 1825: Timothy Callahan (con. 1, lot 5), Dan Connor (con. 10, lot 13), Thomas Nelligan (con. 10, lot 22), John Galvin (con. 11, lot 10), Tim Connor (con. 11, lot 11), in Ramsay Township. Only Nelligan of this group stayed on his land.

Bartholomew Murphy, leader of the Ballygibblins, left his land on the Perth road in the Wolf's Grove area, and Michael Foley from County Carlow, Ireland, took his place (con. 6, lot 13. Michael Foley was a graduate of Trinity College in Dublin and was 29 when

* Former Carleton Place resident, author Douglas Findlay of Ottawa, wrote a novel on this family entitled *Search for Amelia.*

he came to Upper Canada. In the woods of Wolf's Grove he built a home to which poets, artists, and politicians from the United States as well as Canada came in later years. Michael Corkery, one of the 1823 settlers, who located on lot 10 of the 3rd concession of Ramsay, mentions Foley's parents in a letter to the Old Country in 1825. Apparently they were expected to come out with Robinson's emigration of 1825 but did not arrive. Mr. Corkery's letter was addressed to "Honourable Peter Robinson, Superintendent of Irish Emigrants, York or Elsewhere":

> We congratulate you on your safe arrival with all those under your patronage . . . we are doing very well, thank God, and enjoy good health. My daughter is married to an old settler in Lanark but we have got a young son as an increase which makes up the number. We had a good crop last year out of which we sold Mr. Bain six barrels of flour but my eldest's daughter's illness together with buying clothes and necessities for winter prevented me buying a yoke of oxen which are indispensably necessary on a farm. We have a good crop this year also, out of which I expect I can sell about 24 barrels of flour and 100 bushels of potatoes; but as I have no market convenient, nor oxen to convey it, where there is a market, I don't know how to manage. Now as there are some of your later settlers convenient to me who will, no doubt, be supplied with rations, if you would be so good as to cause the above-mentioned flour and potatoes to be bought for them of me, it would favour me to the extreme and enable me to buy a yoke of oxen and other necessaries. . . . My son-in-law, Michael Foley, who you may recollect gave you some trifling money for his father and mother which expected would come out under your banner—you will recollect on the day you were going away at Colonel Powell's Perth—he has got no account from them this year and as they did not come out with you, he is uneasy to know whether they presented themselves, or perhaps you might have a letter from them. If convenient, read a few lines in answer to me. You may direct to Rev. John McDonald, for Michael Corkery, or to Mr. Ben Delisle.
>
> Your obedient servant,
> Michael Corkery.

Michael Corkery's homestead was birthplace of Canon Corkery, curate of the parishes of Huntley and Pakenham for many years.

One of Robinson's emigrants who settled in Pakenham Township, John Dohorthy was confined to the Perth jail in 1825 for "maliciously maiming a cow". A death sentence had been passed by the jury, for in those days the property of others was deemed more important than a man's life. The sentence was passed in August* and in September Mrs. Dohorthy sent a petition to the Lieutenant-Governor, Sir Peregrine Maitland, asking for pardon of the prisoner. Rev. William Bell recorded in his Journals that Dohorthy later escaped from the jail into the woods one frosty evening just before dark. He was wearing no boots when he escaped and before morning his feet were frozen, with the result that he lost all his toes. Perhaps this was considered sufficient punishment by the magistrates at Perth, for records show that he was granted the deed for his land in Pakenham Township in 1826.

Potatoes and turnips were the largest crops produced by the Irish settlers. By 1826 there were only 91 acres cleared of all the land taken up by Robinson's settlers in Pakenham. Considerable lot-trading went on, but many settlers finally had to come to terms with the land and recognize it for what it was—largely unfit for farming. In Pakenham only eighteen of the original settlers remained—the Greens, Boyles, Clahans, Greggs, Mantles, John Dohorthy, George Hanniver, Henry Mahony, and Dennis Shanahan. Of these, the Clahans later left for the United States, the Boyles and Mantles moved to Huntley, Henry Mahony went to Montreal, and the Greggs vanished from the scene.

In the spring of 1826 Peter Robinson sent a return of his emigrants to the Lieutenant-Governor of Upper Canada for the Earl of Bathurst. It showed that as of March that year the following vital statistics† applied to his settlement of Irish emigrants:

| *Township* | *No. of Souls* | *Births* | *Deaths* | *Acres Cleared* | *Bush. of Potatoes* | *Bush. of Grain* | *Bu. of Turnips* |
|---|---|---|---|---|---|---|---|
| Ramsay | 251 | 31 | 11 | 430½ | 3318 | 13130 | 7950 |
| Huntley | 79 | 15 | 7 | 116½ | 469 | 3832 | 1430 |
| Goulbourn | 59 | 2 | — | 96 | 492 | 2307 | 829 |
| Pakenham | 56 | 10 | 2 | 91 | 195 | 1100 | 486 |
| Beckwith | 18 | 1 | — | 26 | 192 | 600 | 150 |
| Lanark | 6 | 2 | — | 10 | 60 | 100 | 200 |
| Bathurst | 8 | 2 | — | 8 | 100 | 400 | 170 |
| Total | 477 | 63 | 20 | 778 | 4826 | 21469 | 11145 |

Total number of Irish emigrants located in the District of Bathurst, in 1823, under the superintendence of Peter Robinson, Esquire—heads of families .......... 182

* Dominion Archives, *Journal of House of Assembly of Upper Canada, 1826-27*, Appendix.

† Haydon, *Pioneer Sketches in the District of Bathurst.*

Present state of settlement:

| | | |
|---|---|---|
| Heads of families now living on their lands | 120 | |
| Locations vacated by deaths | 8 | |
| " " absent without leave, but supposed to be in Canada | 12 | |
| " " gone to United States | 9 | |
| " " absent, but at work in Canada | 32 | |
| " " absent, returned to Ireland | 1 | |
| | 182 | 182 |

There were already Irish Catholic families in the township of Huntley, bordering on Ramsay and Pakenham, and some of these had come from the Richmond settlement. More settlers arrived in Huntley, and Peter Robinson later set aside a lot on the 8th concession for a church to look after the spiritual requirements of his Irish Catholic settlers in both Huntley and Ramsay townships. St. Michael's church was not built, however, until 1837.

During the 1840s a great many more Irish arrived, settling along the Rideau in Montague and North Elmsley townships. An emigration agent's report for the latter part of May 1841 noted among other things "a large number of emigrants from Belfast and other ports in the north of Ireland are going to settle in the Bathurst and Johnstown Districts".*

This immigration trend continued throughout the '40s. Irish names first appearing in the Assessment Roll for Montague in 1841 include: Stephen Brannich, William McGragh, Prosper Denning, Michael Dillebough, Alex, Wm. and Malcolm Condie, James Carr, Serrah Rockey, Patrick Halpen, Martin Larkin, Robt. and Wm. Carter, Patrick Reel, Pat Driscoe, Thomas Dillon, Patrick McAnna, Pat Conlin, Andrew and Thos. Crozeir, Alex Kinninmonth, David Loughran, Thomas Keys. The Assessment Roll of 1841 for Elmsley included: Dan Carrol, John, Pat, Thos. and Michel Kelly, Sam Boyle, Pat King, Robert McClearon, Thos. and Wm. Dudgeon, John Couch, James Moore, William Diemond, Charles O'Hara, Wm. and Pat Develon, Peter Levi, William O'Nealy, John Morin, Laughlan Arthur, Wm. and Joseph Cosgrove, Thomas Mobray, Henry Cullens, Patrick Gilhully, Sanford Dickory, Alex. and Patrick Jordan, William Becket, Richard Chacklan, William Sweney, John Shay, John Garvin, James Finne.

* *Annual Report of Agents for Emigration in Canada for 1841* (London, 1842).

## CHAPTER IX

## THE McNAB LEGEND

At the same time as Peter Robinson's Irish settlers were spreading out into Pakenham, Ramsay, and Huntley, a Scottish chieftain was attempting to set up a feudal state to the northwest and there establish himself as lord of all he surveyed, extracting payment in goods from the settlers on his land as his forefathers had in the "auld" land.

Archibald McNab, last chieftain of the McNabs, had fled his father's estate at Kennell on the banks of Loch Tay in Scotland, to take refuge in Upper Canada with his cousin, the last Buchanan of the ancient house of Arnprior.

McNab's estate in Scotland was mortgaged to the Earl of Breadalbane, and to escape his debts McNab secretly set sail from Dundee for Canada along with Peter McIntyre. Arriving in Montreal he proceeded to Glengarry and thence to York to negotiate with the government for land along the Ottawa River to which he might bring clansmen from Scotland as settlers.

Sherwood, the Chief Surveyor, had recently completed a survey of a township bordering Fitzroy on the Ottawa. McNab, without seeing this land, eagerly accepted it and agreed to the government terms to settle it with his clansmen as in the Glengarry highland settlement along the St. Lawrence River. The latter establishment had already shown itself loyal to the Crown, and no doubt the same strong loyalty could be expected from McNab's settlement. He was given the land for 18 months, at the end of which time the government representative would make a survey to determine how the settlement was working out.

McNab had the power to assign up to 100 acres to any family. He himself was granted 1200 acres which would be increased upon completion of settlement terms. The settlers were to pay McNab interest on any money expended for their needs. Sherwood, the surveyor, had first choice of land in the township in payment for his services, but the remainder was entirely in McNab's hands. In 1824 McNab wrote to Dr. Hamilton in Scotland requesting 20 families. He was to meet them at Montreal and conduct them to their new land.

By January 1825 heads of families signing the bond prepared by the Canadian Attorney-General were: James Carmichael, Peter Campbell, Donald Fisher, Peter Drummond, James Robertson, Alex. McNab, James McFarlane, Duncan Campbell, James McDonald, Donald McNaughton, John McDermid, John McIntyre, Peter McIntyre, Donald McIntyre, James McLaurin, Peter MacMillan, James Storie, James McFarlen, Alexander Miller, Malcolm McLaren, and Colin McCaul.

In April the McNab settlers, 84 in number, embarked at Greenock aboard the *Niagara.* At Montreal McNab and his piper, James McNee, met them. They boarded *bateaux* at Lachine and three days later arrived at Point Fortune. One McLachlin took the contract for bringing their baggage to Hawkesbury on oxcarts and sleds; the settlers walked. At Hawkesbury they took the steamboat *Union* and sailed for Hull. After travelling two days and two nights they reached Chats Lake (now Fitzroy Harbour), where they disembarked and proceeded through the woods. The journey from Montreal to McNab's settlement took 28 days. The newcomers pitched camp at the present Arnprior steamboat landing.

Sketch by the author

THE McNAB

Willis, *Canadian Scenery* W. H. Bartlett

PORTAGE AT CHATS LAKE, 1839

They had been told that the Chief would supply them with a year's provisions but soon found he could not even give them the bare necessities of life. Some after locating on their land were forced to go to work in neighbouring townships in order to earn provisions. Thomas Burns in Fitzroy hired a few of them for harvesting, haying, and potato digging; others went as far as Beckwith Township to work, buying food on credit there.

There were no roads. A pathway through the forest led from Snedden's Inn in Ramsay to Morphy's Falls in Beckwith, but the journey from Ramsay to McNab (as the Chief had named his township) was entirely by water—down the Mississippi to its mouth, up Chats Lake to the mouth of the Madawaska River, and up the Madawaska to the Flat Rapids settlement. Canoes and boats roughly knocked together brought small loads of supplies from Morphy's Falls, and they were carried on the settlers' backs from Beckwith to Snedden's. For the first three years of settlement the newcomers were continually occupied with this arduous method of obtaining supplies.

It was not long before the Chief's malpractices became evident. As early as September 1825, a few months after the arrival of his first settlers, he was being sued by Harvey & Powell, the mill owners at Pakenham, for non-payment of supplies bought and money loaned.

Documents and letters extant in in the Perth Museum reveal that as early as February and April of 1825 McNab was already in financial difficulties and trying to placate his creditors. Other records reveal that the Chief was a regular visitor to the Perth courthouse until his departure from the district in 1842.

It is small wonder that his subjects were continually hounded and enslaved in the interest of refurbishing his lost fortunes. The hardships of the McNab settlers far outweighed those of all the other emigrants, for they were kept in a kind of serfdom, having no rights of their own nor any government authority to appeal to. There were tales of women and children kept alive on a diet of potatoes alone with a little salt, while the men worked outside the township. Settlers had to ask the Chief's permission to take such work and it was not always given. So bad had been their lot in Scotland, however, that the clansmen conformed to the situation almost to a man. Alex Miller, a school teacher, seems to have been the one exception.

It was understood that all the timber in the new township belonged to McNab, but Miller, believing this incorrect, sold some from his location to a lumberman, John Brill. Due to McNab's influence with the governing powers at the time, Brill was forced to pay duty on all the timber he had cut in the township. In 1826 Miller asked permission of the Chief to work in another township in order to provide food for his family. Because of his previous disobedience over the timber dispute his request was refused, and this began a series of persecutions which lasted for 16 years before justice finally caught up with McNab.

Miller had provisions for his family sufficient to last only six weeks and no way of earning more, so he left the township, was arrested *a capias* by order of the Laird for a debt of £80, and taken to the Perth jail. These were Family Compact days when a person could be arrested for debts of 40s. and kept in prison for months without redress.

It was six weeks before the other settlers learned of Miller's fate, but when they did five men travelled the 60 miles through the forest on foot to Perth to stand bail. These were: John McIntyre, James McFarlane, Peter McIntyre, Donald McNaughton, James McDonald. Miller was freed. The settlers engaged lawyer James Boulton to defend Miller. Boulton, brought up in a Family Compact household in York, undoubtedly had more sympathy for the ruling class than for their opponents. The settlers had to pay £50 each to secure Miller's release. He left the township and taught school in Beckwith for many years.

In 1827 McNab wrote to Lord Hamilton in Scotland asking for more settlers, but was refused point blank, for reports and rumours of his actions had filtered back to the old country. Perplexed, he went to Montreal, met some recent arrivals, regaled them with charming tales, and induced the Hamiltons, Wilsons, and David Airth to locate in his township at the rate of one-half bushel of wheat per acre to be paid him and his successors *forever*!

When McNab went to Montreal or York, he always gave lavish parties and entertained in the grand manner from his timber income. And at his home on the Madawaska, Kennell Lodge, he was the proverbial host but never forgave an injury, whether fancied or real. It is recorded that there was little love lost between the Chief and another famous McNab, Sir Allan MacNab of Hamilton. The Laird was accustomed to signing the guest book of any lodging where he might spend the night simply as "The McNab". Visiting Hamilton, the Chief registered that way at the local hotel. Sir Allan MacNab happened to come in later and seeing the entry in the register, wrote his name below it as "The Other MacNab".

In 1831 the Chief persuaded Messrs. George and Andrew Buchanan to come from Montreal to McNab and establish a grist mill. A large dam was put across the Madawaska and the mill built on a small island where a bridge now stands. A saw mill on the east side of the river was completed by 1833 and saw logs driven down the Ottawa. The village boomed. Andrew Buchanan became Justice of the Peace and performed marriages during McNab's absence. Eventually the settlement became known as Arnprior, after the prior of Arn in Scotland where the head of the Buchanan clan resided.

During these years McNab continued his persecutions, and the settlers from time to time drew up petitions and complaints which they sent to public bodies. However, since McNab was a strong Family Compact supporter, not even the Hon. William Morris at Perth was willing to take the word of the settlers against the Chief.

In 1835 McNab engaged in a lawsuit with George Buchanan, and in 1836 the Buchanan business enterprises failed, the whole estate including the grist and saw mills being handed over to Messrs. Gould, Simpson, and Mittleberger of Smiths Falls. Jason Gould took over the little steamship left by the firm, the *George Buchanan*, and ran a regular transport service from Chats Lake to the Cheneux Rapids near Portage du Fort on the Ottawa.

At Perth when the Rebellion of 1837 broke out, Rev. William Bell's son John assumed command of the Leeds Militia and proceeded to Kingston, while in the northern sector of the District, The Laird of McNab, having volunteered his services to the Lieutenant-Governor, was asked to take command. He was appointed Laird Colonel of the 20th Battalion of Carleton Light Infantry, "comprising the townships of McNab, Fitzroy, and Pakenham, with instructions to nominate his officers, forward the list to headquarters, and call the regiment out to muster forthwith".*

On the 25th December, 1837 the whole regiment mustered at Pakenham and were placed under militia law. McNab made a speech, read the names of officers, and gave a general order that they were to muster by companies near the homes of their captains. Settlers from the above-named townships of Pakenham and Fitzroy volunteered, but McNab's own clansmen refused to serve under the Chief and sent a petition to Sir Francis Bond Head declaring themselves true and loyal subjects but pointing out the abuses they had suffered from the Laird under civil law and that they feared to serve him under a more severe martial law.

The Rebellion, however, was quelled before any action was necessary concerning the local rebels. Yet they did not get off Scot free. Trouble broke out along the St. Lawrence River when an American organization called the Hunters' Lodge attacked Prescott under Von Schoultz in November 1838.

Again the Bathurst Militia was called out. Nine hundred assembled at Pakenham, but again the McNab settlers refused to serve under their Chief. Fraser recounts:

> The poor settlers were looked upon by the ultra loyal as rebels, not only to their Chief but to the government; and to punish them severely was now the object of the Irishmen of Pakenham and Fitzroy. Although they numerically surpassed the McNab settlers about five to one, the Highlanders fought bravely. They were compelled to retreat to Mrs. McFarlane's old house, in which they defended themselves with the utmost resolution. Frying-pans, pokers, tongs, kettles, brooms, and every article of any solidity, were used as weapons of war. The fight lasted till night when both parties became tired of the contest; some ugly wounds were given and received; and a man of the name of Porter was so badly injured that he died in ten days after-

* Alexander Fraser, *The Last Laird of McNab* (1899).

> wards. News reached Pakenham that night that the rebels were totally discomfitted, and that Von Schoultz and most of his gang were taken prisoners.

Thus terminated the battle of Pakenham.

The numerous petitions forwarded to the government had made some impact on Lord Durham when he was investigating the affairs of the province. Francis Allan, appointed Crown Lands Agent at Perth in 1837, had been instructed to visit every settler in McNab Township and make a thorough report concerning the practices of McNab toward his tenants. Allan was thorough and business-like and not influenced by the lavish hospitality he encountered at Kennell Lodge. He took four months on his survey and produced a report which plainly showed the tyranny of the Laird. Allan indicated that McNab could not show on paper one shilling he had laid out on behalf of his settlers. The roads in the township, he said, were in such a miserable condition that horses were wading to their knees every few yards in certain places. All the settlers' charges against McNab were shown true by the report which was published and placed in the government archives. It was also published by the Honourable Francis Hincks in his newspaper, the *Examiner* in Toronto, and brought lawsuits from the Laird. The government stepped in, and McNab, seeing his power slipping, offered to sell his land (already sold and rented by him several times over to others!) to the government for £9,000. They offered him £4000 and the final sum agreed upon was £2500.

The feud between McNab and the settlers still continued, although the government proceeded to adjust the settlers' claims and issue Crown grants removing the Laird's feudal power. McNab moved from Arnprior to White Lake. The acts of revenge which he committed are too many to be told here but he finally overstepped his rights by stopping the flow of water to a grist mill belonging to John Paris. McNab not only added to a dam above the mill, stopping the flow of water, but he also started to build a grist mill of his own on the public highway for no apparent reason. The settlers raised enough money to send John Paris to Perth, where he found a lawyer who seized upon a situation where McNab could at last be prosecuted. McNab was charged with creating a "public nuisance" by blocking Her Majesty's highway, since a road had to be built around his grist mill. W. O. Buell, the Perth prosecuting attorney, won the case for his client in 1843 and McNab was fined. The settlers tore down his mill. His fortunes were on a downward trend, and although he continued to sue his former serfs from time to time he lost most of the lawsuits. Perhaps it was his damaged pride which eventually freed the settlers from his acts of revenge. He left the township, going first to Hamilton, where he rented a cottage from Sir Allan MacNab for a short time, thence to the Orkney Islands. He died in 1860 in Lanion, a small fishing village in France.

After he left the township, settlers flocked in and municipal government began to take shape. Roads and bridges, denied improvement before, were altered, and additional ones built, helping further settlement in Pakenham and adjoining townships.

The wilderness cutting Renfrew County off from Lanark was opened up, an immense benefit for both counties; for the lumbering era with its steady traffic to the shanties in both counties was steadily increasing.

Public Archives of Canada

HOME OF THE McNAB, NEAR WHITE LAKE VILLAGE

The headquarters of the Scot who sought to transplant in his own interest the clan system to the Upper Ottawa. The building was dynamited in the 1930s by the female owner who considered herself pestered by historical society members who sought to preserve it.

## CHAPTER X

# DEVELOPMENTS IN LAND SETTLEMENT AND COMMUNICATIONS

In 1826 John Galt, an enterprising Scottish novelist and philanthropist, founded a real estate company known as the Canada Company, later incorporated under the provisions of an Act of Parliament.

The Canada Company contracted to purchase Crown reserves and other land in Upper Canada for the purpose of opening up the country. Some 1,200,000 acres of detached lots, sometimes just separate farms generally containing 200 acres, were bought in this way. Under terms of the contract, the Company were not to sell to anyone suspected of being a speculator, but rather to induce industrious farming immigrants to settle on the land. Special allowances were advanced to settlers for each payment. A title or deed was granted as soon as one-half the purchase price had been paid, and a mortgage was allowed for the remainder.

One of the first acquisitions by the Company was the Huron Tract from Guelph to Goderich, bought at a bargain price from the Crown but under condition that the Company build roads, bridges, schools, and churches and settle the region. The Canada Company also included in its purchases land in the District of Bathurst, advertising its attractive terms in newspapers such as the *Bathurst Courier* regularly. In this way new settlers were attracted to Lanark County. A typical advertisement from the *Courier* reads:

> Lots from 100 to 200 acres each, scattered throughout Bathurst, Beckwith, Burgess, Dalhousie, Darling, Drummond, Horton, Lanark, Montague, Packenham, most of them surrounded by old settlements. By this arrangement the Company dispose of their lands by way of lease, for a term of 10 years, . . . rents payable the first of February in each year, being less than the interest upon the price.

The settler could lease his land for ten years, and at any time pay

Willis, *Canadian Scenery* W. H. Bartlett

LONG SAULT RAPIDS ON THE ST. LAWRENCE, 1839

Archives of Ontario Thomas Burrowes

BLOCKHOUSE AND LOCK AT THE NARROWS, RIDEAU LAKE

cash and become owner. In the interest of the settlers the Canada Company arranged facilities called "Settlers Provident or Savings Bank Account", into which purchasers could deposit money until they had accumulated enough for the cash payment.

Meanwhile the government of Upper Canada was concerned with communications difficulties, both in the interest of progress and because of the still-present American threat from below the border. The Long Sault Rapids in the St. Lawrence was still a hazard to traffic inland, and the St. Lawrence was highly vulnerable to American attack. It was thought prudent, consequently, to have an alternate route for transporting supplies and men to Upper Canada from Montreal.

Colonel John By, an Army engineer, was put in charge of building a canal linking the Rideau lakes and rivers with the Ottawa River, providing a rear route to Lake Ontario and York from Montreal, and linking the strong military fort at Kingston with Lower Canada. This would offer as well a safe route, and one more economical for transporting heavy artillery than by means of the cumbersome Durham boats along the St. Lawrence.

Colonel John By landed in Canada in May 1826 with instructions to complete a waterway having a uniform depth of five feet from the Ottawa River to Kingston. In less than six years he had completed what could be regarded as one of the great engineering feats of the 19th Century—built as it was through virgin forests and untamed rivers, and with such materials as could be found locally from the woods and quarries. In the hot, humid swamps of the Rideau Lakes many workmen died of fever in summer or the extreme cold in winter. On the site of present-day Ottawa there were only one or two small clearings by 1826.

From the Falls at the Ottawa River as far as the present Hogg's Back Rapids, the Rideau was almost impassable. It took the Clerk of Works, John Mactaggart, five days to get from the banks of the Ottawa to Dows Great Swamp. Rough water continued from Hogg's Back to Black Rapids, and from the Long Island sector for four miles; thence there were 23 miles of still water and three small settlements at Burritts Rapids, Nicholson's Rapids, and Merrick Mills. A limestone quarry owned by James Clowes was in operation at Merrick Mills. Small settlements existed along the river at Maitlands Rapids, Edmunds, and Slys. There were no clearings and the river banks were low and swampy.

Just beyond Slys the river dropped 35 feet in 100 yards into a rocky channel about 50 feet wide. Here a settler had built a saw mill and milldam, but no further development had taken place near the site of later Smiths Falls. Continuous rapids followed and there were narrows in twenty-three miles of Rideau Lake—at Oliver's Ferry and Upper Narrows. The trail from Brockville to Perth crossed the lake at Oliver's (now Rideau) Ferry.

Mactaggart's first assignment was to build a bridge across the Chaudière Falls at Hull to the beginning of the canal. He called it the Union Bridge.

Two small villages were laid out on the site of the present city of Ottawa, called Upper and Lower Town, terms still in use by Ottawans. Active work on the canal did not begin until 1827 when two companies of sappers and miners arrived from England to start construction.

Mactaggart in his two volumes entitled *Three Years in Canada* (1829) had only praise for Colonel John By. He called him a "gentleman" who withstood privations with wonderful patience and good humour. That he could run rapids feared by even the Indians, sleep soundly anywhere, and eat anything—even raw pork—proved his superiority of character—and constitution.

Excavation was by hand with pick and shovel, with oxen only

Public Archives of Canada James P. Cockburn

NEAR NICHOLSON'S RAPIDS, RIDEAU RIVER, 1830
Highly typical of river scenery in the pioneer period.

Public Archives of Canada — James P. Cockburn

'MY CANOE PORTAGE, SMITH'S FALLS'

Public Archives of Canada — Philip Bainbrigge

'MEYRICK VILLE, RIDEAU CANAL, CIRCA 1838'

occasionally available from local settlers. Rock was removed by wheelbarrows. A simple hand hoist was used. Flat iron was brought from England and forged by local blacksmiths. Iron castings came from Lower Canada iron foundries. Timber was made into gates by carpenters. There were many accidents and much loss of life. Mactaggart speaks of seeing heads, arms, legs blown in all directions through the improper use of gunpowder. During the summer of 1828 many died of swamp fever. Mactaggart tells of a "blue mist" that seemed to hang over the marshes but at noon it would change to a "quivering" atmosphere—and the smell was nauseous, like an animal in the last stage of decomposition.

Possibly the density of the forest was responsible for ague and consumption, for other writers have spoken of trees so tall and close together that the sun never penetrated the earth. In such verdure prolonged hot weather would produce a tropical, mildew-like atmosphere, pungent with bacteria.

At Jones Falls and Kingston Mills during the summer of 1828 even doctors were ill with ague. Cranberry Lake, one the worst breeding spots for swamp fever, was equalled only by a treacherous strip of forest between Mud Lake and Rideau Lake where in 1830 Colonel By ordered a wide swathe cut through the dense bush in order to generate a current of air so that his men could work.

The Indians they met posed no problem, proving harmless, kindly, and willing to do anything to oblige strangers. Mactaggart comments: "If all the nations of human beings on earth were so good as they it would surely be a blessing bestowed on earth".

In the spring of 1832 the canal was officially opened. Throughout the construction the military value of the waterway was kept constantly in mind. Blockhouses had been erected at strategic points with small contingents of soldiers to man them. At Merrickville today stands one of the two remaining blockhouses of this period.

At noon May 24th, 1832, Colonel By, his family, and fellow-officers set out on the maiden voyage from Kingston in Robert Drummond's vessel *Pumper* which had been renamed *Rideau* for the occasion. They arrived at Smiths Falls (then a village) at 6 a.m. on the 25th. A cannon mounted to welcome them blew up but fortunately no one was injured. A few extra passengers were taken on board there and they progressed slowly to Merrickville and other small villages en route, reaching Ottawa on May 29th.

Now at last there was a transportation link with large centres enabling settlers in this portion of Upper Canada to establish farms along the canal. Indians used the canal frequently, as well as the British Army in conveying troops by barge towed by canal steamers. Sometimes a steam tug would pull as many as ten barges, and these had to be locked through in pairs, so that lockmasters and their men were often on duty 24 hours a day.

Perth was still cut off from the waterway but determined to have access to the canal a group of citizens led by the Hon. William Morris organized the Tay Navigation Company in 1830. Various ways were tried to raise money. Unsuccessful they appealed to the government of Upper Canada which finally granted them $10,000 in 1832. Together with money raised locally and a loan of $5,000 from the Bank of Upper Canada they were able to begin construction on the Tay Canal in the summer of 1832.

In comparison with the Rideau Canal it was a minor undertaking. Four small locks were built, designed by a Perth builder and mechanic, John Jackson. A bitter argument arose between Morris and his fellow-Member for Perth in the Legislature, Donald Fraser, over Cockburn's Island, part of which had been sold to raise the money. Fraser insinuated certain people had profited from the sale, and Morris took up the battle. The government investigated and their report exonerated the Tay Navigation Company. However, two embittered voters submitted a petition to the House of Assembly suggesting Fraser had no right to sit there since he had not attained the necessary freeholder qualifications, a point overlooked by the constituency during his election. A trial was held and Fraser was officially unseated. He contested the next election nevertheless, and was again returned. By this time he had, however, secured the necessary land patents.

The navigation works continued with a further government grant and were completed in 1834. The *Enterprise*, a little steamer built in Perth and commanded by Captain William Richards, began a regular service between Perth, Bytown, and Kingston. Captain Richards was Irish, a sailor who had served in the British Navy during the War of 1812-14, then a free trader to the West Indies and survivor of many fights with pirates. He had had his own boat wrecked by a typhoon and finally settled in New Brunswick, later moving to Perth in Upper Canada. The Tay Canal was not really deep enough to handle steamboats, and after a few years he transferred the *Enterprise* to the main branch of the Rideau where it operated between Kingston and Bytown for many years. Eventually her engines were transferred to one of the steamers built by Jason Gould of Smiths Falls for use on Muskrat Lake in Renfrew County.

An amusing incident in connection with the *Enterprise* concerned the Rev. William Bell. William Morris had been selling shares in the *Enterprise* when she was in the last stages of construction and he persuaded Mr. Bell to invest money in the boat. When the steamer was launched the Presbyterian pastor was horrified to find that a bar had been installed in the lounge. Worse still the steamboat "profaned the Sabbath" by travelling on Sunday. Bell long lamented his action in unwittingly supporting the *Enterprise*.

Early commerce was carried on by the *Jolly Brewer* and *Captain Barney McSherry*, the latter once making a trip to Montreal and back in only 22 days! Steamers travelling as far as Perth in 1835 included the *Bytown* and the *Thomas McKay*.

The feeder canal to Perth was used to transport squared timber, and Perth prospered. Tolls on the Tay were not sufficient to keep the canal in proper repair, however, and it deteriorated; again appeals had to be made to government bodies. For a time it seemed the water route might be further extended. As early as 1834 a notice appeared in the *Bathurst Courier* stating that the inhabitants of Beckwith, Ramsay, Lanark, and Dalhousie intended to petition the Legislature to employ a competent engineer in examining the route from the Rideau Canal through Cockburn Creek. They desired another canal of three miles length to connect the creek and the Mississippi Lake near Carleton Place and provide their townships with boat navigation for 60 miles, as well as acting as a feeder to the Rideau Canal. Nothing came of this pipe dream.

John W. Douglas, born in Perth in 1840, related his reminiscences of traffic on the old Tay Canal during his youth thus:

> You can reach Montreal now in three or four hours. It took a whole day when I was young for the 'Royal Mail' to get to Brockville, and sometimes two or three from there to Montreal. When the mail arrived, the coachman, swelling with importance as he sailed up the street, blew his horn and everyone was at the door to see it lumber up the street and haul up at Glascott's Hotel. . . . Then what a stir the arrival of the *British Queen* and other giant craft which then navigated the Tay canal caused. Merchants then got their goods twice a year. The voyages to and fro were not exactly on a par with those of the old canal man in the United States. In a blow the boat began to rock a little and an old lady tremblingly enquired of the

tar: 'Oh, sir, is there any fear?' 'Oh, yes, mum,' gruffly said Jack 'plenty of fear but no danger'. The boats often struck a snag and went to the bottom, and besides the loss of goods entailed, they blocked navigation, so that goods were often delayed months. No sooner were the boats safe in port, however, in that land-locked harbour that we knew as the 'Basin' than Perth's streets were alive with carts, trucks, and teams of one kind and another unloading the craft. It was amazing the amount of stuff they would disgorge. The sailors had a fat time, if inclined to 'take a horn', as most of them were, for every boat had large consignments of the very best liquors. A gimblet hole on top and another at the end of the barrel, and the supply was inexhaustible. Then we urchins had a good time for sugar always came in puncheons, in which were auger holes, and with us a discarded candle mould did the business, and our fingers and knives yielded a bounteous supply of 'gum' in the shape of pitch from the sides of the craft.*

Early roads improved slowly from blazed trails to wagon tracks. A traveller to Perth in 1820 remarked: "All the roads I have described before were turnpike and bowling green to this".† The road from Brockville at this time was divided into three stages of seven miles each, and the best the party could do was three hours for each stage.

Government roads were the first built—one from Perth to the Richmond military settlement passing through Franktown where there was a government storehouse. This road eventually linked Perth with Bytown. The stretch from Bytown to Richmand was the first sector built and records conflict as to whether the Perth portion was completed before the Duke of Richmond arrived in 1819 or whether his engineers cut a road through to facilitate his journey to the Richmond settlement. In any case the stretch of road between Perth and Franktown was pocketed with swamps, and the Rev. William Bell speaks feelingly and often in his Journals of having to wade through them, carrying his shoes, and being unable to drive over them except in winter.

The first trail out of Perth northward to Lanark was built to set up another government storehouse and carry the Lanark Society settlers and their belongings to the Lanark Depot and thence to their land locations. Money was voted by the government for this road and it was cut through in 1820.

* Perth *Courier*, June 30, 1905.
† Canada Post Office Records.

It was a problem to get wagon trails built even after the townships were partially settled, since all roads, except government sponsored ones, were built by statute labour, each settler being responsible for the part of the road passing his property. There was no one to account for the portions of land set aside as clergy reserves nor for crown land, and community effort was required to clear and build these portions.

The famous Perth Road, portions of which are still in use today, linked Perth with Pakenham at one end and Kingston at the other. Traffic from Bytown also fed into it from the Bytown-Richmond settlement road, and the lower portion of it from Perth to Brockville carried constant and heavy traffic. By the time the Rideau Canal was completed this road was in a state of good repair with comfortable inns for travellers along the way. In 1827, however, parts of it were anything but comfortable. A Perth resident, Henry LeLievre, related his experience on the Perth highway in a letter to Hamnet Pinhey, mill owner and prominent farmer at South March:

> My troubles began after leaving the road leading to Captain Bradley's, opposite Dominic Burk's—I met with a series of troubles which never ended until I had got within ten miles of home.
>
> The first day I did not get within seven miles of Shipman's Mills owing to the number of clearings which I was obliged to go round or have trouble of taking down and putting up at least half a dozen fences in each, which kept me until dark ere I reached the house at which I stopped the night. The next morning I set out at 7 o'clock (after making a hearty breakfast of potatoes and milk, the house not being able to afford anything better), in expectation of being able to reach home that night but it will no doubt surprise you when I tell you that I succeeded in reaching Shipman's Mills—the road being so filled up with windfall trees that I am sure I did not leap over less than fifty, and at last came to such a pile that I was obliged to leave my horse and go about three miles to the first clearing and get a man to return with me and chop the trees out of my way. My poor mare was extremely tired as well as myself. I left Shipman's this morning and arrived here at about 4 o'clock p.m. after getting my mare in a bog and obliged to take her by the tail and help her out.*

And LeLievre begs Pinhey not to send anyone along this road until it has been properly cleared.

A branch of the Perth road ran north to Lanark. The early engineers were forced to build the road along the east side of a black ash

* Letter from Henry LeLievre to Hamnet Pinhey, September 1827.

swamp north from Armstrong's Corners to a narrow point between the 7th and 8th concessions of Drummond where it was possible to cross the north shore of the swamp and continue along the Mississippi River to McIlquham's Ferry, and thence to Lanark village. This was the route taken by the first Lanark, Dalhousie, and Ramsay township settlers. Later another road was opened from Armstrong's Corners northeast to Prestonvale, Ferguson's Falls, and on toward Clayton.

The blazed trails and beaten tracks were later replaced by corduroy roads. The road to Lanark village was one of the first corduroy roads built in Lanark County. The method was to lay tree trunks loosely together side by side over which stages and wagons rumbled and rattled to the great discomfort of the occupants. John Mactaggart described them thus:

> These turnpikes are fancied to resemble that famous King's Cloth, called *corduroy*. When Dante wrote his 'Inferno' the critics blamed his muse for not selecting a proper highway to Pandemonium; but had she been aware of the nature of the corduroy species, there is no doubt that that would have been chosen, as certainly none can be more decidedly infernal.
>
> In passing over them in a lumbering waggon, the poor human frame is jolted to pieces. But out of evil there always comes good; for even the country people to take too much care of their roads, so that the passengers would have no reason to complain of them, then they would receive no aid from the colonial funds towards the trouble. As they are then they will gradually improve, for when the officers of State take a drive or when M.P's travel to their public business, the *Road Bill and Turnpike Act* are strongly forced upon their recollections; the corduroy send in their own petitions in earnest.

By 1835 Perth and vicinity had improved roads, but no assistance had gone out to municipalities in the interior for the improvement of their roads. An April issue of the *Bathurst Courier* carried a letter from the ratepayers at Lanark charging that the lower portion of the Lanark road next to Perth "has been looked after money-wise by the people who want to drive on Sunday, but no money can be found to assist in building a proper upper portion". The letter further pointed out that there were three bridges in the space of no less than three miles—across the Clyde at Lanark village, at Peter Kerr's tannery off the 4th concession, and at lot no. 7 of the third concession. The writer comments that one of the Perth magistrates has said the Clyde was not worthy of notice, but "if he had to ford it, he would need to be encased in leather to his armpits."

Eventually money was voted in Council for the corduroy road to Lanark, and a road was built from Morphy's Falls to Shipman's Mills in Ramsay in 1829. The road from Shipman's Mills to Pakenham ran from the village to the "Tannery" (or Leckie's Corners as it was then called), along the 8th line of Ramsay to Bennies Corners, down a side road to Snedden's Inn, and along the 9th concession line to Pakenham. This road was so bad for many years it could be used only in winter.

In the 1830s a road was built from Perth to Innisville, Boyd Settlement, past Wolf's Grove to Bennies Corners in Ramsay, and from there to Pakenham. This was the upper portion of the "Perth Road".

The corduroy roads were also fire hazards in dry season. William Bell tells in his Journals of a fire occurring on the corduroy road to Lanark which took many volunteers and firemen a long time to extinguish.

Plank roads were introduced into Lanark County in the 1850s, replacing the bone-loosening corduroy. In the 1840s Charles Rice, a later editor of the Perth *Courier*, began writing letters to the *Courier* urging the M.P.s for Lanark and other influential people to do something about district roads. The plank road was then being tried out in Syracuse and Rome, New York, and on a visit to that area Rice had investigated their construction and cost. Lumber was still plentiful in the county and this form of road promised to be more economical than broken stone, an alternative. Rice hammered away at his theme persistently through letters to the editor until some action was taken. A company called the Plank Road Society was formed, and roads paid for by public subscription and local council aid. The first plank road constructed was on the town line between Bathurst and Drummond (the Lanark road) as far as Balderson's Corners, and from there to Lanark village. John Gillies took the contract for providing 3-inch planks at $12 per thousand board feet from his mill at Gillies Mills. When completed the road was considered "excellent" by travellers.

Another plank road was built from Perth to Port Elmsley. In 1850 the city fathers of Carleton Place set about to have one built from Carleton Place to Ottawa. A notice was put in the Perth *Courier* asking for subscribers and indicating that interest would be paid on money loaned. But Canadian winters proved harder on them than traffic and they were only a temporary expedient.

In the early days mail was carried on foot, later on horseback, and then by stagecoach. Sir John Sherbrooke, the Governor-General, ordered a post office opened in Perth in 1816 with Colonel Josiah Taylor first postmaster. Between 1817 and 1822 all mail for Lanark County came via Brockville to the Perth Depot.

In 1830 a Brockville and Perth Mail Stage was established. The coach left Brockville on Wednesday and Saturday at 4 o'clock in the morning, usually arriving in Perth around 6 or 7 o'clock. The driver stayed overnight on Wednesday and left Perth around 9 a.m. On his weekend trip he stayed over Sunday at Perth, returning to Brockville on Monday. Mail from Lanark village, Bytown, and Morphy's Falls arrived on alternate days at Perth to connect with the Brockville stage. By 1846 the stage travelled three times a week to Brockville, and the fare was 10s.

In the late 1830s Josiah Taylor was succeeded by Francis Allan as postmaster at Perth. By 1846 there were still only eight post offices in Lanark County, according to *Smith's Canadian Gazetteer*, indicating that there were still many parts of the settlement cut off from communication with the outside world. At this time postage was still being paid by the recipient, and charges were high. There were no postage stamps—the postage being stamped or written on each letter by the postmaster. Letter-size paper was used for correspondence and folded and affixed with sealing wax on the outer flap. There was no envelope. Long lists of letters awaiting collection were posted regularly in the Perth newspaper, and presumably if the recipient could not afford to pay the incoming postage, the letter went to the Dead Letter Office and was destroyed.

The post offices for the county listed in the *Gazetteer* of 1846 were, with their postmasters:

Perth—F. Hall
Lanark—John Hall
Smiths Falls—G. Mittleberger
Carleton Place—Robert Bell
Franktown—E. McEwen
Kilmarnock—J. Maitland
Pakenham—Andrew Dickson
Ramsay—Jas. Wylie

Postage stamps were first issued by the Canada Post Office in 1851, and other difficulties and inconveniences gradually gave way to our modern system.

# CHAPTER XI

## PROGRESS IN AGRICULTURE

For many pioneer farmers the main source of revenue, and sometimes the only one, was the produce from forest clearing—oak staves, square timber, planks and boards, and potash. These sold to a Montreal market.

During the Napoleonic wars there had been a shortage of potash overseas and by 1808 potash prices in Montreal were as high as $320 a ton. To make potash trees were cut, leaves and twigs being allowed to dry, and then the whole burned. The half-burned logs were reburned until reduced to ashes, which were carefully raked off the top of the pile and put into a container called a *leach*, with lime and water. The lye produced by this mixture was drained through the bottom of the *leach* into an iron pot. The lye was then boiled until it reached a thick consistency and poured into kettle-drum-shaped half-coolers. When cool the substance looked like brown stone and was very hard. The potash cakes of two half-coolers could be fitted into a standard-size oak barrel and shipped that way. A barrel weighed about 700 pounds and sold for around $40.

The flourishing potash market encouraged squatters to ravish the forests. For a down payment on a piece of property, a settler was accorded squatter's rights with no interest charged on the balance of his land as long as he paid his taxes. Lots in Darling and other townships were plundered heavily this way by squatters who cut off all the timber and converted it into potash, and having accumulated some capital left the land.

There was a general economic depression throughout Upper Canada when the land of the first settlers at Perth was beginning to produce grain. Between 1819-1822 the price of wheat dropped from $1 to 50¢ a bushel, livestock values and real estate were reduced to half.

Travelling "Yankees" were then selling American beef to Perth and Lanark. In 1822 the military establishment was discontinued at Perth and the government withdrew its support. However, at Lanark, a superintendent, clerk, doctor and schoolmaster were maintained by the government until 1829. By that year none of the cash advances made to the settlers had yet been paid, and the government was consequently withholding titles to the land. Finally over 300 settlers in Ramsay, Lanark, Dalhousie, and North Sherbrooke drew up a petition claiming remission of the payments. The first petition went out in 1825, and numerous others followed. On August 5th, 1832, the Lanark Society settlers appealed to Sir John Colborne:

> With regard to imports and exports, few places have been more disadvantageously settled than Lanark, cut off as it is from all communications by navigable rivers except at a distance to the nearest front of between 60 and 70 miles, by roads that after the labours of 18 years, between Perth and Brockville, are yet barely passable, and from Perth to Lanark after 12 years, are yet impassable for some time both spring and fall. In Perth and Lanark, no money market has been found for grain. . . . Still the older part would prefer remaining rather than be obliged to seek new homes, knowing that although to stay is comparative poverty, yet to remove is at once destruction of all endearing associations and sure precursor of an old age of indigence and toil. Twelve years has now silvered many a head and enfeebled many a well-nerved arm that during the same period could easily have repaid the advances made had that time and those exertions been expended on generous soil. . . . In conclusion, petitioners would observe that if the past and present have been and is gloomy, the future affords no ray of hope, as the greater part of the land once laid down in grass cannot be made available for any other crop.*

The government finally acted in 1835 and sent Surveyor Rankin to make a report. His survey indicated that much of the land was indeed unfit for farming because of its rocky nature, and found it remarkable that the settlers had been able to eke out a living at all. On the advice of Sir John Colborne, in 1836 the British government cancelled the settlers' debts of some £22,000.

Despite the obstacles to farming in Bathurst District, the position of the Lanark Society weavers and tradesmen was a vast improvement over the conditions they had lived under in the homeland. By 1824

* Bathurst District Papers, Ontario Archives.

Lanark Township alone had a population of 1560, with 275 oxen and 1338 cows in possession of the settlers. Some of the emigrants had their own looms set up and were better dressed than tradespeople in the old land. Food was plentiful once the land had been cleared, for the soil was rich and virgin. The larders were filled with Indian corn, peas, wheat, oats, ham. As a Beckwith settler said: "There were many hardships but it was wonderful not to be under a Laird and to know that the land was one's own."

Hay and oats were required in large quantities by the lumbering industry. Pork and flour had to be imported for many years from American lake areas, for sparsely populated Upper Canada simply could not supply sufficient to keep the shanties up the Ottawa. An excellent market developed at Bytown (Ottawa) and by 1836 it was said to be the best market in all of Upper Canada. Here the farmer could secure cash for his goods.

Oats was the main cash crop in Lanark and Carleton counties. Pork was home-cured for the shanties, and horses and oxen were raised for sale to lumbermen. In the late 1830s and early 1840s oxen were used for "straightening out" the "sticks" in the lumber camps, as well as for hauling logs to river and mill. So greatly had agriculture advanced in the district by 1842 that the same settlers who had asked for remission of land payments were sufficiently affluent to send relief money to distressed parts of Scotland. The following notice appeared in the *Perth Weekly Despatch*:

> In pursuance of a Requisition signed by a number of respectable inhabitants of this place, a meeting was held in Mr. Gillen's schoolhouse at Ramsayville on Tuesday 24th May, for the purpose of taking into consideration the present distressed state of the Operative classes in the towns of Glasgow and Paisley, Scotland, and also of devising the best means of raising a contribution for their relief. William Wallace, Esquire, being appointed Chairman, and J. A. Gemmill, secretary, extracts from several Scottish and Provincial newspapers descriptive of the destitute conditions of the operatives in various parts of the West of Scotland [were read].*

The settlers passed a series of resolutions at this meeting that in "thankfulness to God for their own abundance" they would give to alleviate the sufferings of their kinfolk in Scotland. About £15 was subscribed on the spot, and at the time when the notice appeared in the *Weekly Despatch* about £57 had already been sent to Scotland.

* Perth *Weekly Despatch*, 1842.

During the early pioneer days the colonial government made no attempt to organize agriculture, but local cattle fairs were arranged by interested citizens at Perth and held as early as 1827. Of the first fair held in May the Rev. William Bell commented in his Journals that it rained all day, few people and fewer cattle were present, and very little business was done. During the evening some transients got drunk and kept the streets in a brawling uproar for hours. At the October fair the same year there were more people, animals, and incidents. There was also a horse-race during which one man was killed and another badly hurt. Horse-races had been held in Perth since 1823. Most of the participants at first were ex-army officers, the only citizens who could afford horses, but by 1829 the editor of the Perth *Examiner* could comment:

> We were much pleased to notice the wonderful improvement in the breed of horses which within these few years has taken place in this settlement . . . a few years ago only a solitary horse or so could be found in the township. . . . Now the majority of settlers are supplied with good serviceable horses and in the town there are some first rates.*

After 1827 the Perth Cattle Fair was held semi-annually, the Fall Fair being the more important one as a source of supply for lumbermen wishing to buy teams of oxen or horses.

Horned cattle, horses, and oxen were shown and purchases made. The cattle fair benefited both farmer and consumer, and the farmer no longer had to depend on a local butcher or drover for a market. Competition assured him he would get almost what his stock was worth. He received cash payment, and this in turn benefited the merchant who had goods to sell. The drover also profited, for he could appraise much livestock without having to make tedious trips to back concessions; and he could hire boys at the fair to help him drive his wares to an urban market. Often several drovers branded their cattle and then drove and pastured their herds together as they travelled to market at Brockville or crossed the border to the United States.

With the exception of the Trent Valley, the Ottawa Valley was the only area of Upper Canada where agriculture and lumbering complemented each other, one supplying food and labour and the other employment and cash payment. In other districts of Upper Canada at this time lumbering was carried on principally by farmers clearing

* Perth *Examiner*, 1829, Perth Museum.

their lands and supplying local saw mills. Most lumber in such cases was absorbed into the local scene for construction purposes.

Large quantities of American livestock came into Upper Canada free of duty, to be slaughtered for food or sold to farmers at border towns such as Kingston. Because of the abundance of American livestock many farmers in the interior hesitated to invest in stock-raising on a large scale, since their well-established American competitor already had the edge on the market.

Courtesy Mrs. John McGill, Sr.

HORSEPOWER THRESHING

Agricultural societies were formed to change the situation and encourage the raising of livestock and improvement in quality of animals raised. The Bathurst District Agricultural Society was organized March 20, 1832. At the first fairs they offered prizes under $10 for the best livestock, ploughing, wheat, oats, corn, peas, barley, potatoes, flax, hemp, maple syrup, and cheese. The distaff side was not forgotten, and prizes were given for "the best 20 yards of flannel", "the best twenty yards of linen", and other domestic manufactures. By 1834 there were fairs at both Perth and Bytown. Extending competition, in the *Bathurst Courier* of September 1834 it was advertised that "a premium of five pounds will be given to the farm servant who has resided the longest time with one master and can produce the best testimonials as to character". But many attended fairs for no good reason whatever, as pointed out by W. P. Lett in his *Recollections of Bytown* in verse:

*'Twas not to buy or sell they came*
*From far and near, the blind the lame,*
*The grave, the merry, and the gay*

*Upon that old eventful day:*
*They all assembled, wild and free,*
*To have a ranting, roaring spree.*

Another agricultural society soon took shape. In June 1835 a letter appeared in the *Courier* signifying that farmers in Ramsay, Dalhousie, and Lanark townships had sent representatives to Lanark village in the interest of forming an agricultural society "to encourage circulation of useful tracts on practical husbandry, to procure seed corn of various kinds from the best market and resell to members at cost prices, and to aid by most efficient means the destruction of wolves". A general meeting was held at Lanark with Donald Fraser presiding. The result was the formation of the Lanark County Agricultural Society.

Prizes were now offered for improved methods of clearing land, successful methods of crop rotation, and better implements. A new implement entered had to have endorsement by farmers who had tried the invention. There were also plowing matches with special concessions for those who ploughed with oxen. Plots were given numbers, and directions given that judges were not to appear on the field until the plowing had been completed so they would not know whose work they were viewing. Horses or oxen could be used but only one driver to a team. The time for plowing was between 10 and 3 p.m. Plots were drawn by lot, and only members of the agricultural society could compete.

In 1840 a North Lanark Agricultural Society was formed at Carleton Place with James Wylie of Ramsayville (Almonte) as president, Francis Jessop of Carleton Place secretary, and Robert Bell of Carleton Place treasurer; it too held an annual fair at Carleton Place until the 1850s, and then at Almonte. The Beckwith Township Agricultural Society continued to hold fairs at Carleton Place for some years. Robert Bell was secretary and treasurer of the United Counties of Lanark and Renfrew Agricultural Society from 1845 to 1852.

In 1846 an Agricultural Association of Upper Canada was organized to coördinate the activities of local agricultural societies throughout the province. The same year the Perth Society was reorganized and renamed the South Riding of Lanark Electoral District Agricultural Society—later shortened to South Lanark Agricultural Society. The organization spent most of its funds in introducing improved breeds of sheep, hogs, cattle, and horses. A later offshoot of the agricultural fair was the turkey fair held at Smiths Falls, attracting buyers from as far off as New York state. At one time it was called "the greatest poultry fair in the world".

The early fairs were not only occasions of competition and commerce, but of social events of great importance to all ages. Donald Fraser, writing in the Perth *Courier* in 1905, recalled the Perth Fair of his boyhood in vivid detail:

> With improved transportation facilities, the old Spring and Fall Fairs in Perth have become a thing of the past. I think, however, the Perth boy who has had no experience of these old fairs is to be pitied. We thought of them for weeks ahead; we had no money to save up for the occasion, but that did not interfere with our enjoyment for a moment. We had all our faculties and what more does a healthy boy need? Holidays were not given then as now, on every possible occasion. But there was no school for us on Fair Day.
>
> We rose early to wash our faces and take breakfast . . . but it did seem an awful waste of a boy's precious time. We were afraid something would come into the fair without our seeing it. We had to be on nearly all the leading roads at once, and see everything as it came in. What a comparing of information went on and how quickly wonderful reports had to be confirmed by personal investigation!
>
> By ten o'clock the market square was covered with cattle and rows of waggons along the street line. The apple waggons and the honey waggons, what boy can forget them? Think of one of Mrs. Allan's ginger cakes and a whole copper's worth of honey on it. And her ginger beer in stone bottles; there never was before and there never will be again any half so good.
>
> The cattle buying began early. McShane of Montreal; Murdock of Kingston; James McFarland and his two sons, John and James, were busy men. How quickly the bargains were made! No haggling, the cattle marked and driven off, every hoof sold by four o'clock, the farmers well satisfied and a good many dollars in their pockets. When this was over horse-racing began. In very early days the course was at the far end of the old burying ground bridge at the foot of Brock Street in the neighbourhood of James Murphy's. Latterly the course was from the White House to Matheson Hotel on Drummond Street. . . . Towards evening, I am afraid the faithful historian would have to record a few sanguinary contests; old grudges had to be settled, . . . good old Father McDonagh could restore peace and quietness quicker than a score of policemen nowadays. His presence was sufficient, but occasionally the old gentleman caught the spirit in the air and wielded his heavy cane in true Connaught style.

> Next day we took our corporal punishment and made no complaints. But wasn't it a shame to punish little boys who had been so happy and took so lively an interest in such important institutions as the Fair days in Perth.*

John W. Douglas in the same issue of the *Courier* recalled the fair days somewhat differently:

> It always seemed to rain on or just previous to fair day. The roads were horrible and farmers at any distance had to start the day previous with any cattle and horses they had to sell. As a consequence, lanes and even the main streets were clogged with hundreds of vehicles. Meeting each other, old soldiers fought their battles oven again. Whiskey flew and many an old grudge eventuated in free fights which everyone viewed as a matter of course.
>
> One of these I particularly remember. It began just opposite Matheson & Balderson's law office, and soon a dozen were in it, with a crowd of between five hundred and a thousand people excited and yelling, many anxious to take a hand in. Soon Sheriff Dickson appeared on the scene and being a very powerful man, he worked his way in and grabbing the two chief belligerents, he 'yanked' them off to the jug, but not without getting many a dig and sly kick from sympathizers of those taken in limbo.

An old scrapbook clipping, undated, reports an early Smiths Falls fair held at Ward's barn on the first Friday in October. Farm produce and ladies' work were shown, judging and selling being completed by noon when the crowds congregated on Beckwith Street between the bridge and William Street for the social events:

> At the corner of Main and Beckwith was a man with cure-all medicine and 'Cheap John' with his jewellery. Here were waggons drawn up, loaded with apples, plums and all sorts of vegetables. The centre of attention was the honey waggon. On the corner opposite then Shaw's store, was William Code known as 'Honey Code', his waggon loaded. For years he served youngsters who had a copper with a chip of honey known as 'honey on the chip'.
>
> John Barleycorn would begin his work as the day wore on and fights began. . . . Ed. Gilroy was Chief Constable and his staff of probationers would begin to fill the 'lock-up'. . . . In those days entrance fee to the fair was 3 pennies, later raised to 25¢. Edward Chalmers was secretary of the fair.

* Perth *Courier*, June 30, 1905.

# CHAPTER XII

## THE GROWTH OF PERTH AS COUNTY SEAT

The political and judicial divisions of Upper Canada during pioneer days changed periodically. In the case of the area with which this history is concerned, so many changes occurred that some clarification is here necessary.

In 1792 the Legislature of Upper Canada divided Upper Canada into four districts—Eastern, Midland, Home, and Western. The Eastern District comprised all of present eastern Ontario as far west as the Gananoque River. The same year John Graves Simcoe, the Lieutenant-Governor of Upper Canada, issued a Proclamation further dividing the districts into counties and Carleton County was outlined as all that land now occupied by Carleton, Lanark, and Renfrew counties.

In 1798 the Eastern District was further divided and Carleton, Grenville, and Leeds counties were to be called the District of Johnstown.

The Rideau Settlement began as a loose appendage to the District of Johnstown. As the land was surveyed and settlers flocked in it was necessary to make further adjustments. In 1821 an Act of the Upper Canada Parliament was passed placing the townships of Goulbourne, Beckwith, Drummond, Bathurst, March, Huntley, Ramsay, Lanark, Dalhousie, and North and South Sherbrooke in Carleton County. By this Act the Governor, Sir Peregrine Maitland, was given power to further divide this District as he saw fit, and in January 1823 a further alteration was made. The Governor's proclamation named the County of Carleton as separate from the Johnstown District, to be called "The District of Bathurst", and Perth became the judicial seat, a position it was to hold for many years.

Another Act in 1824 divided the Bathurst District into the counties

A MAP
of the Province of
UPPER CANADA.
describing
ALL THE NEW SETTLEMENTS, TOWNSHIPS, &c.
WITH THE COUNTRIES ADJACENT, FROM
(Quebec to Lake Huron.)

Public Archives of Canada

James Wyld

UPPER CANADA IN 1841

Archives of Ontario Thomas Burrowes

PERTH FROM THE NORTHEAST BANK OF THE TAY, 1828

Courtesy Perth *Courier*

VIEW FROM THE BRIDGE, PERTH, 1962

of Lanark and Carleton. By this Act, Lanark County comprised the townships now within its boundaries with the exception of Montague, North Elmsley, and North Burgess. They remained part of the Johnstown District and Leeds County until 1844 when they became part of Bathurst District. Lanark County was also to include all the unsurveyed land to the north, now the County of Renfrew.*

Shortly after the 1823 Proclamation was issued, a special session

* In 1842 Carleton County was detached from Bathurst District and given the name Dalhousie District. The Municipal Institutions Act of 1849 divided Bathurst District into Lanark and Renfrew counties.

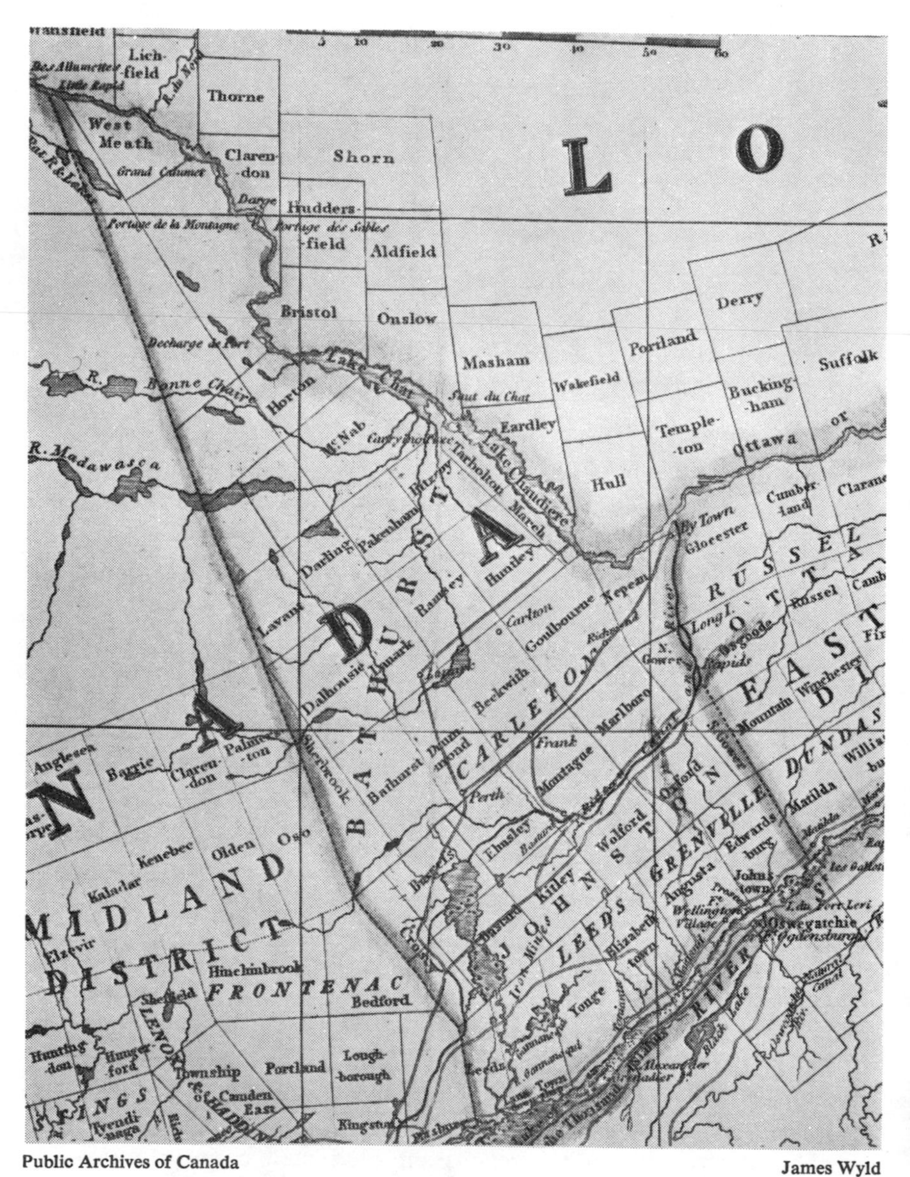


Public Archives of Canada

James Wyld

MAP SHOWING BATHURST DISTRICT IN 1841

of magistrates was called at Perth for the licensing of public houses. The following magistrates gathered at the courthouse: Alexander Thom, William Marshall, G. Bourke, John Watson, Joseph Maxwell, George J. Joynt, James Weatherly, Alexander McMillan, Francis Cummings, Alexander Fraser, Roderick Matheson, and Henry Glass. Dr. George Hume Reade was the first Clerk of the Peace appointed. Licenses were issued for William Matheson (the gaoler whose hotel was at the corner of Foster and Drummond streets); John Balderson at Balderson's Corners; James Armstrong who kept the Drummond Arms Hotel at the cross-roads north of Perth known as Armstrong's Corners.

The first lawyer for the new county seat arrived the same year. This was James Boulton, son of the Honourable Henry John Boulton, Attorney General of Upper Canada at York. James soon purchased land originally granted to Captain William Greig on Drummond Street near the Tay River and built an elaborate residence patterned after "The Grange" in York (then belonging to his uncle, D'Arcy Boulton, and now part of the Art Gallery in Toronto). It was surrounded by a sturdy stone wall. This building now belongs to the Society of Friends.

Thomas Radenhurst was Perth's second lawyer, arriving six months after Mr. Boulton. Radenhurst had been educated at Dr. Strachan's school at Cornwall and afterward studied law in York. He commenced his practice in Kingston, then moved to Perth. He married Edith Ridout, daughter of Surveyor-General Ridout of York, and in 1832 bought a fine stone residence in Perth, earlier built for the Reverend Michael Harris. Here his daughter Sarah-Louise grew up and later married William Morris, son of the Hon. William Morris of Perth. (Mr. Radenhurst later represented the County of Carleton in the Upper Canada legislature, and was nominee of the Reform Party but an unsuccessful candidate for Lanark County.)

Daniel McMartin was Perth's third lawyer and proved himself one of the cleverest at court. He was an American and when in 1834 he built a red brick mansion at the corner of Gore and Harvey streets he brought all the materials for it from the United States. He was a man of pronounced opinions and retained his American tastes and prejudices. He became a very prominent lawyer in the District.

The courts of Quarter Sessions were always well attended. One writer has spoken of how "the walls resounded to the orations of Radenhurst and McMartin and the pompous but efficient High Constable, Anthony Wiseman".

Sketch by the author

JAMES BOULTON'S HOME, DRUMMOND STREET, PERTH
It was erected in 1823.

Boulton disliked McMartin and their public quarrels became legendary in Perth and district. Rev. William Bell recorded the more dramatic ones in his Journals. One of these occurred in April 1827 when McMartin challenged Boulton to a duel; but Boulton declined to fight as he had "no chance of hitting his opponent, he being no thicker than a broomstick".

McMartin then placed a notice in the Post Office calling Boulton "a liar and a coward", and signing his name. Boulton disliked fighting with pistols but had no objection to verbal onslaughts and responded by placing another notice in the Post Office beside McMartin's, intimating that his opponent was, among other things, "illegitimate". Crowds thronged the Post Office to view the notices and both posters were torn down. Mr. Morris slyly offered to supply brooms to the antagonists "if they had not fixed upon weapons", but the quarrel fizzled out.

These young lawyers occupied the most imposing homes in Perth at the time. They moved in an élite society consisting of half-pay

Sketch by the author

RESIDENCE OF THE REV. MICHAEL HARRIS IN 1824
An excellent example of Colonial Georgian architecture. It has long been known as the Radenhurst-Inderwick residence in Perth.

officers, government officials, and leading businessmen. To ordinary folk, in and out of town, their quarrels were highly amusing.

Boulton was involved in another dispute with Radenhurst early in the summer of 1830, and this culminated in an agreement to a duel. Neither wished to incur the long arm of British law (duelling being outlawed at this time in Canada), so they crossed the St. Lawrence River to New York State "where they expected to have the pleasure of shooting one another without molestation. But this like all former affairs of the same kind", reported Mr. Bell, "ended in smoke. One of them, indeed, it is reported, heard or thought he heard a bullet whiz past his ear. But they came home without any holes in their skin, to boast of their heroism and talk of their hairbreadth escapes in flood and field."

A more serious affair took place at Perth in 1833 which took the edge off duelling in the county for all time to come. Young John Wilson, eldest son of North Sherbrooke pioneer Ebenezer Wilson, was a law student in Boulton's office and lived with the family. Radenhurst

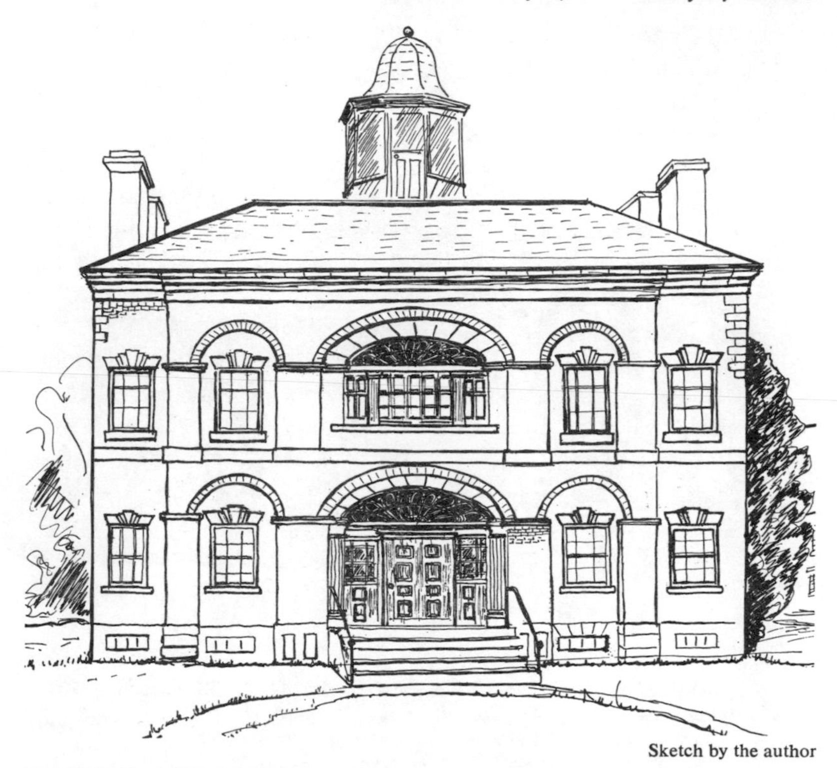

Sketch by the author

DANIEL McMARTIN'S HOUSE, CORNER HARVEY AND GORE, PERTH
He was an American with strong prejudices and ordered all materials brought from the U.S. for the building of this house in 1839.

had as law student in his office his nephew, Robert Lyon, whose father was one of the founders of the Richmond settlement.

A former governess in the Boulton household, Miss Elizabeth Hughes, was the cause of the dispute. Scarcely a year before, on the way to Perth, her father, a Unitarian minister, had died of cholera in Lower Canada, leaving her, her sister, and a brother aged 12 orphans. A family named Ackland adopted them when they arrived in Perth, and at the time of the duel Miss Hughes was teaching in Mrs. Ackland's School for Young Ladies. Wilson had been courting Miss Hughes.

The young law students were often in each other's company as they both attended Court Sessions out of town. On one of these occasions Lyon made an uncomplimentary remark about Miss Hughes. Young Wilson repeated the remark in a letter to Mrs. Boulton and eventually it reached the ears of another young lady whom Lyon was courting. She in turn treated Lyon coolly when next they met. Upon learning the cause of his rejection Lyon assaulted Wilson the next time he found him outside the Court House. Wilson, humiliated, consulted his employer and eventually challenged Lyon to a duel.

Since similar affairs had come to nothing in the community, the same might have happened on this occasion but for an interested third party, Henry LeLievre. He was the son of a French republican, Commander of a French frigate, who had deserted to the British when Napoleon came to power. In due course Colonel Tito LeLievre was sent to Canada to take part in the 1812-14 War with the Americans, after which he settled with discharged soldiers in North Elmsley Township, near Perth. The LeLievres were French Huguenots and a branch of a family named LeBreton, related to the famous English actress, Lily Langtry.

Henry LeLievre was a man of powerful frame, handsome, reckless, and untroubled by scruples. He had hitherto unsuccessfully wooed Miss Hughes himself. He knew Lyon's reputation as a crack shot. Whichever way the duel went, there would be one less contestant for the attentions of the lovely young lady. LeLievre fanned the flame of pride and "honour" in both young men, using his persuasive powers to keep the issue alive. A time and place was set for the duel, and on June 13th the parties met by the Tay River, just outside the town.

There were five men present—Wilson, Lyon, Wilson's second Simon F. Robertson (another law student), LeLievre, and Dr. Hamilton. Pistols for the occasion had been unobtrusively secured from a local store and were returned anonymously afterward. The first round of ammunition proved harmless. Some said the pistols were loaded with blank cartridges but another spectator claimed Wilson's temple was grazed. Robertson and the doctor did their best to put an end to the affair then and there, but LeLievre ordered the two to reload.

Again they took their positions and on command wheeled and fired. Both pistols went off at the same time. Lyon's shot missed Wilson but Wilson's penetrated Lyon's heart. He died instantly.

The body of young Lyon was carried to the home of his uncle, Thomas Radenhurst, where the distraught and enraged lawyer cursed the whole Boulton household and threatened to shoot either the lawyer or his apprentice if he found them within range.

A few days later a solemn procession left the Radenhurst mansion with the remains of the young law student. The funeral cortege proceeded to the Craig Street Cemetery and lowered the body into a grave near the Radenhurst family plot. Later Lyon's friends in the town subscribed money to erect a simple headstone.

Wilson and Robertson, horrified at the outcome of the duel, gave themselves up and were lodged in the county jail at Perth for three months until the next assizes were held at Brockville. Both were tried before Chief Justice John Beverley Robinson. Both young students defended themselves so ably that the Chief Justice commended them. Impressed by their calibre, he called the attention of the jury to the fact that Wilson did not desire to fight the duel, had consistently hoped for a reconciliation, that he was of humble origin and had had to be more aggressive to establish his character and reputation for a future in law. The sympathy of the Judge and Wilson's own pathetic "I closed my eyes and the deed was done" won the jury. Both students were acquitted.

Sketch by the author

TOMBSTONE IN CRAIG STREET CEMETERY, PERTH

The duel occurred in June, and Boulton after this sad affair had no heart to practice in Perth. By October he was preparing to leave the town and his gracious brick house overlooking the Tay. The evening of his departure some young people purportedly organized by McMartin drove along the street with a gibbet from which hung a figure representing the departing lawyer. This they later burned in front of the Boulton house. His friends tried to stop the parade, put out the fire, and scattered the actors. It was an unhappy ending to the young lawyer's career in Perth. He left for Niagara, where young Wilson later followed him to continue apprenticeship in his office.

The Rev. William Bell commented in his Journals that "there was a vindictive spirit manifested among the members of the Bar, not only at one another but by the public against the whole of them, which showed they were no favourites". LeLievre fled the district and for a time was a fugitive, finding his way back to Ottawa and Montreal where some LeBreton relatives lived. Later he went to Australia. E. John Hubbell arrived late in 1834 to take over Boulton's office as attorney.

Justice at this time was patterned after the British law. Lawyers collected large fees for settling line fence questions because the original surveys had been often too hastily made. Correct locations of line fences and roads required examination of records and documents and much legal interpretation. Sometimes a whole concession would be involved.

Litigation formed a mainstay for lawyers. Defamations of character and trespassing on property were popular causes for suits, but old records show that there were also breaches of promise and suits for bastardy. The latter generally involved the "master of the manor" and the hired girl. Collection of debts accounted for a great many court cases and the vicious hanging for debt law was still in force until 1835, when it was abolished.

There was, of course, in such a society no protection for animals. Mr. Bell in his Journals laments the brutality he observed among settlers. In one case a poor old horse "mere skin and bones" was beaten by his owner because he could not or would not pull a sleigh loaded with heavy hardwood. He related that there was a law in existence regarding animals by July 31, 1825, but it was so brutal and severe that people connived in not carrying it out for the punishment was hanging. It also covered domestic animals which were valuable during the pioneer period.

During the 1820s Perth grew steadily to accommodate the influx of settlers to the county and the steady traffic to and from the town on legal or other business. There were plenty of general stores. Along with those of Morris, Delisle, Matheson, and Watson, early merchants of the military settlement, were others owned by Alex Wylie, John Ferguson, and John and William Bell, Mr. Bell's sons.

Mr. Ferguson was one of the Scotch Line pioneers and had been the first assessor with Sam Purdy in 1817. He was also an early magistrate. He not only had a store, but also operated a distillery and manufactured a reputable whiskey called "Craigdarroch". Ferguson later ran a tavern called the Waterloo.

In 1828 the Bell brothers opened a store bringing "13 loaded trains" (wagons of goods) from Montreal. They also changed the business methods for general merchandising. Before their arrival on the scene it had been customary for merchants to keep their prices at a certain level. The Bell Bros. store proposed to take less profit and offered their goods at lower prices. They prospered and a year later opened another store at Morphy's Falls in Beckwith. The usual mechanics shops, shoemakers, harness makers, and blacksmith shops were found in the growing capital.

The ague and fever hit the settlement in the late 1820s and early 30s affecting most people and some fatally. Whole families were attacked by ague, leaving them weak and sickly for months. Fortunately another doctor arrived at Perth in 1827 to assist in ministering to the sick. This was Dr. James Stewart Nichol who, like Dr. Wilson, was a graduate of Edinburgh University. Dr. Nichol had a very accomplished wife, the daughter of the German composer Mueller.

Work was commencing about this time along the Rideau River on the construction of the Rideau canal, and when this was completed many of the mechanics and labourers migrated to Perth and vicinity, there to set up shops or engage in farming.

In the early days the settlement could not support a newspaper. Those who could read and desired news of Canada and the world, subscribed to Brockville, Kingston, and Montreal newspapers. Often these were paid for by one person and shared with neighbours and friends. The Rev. Dr. Gemmill, who came to Lanark with the Lanark Society settlers in 1821, brought a knowledge of printing and a small printing press with him. Specimens of his work are now in the Perth Museum. There was no newspaper, however, until John Stewart teacher of the first District Grammar School, ordered a press from Montreal. It arrived in March 1828, was set up in Adamson's Red House, and Stewart began publishing a small 20 by 14-inch tabloid which he called the *Perth Examiner*. In 1829 he changed the name to *Independent Examiner*. The Rev. William Bell recorded in his Journals that Stewart came from Ireland and had taught in a school between Prescott and Brockville for some time. He had edited, "if we are to believe him", the Brockville *Recorder*. Jonas Jones, an influential lawyer and later Judge at Brockville, recommended Stewart to Bishop Strachan when the first Bathurst District Grammar School opened at Perth in 1823. Stewart seems to have had an inflammable nature. He and Mr. Bell early fell out over religious practices, eventually leading to lawsuits.

Stewart used his newspaper to talk back to certain elements in the community which he disliked, and included Mr. Bell. An entry in Bell's Journals dated 1825 indicates the sentiment then existing between the two men. Bell recorded that he had heard "Stewart, my arch enemy, had fallen and bitten his tongue so badly that Dr. Wilson had to sew it".

"Profanation of the Sabbath" was one Bell's frequent complaints from his pulpit, and John Stewart early published an article encouraging such profanity. Bell recorded the upshot of this brazen journalism on February 8, 1829:

> A great number of sleighs, filled with company drove about the streets in a shameful manner. At one time, 18 of these carriages might be seen . . . providing noise and setting an example very annoying to the peaceable and orderly part of the inhabitants. Amongst them was the carriage of Mr. Morris, our M.P.P., as well as that of the Sheriff and several of our magistrates. When the very men whose duty it was to suppress these disorders set the example, what could we expect from others.

Mr. Bell sat down and wrote an article on the conduct of those who profaned the Sabbath and sent it to the *Independent Examiner*. The accused responded with two articles of an "abusive description". Bell then wrote a letter to the trustees of the District Grammar School complaining of Stewart's influence on the young people whom he taught. Stewart sued him for libel. At the next Court of Quarter Sessions, the Stewart *verus* Bell case came up and, although the jury had been "laced with rum" by Stewart and one at least was "very drunk", after listening to Radenhurst's eloquent plea on behalf of Bell, the jury returned a verdict of £5 damage instead of the £500 for which Stewart had sued. Bell paid.

Meanwhile a vitriolic pamphlet dissecting Mr. Bell's character and conduct appeared, anonymously signed "A Presbyterian". Since Stewart professed no faith, the writer was thought to be the Hon. William Morris, the M.P. for Lanark, for the pamphlet had obviously been written by someone skilled in the use of language. This invective spared no words of condemnation. Much of it was false, such as the accusation that Bell cared nothing for the poor settlers outside of Perth and never left his own fireside.

The pamphlet was delivered through the Post Office free to all who came for their mail. The treatise hurt the pastor deeply, since part of it was unjust and the remainder unacceptable. He sued Stewart. The case was postponed for a year and finally brought before the Supreme Court at York in 1829. Stewart had to pay court costs amounting to around £200 but no damages.

Malcolm Cameron who later owned the Perth newspaper, the *Bathurst Courier*, was a friend of Stewart at this time. He was 21, an impressionable age, and seems to have been influenced by his associates, for in 1828 he had written a slanderous address to the Hon. William Morris signing it "James Robertson", and had it printed and circulated among the electors of the county. Morris was apparently not affected by the pamphlet for he proceeded to carry the polls at the next election. The pamphlet later came up in a lawsuit between Morris and Cameron in the 1840s.

There were other sports besides lawsuits in the early community however. One of these was horse-racing. In June 1823 the first horse race was held at Perth and attended by most of the military heroes of the village. William Bell, commenting on the occasion, remarked that he saw an old woman of nearly 90 years creeping along with her walking stick to the races. Whereupon he spoke to her and suggested it would better for her to prepare herself for the "Hereafter". This was Mrs. Hunter, said to be the oldest person in the settlement at the time. She died in December of the same year. For the races, drivers assembled at the old Patterson hotel at the corner of Drummond and Harvey streets, racing from there to the end of Drummond Street.

Another amusement was the cattle fair held after 1827 twice a year—in May and at the end of the summer. Fairs were occasions for drinking and brawling, and as there were no police officers to keep the peace the right of might prevailed. Sometimes horse-racing topped off fair day. In 1829 the Bench of Magistrates at the recommendation of the Grand Jury made horse-racing illegal, but on the first day of the fair that year there was racing as usual with the magistrates present and betting eagerly.

An early colourful figure of the community was Anthony Wiseman, Town Crier and walking newspaper. Appointed High Constable in 1826, his duties included perambulating around the streets and announcing events. At specified locations he would halt, ring the large bell he carried, and when a crowd had assembled he would make his announcements and proceed on his way. He also sold "Hot mutton pies! Ginger beer!" and other delicacies, calling his wares as he went along the street—very popular with small boys.

In the 1830s another lawyer arrived. John Glass Malloch came from Brockville to set up a practice and later married a daughter of Mr. Bell. Mr. Malloch was a teetotaller, which naturally put him in the good graces of Mr. Bell, who seems, however, to have had some difficulty in persuading his own sons of the evils of drink. A Temperance Society was in full swing but it was long before John and William Bell joined it. Mr. Malloch purchased the Bell 25-acre park lot known as "Sweetbank" and here erected one of the finest private residences in eastern Upper Canada, its only rival being Rideau Hall at Bytown. This was called "Victoria Hall" and later became part of the Perth and District Memorial Hospital. Malloch succeeded Judge Armstrong as judge of the Bathurst District Court in 1842.

Dr. Thom sold his saw mill in 1833 to John Haggart, Sr., a native of Breadalbane, Scotland. Haggart built an oatmeal and flour mill on the island, later known as Haggart's Island. John Graham Haggart, his son, born at Perth in 1830, was the town's first mayor in 1867.

A foundry was established in 1835 by C. Miller, at first blast-driven by two horses. This proved very expensive and Miller later obtained a rotary engine. Ploughs for farmers were the first item of manufacture.

The first trading-post at Perth was apparently set up in 1835 when David Hogg, Bailiff for the tenth division of the District, began an auctioneering business. The Bathurst *Courier* reported:

> He is fitting up part of that large and commodious dwelling in which he now resides for the purpose, and will have a sale every week during the winter of articles adapted to the season and wants of the place.

Walling's *Directory of Lanark and Renfrew*, 1863

VICTORIA HALL, RESIDENCE OF JUDGE MALLOCH, PERTH

*Illustrated Atlas*, 1880

HICK'S HOTEL, PERTH

Part of this building was once Glascott's Hotel.

At his first sale in December stoves, fur caps, boots and shoes, dry-goods, ladies' bonnets, and a wide variety of other goods were offered. A shed and stables were available on the premises if farmers wished to sell horses or cattle or barter livestock.

Perth, which had but little to do with the Rebellion of '37, was also cheated of a chance to celebrate its end.

> The Rebellion now being suppressed [Bell wrote in his Journal] the Governor appointed a day of thanksgiving to be observed for this mark of Divine favour. He gave us no official information and the day was past before we received information by any other means. The Presbytery noted this in their next meeting and wrote to the Governor's secretary saying they regretted this, 'it being their wish to observe all appointments of this kind seriously'. . . . In answer His excellency said he regretted the short notice but as he was shortly to leave the Province he wished to observe this important duty before he went.

In November 1838 news of the Patriot raid near Prescott reached Perth, and John Bell received orders to call out his Company of Leeds Militia and march to Brockville, where they remained the winter. The Bathurst militia was likewise called out but not required.

The Hon. William Morris was appointed to the Legislative Council in 1836, an indication that he was in good standing with the governing body at York. For three months Dr. Thom took his place in the Legislative Assembly but was defeated in the next election by Malcolm Cameron. Dr. Thom died in 1846 or 1847.

The Perth newspaper, the *Independent Examiner*, was a four-page effort in 1834 when Stewart sold his "instrument of destruction" to John Cameron, a brother of Malcolm. The same year Stewart lost his position as teacher of the District Grammar School after a dispute with the trustees, and left for Stratford. Cameron changed the name of his newspaper to the *Bathurst Courier* and gave notice that he had no political line to follow and did not intend to be "slave or tool of any political party". His reign as editor was short-lived, for the same autumn he contracted scarlet fever and died. Malcolm Cameron, then angling for political nomination, took over the *Courier* and hired James Thompson, a young man of 22, as journeyman, foreman, local editor and many et ceteras which the editor of those days had to assume since the printing office staff generally consisted of two people—an apprentice and the editor himself. Thompson, a native of Newton-Gore, County of Leitram, Ireland, had come to Canada at the age of 7 and learned the printing trade in Montreal. Cameron sold the *Courier* to his printer in September 1835 but continued to influence the newspaper after his election to the legislature in 1836 and apparently even after he had left the community for Sarnia as late as 1841.

Newspaper life in those days was distinguished by hard work and little financial return. Often the editor was paid for subscriptions by goods—cordwood or farm produce, for currency was scarce. The following notice appeared in an early issue of the *Courier*:

> We wish to inform those of our subscribers who intend to pay in advance, that we will receive no subscriptions as such after the first of the ensuing month. We would appreciate a few cords of wood by way of an anchovie, to keep our ink from freezing.

One writer has called Thompson a "courtly, polished gentleman of the old school", and it is supposed that his pleas for payment were always merely gentle reminders.

The Rideau Canal opened in the 1830s and by the 1840s a steady stream of river traffic plied to and from Perth bringing in supplies and taking out lumber, potash, and a few other exports.

Smith's *Canadian Gazetteer* for 1846 reported that the town then occupied 400 acres of land and had a population of 1800. "Matheson's" was then the principal tavern, and there was a stage running three times a week to Brockville. A jail and a courthouse built of white freestone were then under one roof. Barges were plying the canal with produce for the export market and towing rafts of timber bound for Montreal or Oswego. There were numerous industries, indicating that Perth was a lively commercial centre:

Foundries—Shaw's, Miller's, Lillie's
Blacksmiths—Tom Farmer, Cornelius Farmer, Tait's, Felix Harrishaw, Jas. Lafferty, Lett James, Walter and Thomas Hunter, John Bell.
Breweries—Wm. Lock & Wm. Wordie, Robt. Gemmill, Canwith.
Shoemakers—Wm. O'Brien, Wm. Brown.
Carding Mill—Richard Code.
Waggon Makers—Geo. Cox, Thos. Patterson, Geo. Publow.
Harness & Trunks—Thos. McCaffrey, Mr. Halliday, Mr. Jamieson, Ned Dougherty.
Inn-Keepers—Wm. Glascott, John McCallum, Wm. Wordie.
Axe-Makers—Neil Campbell, Mr. Korry.
Pork Packing Establishments—Dick Walker, John Rodger.

Bakers—James Allan, J. K. Fairbairn.
Painting—John Hart & Son.
Tinsmiths—Wm. Butler, John Campbell, Mr. McLeod.

In 1841 the Act of Union was passed "to provide for the better internal government of the portion of this Province which formerly constituted the Province of Upper Canada by the establishment of local and municipal authorities therein." The first Municipal Council for the District of Bathurst met at Perth's Court house on February 8, 1848. By this time Carleton County had become the District of Dalhousie with its own capital at Bytown. Perth continued as capital, as it is today, of the County of Lanark.

*Illustrated Atlas*, 1880

THOMAS BROOKE

Born at Halifax, settled at Perth in 1818. Clerk for several townships and County Clerk for many years.

## CHAPTER XIII

## EARLY POLITICAL LIFE

In 1816 the Parliament of Upper Canada sat at York. The governing body comprised the Lieutenant-Governor, a military officer appointed by the British government and their representative in Upper Canada; a Legislative Assembly; a Legislative Council; and an Executive Council. Of these only the Legislative Assembly was elected by the people, and it was chosen by those who owned land. The Legislative Council was appointed by the Lieutenant-Governor for life, and members were often promoted from the Legislative Assembly to this august body. The Council also included clergymen, judges, and other important personages. The Executive Council was selected by the governor but had to be confirmed by the Colonial office in London. Frequently the same persons held several government positions and did very well financially.

By June 1819 the magistrates, half-pay officers, and other inhabitants of the Perth Military settlement had drawn up a petition in which they pointed out that the population of their community already exceeded 5000, was rapidly growing, and should be represented in the Legislative Assembly of Upper Canada.

After due consideration the Upper Canada government accepted the petition and appointed Roderick Matheson as Returning Officer for holding the first election in the settlement on or before the 24th of July, 1820. In June land deeds were issued to settlers who had stayed on their land three years or more and had fulfilled the specified requirements.

For the July election six candidates presented themselves, but by the time election day arrived the number had dwindled to two—William Morris and Benjamin DeLisle, both shopkeepers at Perth. As to eligibility very little is known personally about DeLisle, but of

Morris reports and records indicate that he was a well-educated, successful business man. The Morris family have left their mark on Canadian politics and public affairs.

William Morris, born at Paisley in 1786, had emigrated with his parents at the age of 12 to Lower Canada, settling near Montreal. William took part in the War of 1812 and in 1816 he proceeded with the settlers to the Rideau area, locating in Perth and opening the first general store. With his brother, Alexander, he formed a partnership in mercantile trade, his brother opening a similar store in Brockville. Later another brother, James, joined Alexander in the Brockville business.

On Monday, July 10, 1820, crowds began to pour into Perth at an early hour for the first election. By 10 o'clock a number of men proceeded to Mr. Matheson's house and accompanied him to the hustings.* The business had just begun when the floor gave way and fell to the ground. Other than a few splashes of ink over the dresses of the ladies no great damage seems to have occurred. Mr. Bell reported in his Journal: "Plenty of carpenters being at hand, the hustings were speedily repaired and business commenced".

The freeholders (only those who had received their land deeds by this time were eligible to vote) were requested to divide, those for Morris to the right and those for DeLisle to the left. Loud cheering followed the choice of the majority to the right for Mr. Morris. But Mr. DeLisle demanded a poll. A. Murdock (later Inspector of Schools for Lanark County) and Alexander Cameron were the polling clerks. Voting lasted until 4 o'clock when it was adjourned until the following day. The poll then stood at 56 for Morris and 36 for DeLisle.

The method of voting required some courage on the part of the electorate. The candidates generally stood at either side of the polling clerks with their record books. As each voter stepped up he was asked to name his candidate in a "loud clear voice". The polling clerk then recorded his name in the appropriate column. Once at a later election when the voting was exceptionally close a last-minute voter was produced. He had worked for one of the candidates, who undoubtedly expected to get his vote. Instead he spoke the name of the other candi-

* The word *hustings* is often used erroneously to mean *a meeting for the purpose of voting*. The plural form actually means a platform constructed to hold candidates for election and the polling clerk. The cartoon depicting the 1828 election is a somewhat exaggerated version of the hustings. Small wonder they gave way!

Douglas Library, Kingston F. H. Consitt

1828 ELECTION CARTOON, PERTH

This cartoon shows the hustings with rival candidates, William Morris and Dr. Alex. Thom.

date in a "loud clear voice" and so aroused the temper of his former employer that the man took a swing at him. The voter ducked and the blow landed on the opposing candidate. A free-for-all followed!

Mr. Bell reporting the first election in his Journal remarks:

> It was painful to observe that during the day, rum and other liquors were served out in abundance by both parties so that in a short time many of the people were drunk. Some ludicrous scenes occurred and several battles were fought. At 5 in the evening, I and 18 of Mr. Morris' friends dined together at the head inn.

Next morning, DeLisle resigned his pretensions and Morris was duly elected. His friends bore him aloft down the main street of Perth, cheering and singing patriotic songs while the inhabitants plied them with "spirits". Afterward the evening was spent in lively rejoicing.

On his arrival in Parliament Morris lost no time in informing the Legislative Assembly of the needs of his settlement. At his first session in 1821 he introduced and succeeded in having passed an Act to Establish a Public Market in Perth.

# To the Settlers and Proprietors of Land in the Perth Settlement, and adjoining Townships in the County of Carleton, Upper Canada.

***GENTLEMEN,***

*It being extremely probable that you will be admitted to the important privilege of electing a Member, to represent you in the Parliament of Upper Canada, I take this early opportunity of soliciting your Votes and interest, to place me in that honorable situation; and you may rest assured it will always be my anxious care to watch over the interests, and promote the prosperity of* our Infant Colony.

*I have the honor to be,*
*Gentlemen,*
*Your very Obedient Servant,*

WILLIAM MARSHAL, J. P.
*and Capt. late Canadian Regt.*

Montreal, (Lower Canada)—Printed by W. Gray.

Douglas Library, Kingston

EARLY ELECTION POSTER

In 1823 he introduced a Bill for education, requesting financial support for a grammar school, common school, and a salary for a Sheriff. The bills seem to have taken some time to get through the two Legislative Houses but eventually were passed separately.

Mr. Morris early espoused the cause of Presbyterianism in Upper Canada and in 1823, backed by fellow Presbyterians in the Assembly, he moved and carried a resolution declaring that the Church of Scotland in Upper Canada was on equal footing with the Church of England with respect to clergy reserves. The Legislative Council threw the resolution out, but Lord Bathurst in England upheld the Assembly's interpretation.

Thereafter Morris was acknowledged head of the Scottish Presbyterian interests in Upper Canada. His stand against such powerful political figures as Sir John Beverley Robinson, who championed the cause of the Church of England, apparently did not damage his standing with his peers, for he was later appointed to the reigning body—the Legislative Council (a life appointment)—and even became its president. In 1825 he was re-elected, and the next year the British government recognized the claims of the Church of Scotland to the extent of granting them £750 from public funds. Nothing, however, was done about the vast acreage of clergy reserves all over Upper Canada still in the hands of the Church of England.

Another problem at this time was lack of educational facilities in Canada for Presbyterian students wishing to train for the ministry. The Anglicans had their King's College under Bishop Strachan, the Methodists had a seminary at Cobourg in the 1830s, Roman Catholics could attend Regiopolis College at Kingston, but the Presbyterians had to go to Scotland for a divinity course.

Bishop Strachan further provoked Presbyterians by publishing an "Ecclesiastical Chart of the Province in 1827" in which he referred to a Church of Scotland clergyman who had brought his sons up in the Church of England "of which they are now parish priests".*

Morris replied to Strachan in an open letter in the *Patriot* and followed this with speeches and pamphlets. Petitions were presented to both Houses of Parliament and to the Governor-General. In 1827 the British government passed an Act authorizing the sale of parts of the clergy reserves. This may have benefited the farmers whose land adjoined these waste tracts but it did nothing for the Church of Scot-

* He was the Rev. Mr. Bethune of Brockville who had been unable to bear the expense of sending his two sons to university in Scotland.

land since the proceeds from the sales went into the Church of England coffers. By 1837 some 450,000 acres of clergy reserves had been thus sold.

In the election of 1828 the Hon. William Morris defeated Dr. Thom. By 1829 the population of Bathurst District had increased to such an extent that it was entitled to two representatives in the Assembly, and Donald Fraser, pioneer and ex-Army officer, was elected as Mr. Morris' colleague. The Parliament of 1830 dissolved when King George IV died and another election was called at which Fraser and Morris were again elected. In this election Mr. Tully opposed Mr. Morris. The Bell Journal recorded:

> At 10 the crowds began to pour in; at 11 the Returning Officer with numerous attendants mounted the hustings and read his authority for holding an election. At 12 the two candidates Mr. Morris and Mr. Tully began making speeches and abusing one another. At 1 the polling commenced and at 4 it was over, Mr. Morris being chosen by 226 votes to 21 for Mr. Tully.
>
> At 5, I and about 20 more of his friends dined with Mr. Morris at his own house. In his address on the hustings, Mr. Morris had called Mr. Mackenzie a *revolutionary scoundrel* but he now said he was sorry he had done so.
>
> Mr. Tully in his address said, speaking of Mr. Morris, 'Let him come on with all his *Banditti*.' Mr. Morris said he did not think it right to call the Yeomanry of the country who were his supporters, *Banditti*. Then, said Mr. Morris, you must mean my supporters in this town—magistrates, half-pay officers and clergymen. No, said Mr. Tully, I mean Patrocles, Pat O'Shaughnessy and other blackguard writers who have appeared in the Perth *Examiner*.
>
> It was pleasing to observe that there was no treating till the election was over so that those disgusting scenes of drunkenness were avoided and most of the people went home sober.

This was the year when the Reform member, William Lyon Mackenzie, provoked the Legislative Assembly with such an avalanche of grievance reports that they voted to expel him. Although Fraser was the Reform candidate, anything resembling rebellion against the Crown was abhorrent to him and on one occasion he moved a resolution to expel Mackenzie. Mackenzie was ousted and took his case and grievances to England. Colonel Fraser was one of the discharged military men from the War of 1812, and had settled first along the

Scotch Line, then later moved to a farm on the edge of Lanark Village.

Politics was one of the sports of pioneer life, and the next election in 1832 was a lively affair since the Reform Party was now gaining popularity with supporters all over Lanark County. Mr. Morris was again elected without much opposition but the choice of the second Member was a violent contest. Morris himself supported Captain Alex McMillan (Registrar for the District of Bathurst) whose Conservative view corresponded to his own, but again Fraser secured the seat. Voting went on for a week, tension mounting, and as Bell says in his Journal "both parties sent out sleighs in all directions to bring in voters, and the night was busily employed as the day had been". By Friday Captain McMillan had resigned. Mr. Morris discovered, however, that Fraser had not taken out the necessary property deeds to qualify as a political candidate six months previously, and the Assembly declared the election null and void. In a new election Dr. Reade opposed Fraser.

Meanwhile the necessary land deeds were obtained. A grandson of Colonel Fraser, Donald Fraser of Victoria, writing in the Perth *Courier* of 1905 recalls: "Malcolm Cameron in making the nomination on the hustings literally covered himself with the documents. The effect was wonderful, the people were aroused to the highest pitch of excitement, the voting was all done in Perth". Bell reported: "Several battles took place among the Irishmen of whom a great number were present, and more than one got dreadfully beaten". Dr. Reade was defeated and Fraser resumed his seat in the Legislative Assembly.

In the 1834 election Mr. Morris and Colonel Josiah Taylor were elected. Taylor was Postmaster at the time. Several other candidates were proposed for this election: Dr. Thom, Colonel Taylor, Daniel Shipman, William Tully, and John McNee. Mr. Morris was not originally nominated and the Bathurst *Courier* gave a somewhat humorous account of the whole proceedings. As the candidates were nominated, each was introduced with a promotional address.

> Mr. Morris then made an address, commenting on the previous addresses and ending on a pathetic note of farewell to the electors saying he had served them for 14 years, and citing the Acts he had had passed, the things he had done for the settlement and asked them to join him in three cheers for the King, which they did enthusiastically. Then a respectable farmer rushed up to the hustings and

> said: 'Fellow electors, if we *loose* Mr. Morris, we *loose* our right arm in Parliament. Let us return him again.' Some said he did not wish to serve but Mr. Morris explained this was not so. Mr. Montgomery who proposed him, said Mr. Morris had grown grey in the service and all who appreciated his services should now turn to the right—when a large majority of the electors present cheered for Mr. Morris and it was proposed to call an election without a poll but as a poll had been called for, it immediately opened.*

By Tuesday, the polls stood thus: Morris—390, Taylor—252, Thom—146, Fraser—22, Tully—1. There were no votes for either Shipman or McNee, and both resigned on Wednesday. The *Courier* reported:

> Great praise is due J. A. H. Powell, Sheriff, for his impartial conduct during the election as Returning Officer. Several attempts were made to interrupt some of the speakers but he instantly stopped them and threatened committal as he insisted every freeholder had a right to speak while the majority were willing to listen.

By the end of the week Morris had 436 votes, Taylor, 335, Thom, 200, Fraser 29, and Tully still only 1. Obviously Mr. Morris' popularity had not waned during all his years in the Legislative Assembly, and he and Colonel Taylor proceeded to the next Session.

The election of 1836 brought a new political figure to the scene. But for some personal idiosyncrasies he might have engraved his name on Canadian history. This was Malcolm Cameron. Born in 1808 in Lower Canada, he came to the Perth settlement in 1816 with his parents. Here his father, Angus, a disbanded sergeant, was granted land in Drummond township on the banks of the Mississippi, and opened one of the first inns.

His father died in 1822 and Malcolm went to Montreal and hired himself out as a stable boy, saving his money to invest in business. Several years later he returned and opened a general store in Perth in partnership with his brother-in-law Henry Glass, a partnership which dissolved in 1829. Cameron was later associated with Robert Gemmill in the lumbering business.

By 1836 Morris had been called to a seat in the Legislative Council by the new Governor, Sir Francis Bond Head. Dr. Thom took his place in the lower House temporarily. The election of 1836 lasted six days, and Malcolm Cameron polled 559 votes, W. F. Powell 552, Dr. Thom 515, and Thomas Radenhurst 384.

* *Bathurst Courier*, October 10, 1834.

Public Archives of Canada

HON. MALCOLM CAMERON

Cameron bitterly opposed Sir Francis Head's government from 1836 to 1838 but he took no active part in the Rebellion of 1837. Meanwhile he became interested in real estate in Western Ontario, buying up a tract of land where Sarnia now stands and laying it out in town lots. The surrounding forests of hickory, walnut, and oak, valuable hardwood, promised a solid financial future, and to this area Mr. Cameron induced a group of adventurous Perth people to migrate. James Porter who had been in the lumbering business with Mr. Gemmill was one of these, and another was George Durand, a man of means and enterprise. Most of these pioneers were Scotsmen and Radicals who supported Mr. Cameron's political views.

Morris, now in the Legislative Council, was still carrying the Presbyterian banner. In April 1837 delegates from several Presbyterian congregations met at Cobourg and drew up a statement of their rights as established by the Act of Union between England and Scotland in 1707. Morris was chosen to "bell the cat" since he had political standing in Upper Canada, and was generally recognized as a man of sound character, education, and means. He sailed for London and presented his case to the Colonial Secretary Lord Glenelg. Mr. Morris' mission was largely successful. Sir John Colborne's action concerning the clergy reserves was pronounced illegal by the Home government, and Sir Francis Bond Head was instructed to nullify the land grants.

Meanwhile a promise had been received from the Presbyterian Synod in Scotland to assist in the setting up of a suitable college in Upper Canada. Sir George Arthur had succeeded Sir Francis Bond

Head in 1839 as Governor, and when the Legislative Council sat that year under the new Governor, the Hon. William Morris introduced his Bill for establishing a college in Upper Canada for the Church of Scotland. The members stalled on Mr. Morris' bill, deferring it from week to week, month to month, until 1840. Finally the Bill to establish Queen's College at Kingston was passed. This was Mr. Morris' major political triumph.

Funds had already been collected through his efforts the previous year. In 1841 a Royal Charter was granted and Morris was suitably chosen as the first Chairman of the Board of Trustees. There were to be 27 trustees of whom twelve were to be ministers of the Presbyterian church and fifteen laymen. Although there was naturally a Presbyterian divinity faculty for students wishing to train for the ministry, this was the only theological discrimination, for written into the Charter were words of religious freedom: "that no religious test or qualifications should be required of, or appointed for any persons admitted or matriculated, within said College".*

The year 1841 brought many changes. The Act of Union was passed. The seat of government moved from Toronto to Kingston, and the latter overflowed with militia, members of parliament, government officials, and their entourage. Queen's College began its life in a small two-storied frame building called "the hospital" with a class composed of only seven pupils of whom the Rev. William Bell's son, George, was one; in fact he was the first Divinity graduate from Queen's some years later.

In 1844 Mr. Morris was appointed a member of the Executive Council under Sir Charles Metcalfe's administration and became Receiver-General of the province. He was a logical, forceful speaker with an extensive knowledge of parliamentary law and procedure and exercised a beneficent influence on the Executive Council.

In contrast with him, Malcolm Cameron was "small of stature, insignificant in appearance, and his oratory was marred by want of education and an unmusical voice," says John C. Dent in his *Canada Since the Union of 1841*. Mr. Dent further remarks: "He was an honest, earnest and upon the whole, a well-meaning man who did a great deal of useful work in his day and attained much reputation as a Member of Parliament, but he was not always easy to manage and was restive under discipline".

* *Documentary History of Education in Upper Canada from the passing of the Constitutional Act of 1791*, by J. George Hodgins (1894).

There was also another side to Cameron as revealed in a lawsuit which William Morris brought against him in 1844. Mr. Morris in correspondence with Sir Charles Metcalfe's Secretary, J. M. Higginson, has referred to Cameron as a "mischievous man . . . in the course of my life, I have never met his match. The appointments made in the Bathurst District gave him a firmer footing than ever and did great injury to the public".* William Morris had some justification for his remarks. In an early election Cameron had circulated a libellous pamphlet against him, signed anonymously. Cameron was fond of writing anonymous letters and seems to have had much to do with creating conflict between Mr. Bell and Mr. Morris. He seems to have been mercurial in temperament and not very dependable despite his sincere interest in the common people.

Under the Act of Union the combined counties of Lanark and Renfrew were limited to one Member in the Legislative Assembly. William Bell gives a revealing report of the 1841 election at Perth in which Malcolm Cameron was opposed by John A. H. Powell, then Sheriff of Bathurst District:

> Our people had been at great pains to provide flags and music which they sent out to meet the sleighs which soon began to arrive from all quarters well loaded with electors. At 10 an immense crowd being assembled round the hustings, the business of the day began. Mr. Playfair in his speech of some length, proposed Mr. Powell. He began like most other Methodist preachers by relating his own history. Then he abused the Americans, then the other candidates; and in this, most people thought he did not *Play fair*. . . . he accused Mr. Cameron of disloyalty, of being a democrat, and almost of everything bad. He concluded by recommending Mr. Powell, as a complete gentleman. . . . Mr. Powell now came forward and made his address which was remarkable only for its length and the want of point . . . it abounded in invective and was sadly deficient in truth. . . . Mr. Radenhurst in proposing Mr. Cameron repelled with indignation the charge of disloyalty, explained the word *Democrat* and answered all the objections of his *learned* friend, as he termed him. . . . Our William seconded this nomination, reprobated the conduct of the family compact, and showed the necessity of reform . . . he said if Mr. Powell was a gentleman, Mr. Cameron was what was far better, namely an *honest* man. . . . Mr. Cameron began his address by saying that he found himself rather awkwardly situated.

*Letter from Morris to Higginson, dated August 19, 1844. Courtesy T. B. Higginson.

> As an Irish friend of his observed, after all had been said that could be said, he had to say the rest. He then explained his past conduct and refuted the objections brought against him.
>
> The polling began at 3 and continued till 6 when the votes stood for Powell 47, Cameron 88. During the night the town was crowded with men and horses. Powell's people were very noisy but as Cameron's got no liquor, all was quiet in their quarters. . . .
>
> Next day the contest was carried on with great spirit but there was no volume till the afternoon when the rabble finding they were losing ground had recourse to the old method of intimidation and tearing clothes. The coat of a poor Irishman that voted for Cameron they tore to rags. So great was the confusion that the Returning Officer closed the poll till order was restored. . . . The contest continued till Thursday morning when Mr. Powell gave in, his opponent having a majority of 266. . . . Before Mr. Cameron left the place, he gave an address at a meeting of the Temperance Society which caused a great accession of members to the association.

At this time, Malcolm Cameron was residing in Sarnia. He continued to represent Lanark and Renfrew counties until 1848 when he took his seat as representative for Sarnia.

In later years he was Minister of Agriculture and Postmaster General. He was regarded as one of the leaders of the "Clear Grit" party and assisted William McDougall in founding the *North American*, the organ of that party. Among the reforms which Mr. Cameron was instrumental in effecting during the time he represented Lanark were those related to the Canadian canal system, the Homestead Exemption Law, the abolition of imprisonment for debt, the right of married women to hold real estate, Municipal Institutions Act, securalization of clergy reserves, the government railways measures, and the Ballot Act.

In the election of 1848 the Reform Party gained control. Robert Bell of Carleton Place, son of Mr. Bell of Perth, was elected as Reform (Liberal) Member, to represent Lanark and Renfrew counties in the legislature. His opponents in this election were Thomas Radenhurst and Daniel McMartin, lawyers at Perth. Robert Bell had been a merchant in Carleton Place for many years and had been prominent in municipal affairs. In fact, Bell had held almost every office open to the ordinary citizen, at one time or another, and his was a remarkable record of public service from Justice of the Peace to Member of

Parliament. His offices included: Chairman and Secretary of the organized "Loyal Village Guards" of 1837-38, President of the Bathurst Total Abstinence Union, Secretary and Treasurer of the United Counties of Lanark and Renfrew Agricultural Societies (1845-52), Warden of the United Counties of Lanark and Renfrew (1847). He was also prominent in the St. Andrew's Society in Carleton Place, the Brockville and Ottawa Railway scheme, and other community enterprises.

When Bell took his place in the legislature, Parliament was sitting in Montreal, having moved there from Kingston. He was in the Parliament Buildings in Montreal when they were destroyed by fire, and he escaped by a ladder. In the aftermath loyal delegates from Beckwith and Ramsay townships went to Montreal and presented a resolution prepared at local meetings to Lord Elgin, then Governor-General, supporting his reforms and condemning his opponents.

With the redistribution of seats following the census of 1851, Lanark and Renfrew were given separate representation. Lanark was divided into North and South Ridings, and in the next election, Robert Bell was elected for North Lanark and James Shaw for South Lanark. (James Shaw was one of the original officials of the Lanark Depot when he served as Clerk while Lanark Society immigrants were being registered and settled on their lands. He moved to Smiths Falls later and became a prominent merchant. He was one of the first appointees to the Senate from Lanark County.) Bell continued to serve in Parliament until 1866, when he was appointed Inspector of Canals.

The year 1850 brought changes in municipal government, too. Up until 1841 the magistrates had formed the governing body, holding Courts of Quarter Session where legal matters were settled and expenditures voted for roads, property, bridges, and other purposes. In 1841 District Councils were established throughout Upper Canada and each township then had a representative—or two if over 300 population—elected to it. A warden was appointed by the government for each District. The District Council met four times a year, its members being elected for 3-year periods.

The municipal Institutions Act of 1849 abolished this system and established instead County Councils elected annually, with one warden, and reeves with deputy reeves for each township. A joint County Council for Lanark and Renfrew met at Perth early in 1850, the following reeves representing the township:

| | |
|---|---|
| Bathurst and South Sherbrooke — | Josiah Richey |
| Beckwith — | Robert Bell |
| Burgess — | John Doran, Jr. |
| Dalhousie, North Sherbrooke and Lavant — | John Kay, M.D. |
| Drummond — | Murdock McDonnell and Pat Dowdell |
| Elmsley — | James Shaw, Sr. |
| Lanark and Darling — | Andrew Stevenson |
| Montague — | R.E. Matheson |
| Pakenham — | Wm. McAdam |
| Ramsay — | John Robertson |

Robert Bell was elected Warden. Under the new system each township also had a council composed of the reeve and five councillors, elected annually.

By this time Division Courts had also been set up throughout the county making it unnecessary to make the long journey to Perth for all court cases. It is not known when each of these was established but by 1850 the following Division Courts were in operation, presided over by John G. Malloch as County Judge:

| | |
|---|---|
| First Division — | Perth |
| Second Division — | Lanark |
| Third Division — | Carleton Place |
| Fourth Division — | Smiths Falls |
| Fifth Division — | Pakenham |
| Sixth Division — | Renfrew |
| Seventh Division — | Near or at the third Chute of the Bonnechère River in the township of Bromley, Renfrew. |
| Eighth Division — | Campbelltown, Renfrew. |

# CHAPTER XIV

# LUMBERING ALONG THE RIVERS OF LANARK

By the close of the war of 1812 lumbermen were already floating timber down the Ottawa River to Quebec, and by 1830 dams and timber slides were being constructed along tributaries of the Ottawa. By 1837 lumbermen had travelled as far as Lake Temiskaming. By the 1840s the small lumbermen were being supplanted by lumber "barons"—big operators with extensive timber holdings and hundreds of lumberjacks in their employ.

Anglo-Saxon and French-Canadian lumberjacks went in the autumn, some long before snowfall, to remote camps and spent the winter cutting and squaring timber, which they "drove" down the rivers in spring. Food and supplies for the men and their horses or oxen were furnished by the operator. Because the camps required large quantities of food, managers preferred to have good land and good farmers near their timber limits where they might buy hay, oats, peas, and potatoes more cheaply than they could import from the markets of Lower Canada.

When the timber capitalists moved into the Madawaska Valley and the District of Bathurst many settlers took their teams to the shanties and worked there all winter, leaving the farm chores to the women and children at home.

Saw mills erected by men with capital, often Americans, were scattered throughout the region long before lumber-driving got under way in the 1840s. In the early days these saw mills took care of excess lumber. During the 1840s timber limits were leased in the upper reaches of the county, and there were two waterways for the timber runs.

One was from the Clyde which feeds into the Mississippi, down the Mississippi to the Ottawa River, and on to Quebec. This route

*Picturesque Canada*

LUMBERMEN'S CAMP

begins beyond the present boundaries of Lanark County, draining South Canonto and Blythfield townships to the northwest. The Clyde River and its tributaries traverse Lavant, Darling, Dalhousie, and Lanark townships emptying into the Mississippi near Lanark village. The Mississippi River itself also begins beyond Lanark County in Palmerston Township and traverses, with its many lakes and tributaries, North and South Sherbrooke, Dalhousie, Bathurst, Drummond, Beckwith, Ramsay, and Pakenham townships, heading out into Fitzroy where it empties into the Ottawa River at Galetta.

The second timber route was down the Tay River and canal to the Rideau waterway, a system draining the lower part of Lanark County, through Bathurst, Elmsley, Burgess, Montague, and part of Beckwith township. The Mississippi system carried by far the greater volume of timber, circuitous as the route was, for despite its meanderings it did not have the passenger and freight traffic which the Rideau system acquired after the Rideau Canal was built.

By 1835 shanties had already been established in Ramsay Township by George Bryson and Simon Dunn and a timber slide built at Shipman's Mills. George Bryson moved to Fort Coulonge, Lower Canada, and went into the lumbering business with his brother Robert on the Coulonge and Black rivers in the 1840s. George was also a promoter of the Upper Ottawa Improvement Company and for many years a director of the Bank of Ottawa.

Sons of two pioneer settlers of Lanark Township were to become the principal lumber barons of the county. Alexander Caldwell, son of William Caldwell who pioneered on the edge of Darling Township, was already "running logs" on the Clyde at the age of 12. Sixteen years later in 1846 he was well established in business and had built a fine stone residence in Lanark village known as "Clyde Hall". In later years the interests of Alexander Caldwell & Son extended as far as the Trent River, where from his timber limits he cut from 200,000 to 300,000 square feet annually besides 30,000 logs. From their mills along the Clyde at Lanark the company's powerful horses drew immense loads to Perth during the summer months. Much of the timber passing through Perth went down the Rideau route to Kingston and across Lake Ontario to a steadily increasing market at Oswego.

Alexander Caldwell was among the great river captains. He believed in personal direction, and being a natural leader he commanded loyalty and respect from his men and feared no one, not even the rival gangs on the Trent River system where competition was keen and many a fight took place during the spring drives.

Battles likewise occurred on the Mississippi between gangs of McLaren and Caldwell in later years. The Rev. Joshua Fraser grew

*The Ganaraska Watershed*

WOODSMEN SQUARING TIMBER

up with Alexander Caldwell's son, William C. Caldwell, at Lanark village, and worked in the Caldwell shanties. He describes his experiences in his book *Forest, River and Shanty Life* (1883). Here is his description of Alexander ("Sandy") Caldwell:

> He is often spoken of as the pioneer lumberer of these backwoods, though in strict accuracy he was not so, as the Yule brothers were before him and also the Americans who drew timber out of Calabogie Lake as early as 1812 and gave their name to the bay of that Lake, . . . but he was the first who reduced the business to a thoroughly systematic and profitable shape.
>
> Nearly sixty years ago he commenced life in the woods at the age of 12 and until within a year or two of his death, three-quarters of his time was spent in the woods and on the river sharing the discomforts of the gang in the heaviest and most dangerous work that had to be done. He shirked nothing that any man could do and did many a thing that the boldest and hardiest wouldn't dream of attempting. He loved the work and the work loved him; it never soured and aged his temper, but fostered in him all that was kind and genial and manly. . . .
>
> He worked his men harder than any 'boss' on the river, and yet he was better liked than any other on it, for when the work was done and the press over, he was most kind and considerate, and would allow his men every indulgence and join in with them in any frolic or amusement that was going on. . . . He was a first-class shot . . . though he was a merciless despot at getting us up in the morning and off to our posts, still when the hunt and business of the day was over, he was the youngest and keenest among us in any frolic or athletic game that we indulged in. . . .
>
> He had a great dislike to profane language, especially of a blasphemous character. His reverence for the name of the Creator was most profound and he had no hesitation in checking and rebuking a man when he heard him uttering these profanities.

Of his legendary fearlessness Fraser tells a tale of one instance:

> On one of his visits to town while lumbering on the Trent River, he was robbed of $1,600. He had visited several hotels and spent lavishly and freely as usual. He talked the matter over with the hotel clerk and they both decided that it was a notorious bully and desperado of the town who had robbed him, an ex-convict from the penitentiary, a man of immense stature and strength. They started for the man's house, Sandy arming himself with a large

carving knife, from the dining room. Getting the man out of bed, they accused him. He went to get his gun but Sandy intercepted him with the knife. At this point the wife called out that he might as well surrender the money which was hidden in the tick of the bed they were sleeping in.

The clerk appeared at the door and the desperado seeing himself surrounded confessed. When the money had been returned to him, Sandy feeling sorry for the fellow, gave him $10 and asked him to mend his ways. Fraser's final comment: "Take him, all in all, Sandy Caldwell was as noble a type of humanity as ever lived or toiled in the Ottawa Valley".

On the Mississippi the Gillies, the Caldwells and the Gilmours were cutting timber in the 1840s. When he came of age John Gillies had left his father's homestead near Lanark village for a location on the Clyde River, now known as Herron. Here he cleared land and in 1839 married Mary Cullen Bain, daughter of another settler. On a portion of his land he erected a small saw mill with wooden frame and single upright saw weighing 90 lbs., carrying the saw from Brockville on his back—a distance of 55 miles. In 1842 he began cutting logs, at first from his own and his father's farm. These he turned into lumber selling to local trade at $6 or $8 per thousand feet.

*Illustrated Atlas*, 1880

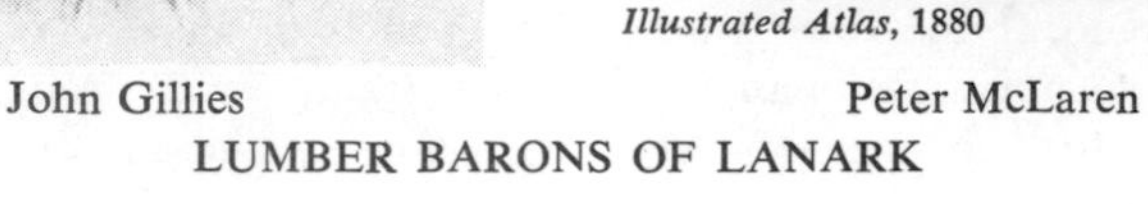

John Gillies Peter McLaren

LUMBER BARONS OF LANARK

The same year as John Gillies began his enterprise the Gilmour Pollock company, a powerful Scottish firm already operating from Miramichi (now Pembroke) to the Upper Gatineau, was cutting large quantities of timber from their limits along the Mississippi River and running a saw mill at Carleton Place. Later as the Mississippi Company they purchased the slide at Almonte.

John Gillies added a grist mill and an oatmeal mill to his enterprises, then later a custom carding woollen mill across the river. Here the settlers brought their lumber for sawing, their grain for grinding, their wool for combing, carding, and spinning, and a community grew up known as Gillies Mills. A millay and a circular saw gave the saw mill more utility, and the Gillies began to take on contracts for special orders such as sawing boards for a plank road from Lanark to Perth. John Gillies then leased timber limits higher up along the Clyde and Mississippi rivers, across the height of land into the Trent watershed, and went into the square timber trade, rafting his produce down the Trent River to Lake Ontario, the St. Lawrence, and Quebec.

Later, also like Caldwell, he teamed square timber from the upper reaches of the Clyde to Oliver's Ferry, shipping it to Kingston and across the lake to the Oswego market.

Another Lanark businessman was also engaged in the square timber trade. This was James Mair, merchant in Lanark village, who leased limits along the Clyde and Madawaska rivers. His son Charles, after a year at Queen's University, left and went into the square timber business with his father and brothers. Mair recalled in later life:

> I loved the river life, the great pineries in winter where the timber was felled and squared, the 'drive' in spring and the 'rafting-up' at Arne Prior or elsewhere, the timber being formed into cribs, securely withed and chained, and united into enormous rafts which were floated to Quebec, to berth at Wolfe's Cove or Cape Rouge or some other shelter. They were there sold to timber dealers, broken up, and shipped to England in large sailing fleets which came for it twice or thrice a year.
>
> The business had its excitements in these swift tributaries. Real peril there was in 'jams' at unslided chutes, where the timber piled up to a great height, and the lock-sticks had to be cut to set the jam going. This was very dangerous volunteer work, and sometimes fatal. I remember an expert, when the jam broke at a chute on the Madawaska, passing clean under it and landing unhurt on shore. These raftsmen were nimble on timber almost beyond belief. Today

> when it is mainly sawlogs that are cut, the fully improved streams make the drive easy; but in the old days I speak of, the unimproved streams were very dangerous, and not infrequent graves were noticeable along their banks.
>
> To us youths, the river life, the canoeing, the chutes, the running of great rapids like the Carillon and the Long Sault, the latter more dangerous than the Grand Rapids of the Saskatchewan, which I have repeatedly run in a bark canoe, and very much longer; the braving of the fierce storms of Lake St. Peter, where many a 'gallant raft' was blown into single sticks, were the most enjoyable things imaginable. The trade, however, regarded financially, was full of ups and downs, showing big profits in some years and dead losses in others; but notwithstanding its uncertainties in those early days, it had for all and sundry an irresistible fascination.

Shanty life and the drives down the rivers spelled excitement and adventure to the young men of Bathurst District in those days, and it was the height of their ambition to take part in the dangerous spring drives. The camaraderie of the camp appealed as well as the hard and challenging work. Many were better fed in the shanty than they were at home, with pay to boot.

One of the most important men in the camp was the cook, who along with the foreman commanded the highest wages. Woe betide any employee who antagonized the cook! Drivers were plentiful but good cooks were scarce and to be handled carefully, unless they proved wasteful—an unforgivable sin for which they might be dismissed without notice. The cook was king of the *camboose*—a slightly raised section of the shanty floor, filled with sand over which the fire for cooking was built. The hot sand was used for baking and what an oven it was! Here the cook buried immense pots of bread and covered them with hot ashes. The finished product was a marvel of flavour and goodness.

> It is all condensed in the bread. When it is strong and firm, and yet—and this is the mystery to me—it is light and porous as that of any first-class housewife's. And what shall we say about the beans? They are simply *par excellence*. They are baked in the same kind of pot as the bread, the lid being hermetically sealed to the rim by dough, and then buried in the hot ashes. The beans are first thoroughly sifted, washed and boiled; and then large slices of fat pork mixed with them. The pot then placed in its deep bed of hot ashes . . . . for succulency of flavour and savory richness of nutrition,

> [this] will completely throw into the shade the famous pottage of Esau bartered for his birthright. . . . It is strong food of course, the very strongest, I believe, in the world. A person who is accustomed to the ordinary dishes of domestic cooking must be cautious how he attacks it at first. If he takes too heavy an allowance, as he is strongly tempted to do on account of its savoriness, he will very likely throw his stomach into convulsions. But it is the grandest food in the world for shantymen whose vigorous open-air exercise in the keen oxygenated atmosphere enables them to digest food which would upset and demoralize the stomach of a town or city man. . . . In proportion to its nutritive power its bulk weight is the most portable in the world.
>
> Years ago, pork, tea and bread were the sole food of the men, and sometimes not too much of that, nor the best quality either. . . . Compared to other laboring classes, our shantymen fare sumptuously every day. What do you think of such a bill of fare as this, which constitutes the daily routine of my friend C's menu: Mess pork; fresh beef; bread; tea; dried apples, stewed; beans; potatoes; sugar; often butter and fish?*

Fraser describes one particular cook called Ned, a small "fiery-eyed old Frenchman", who ordered about great hulks of men as if they were children. "Go and wash your hands" he would tell some forgetful fellow "who presumed to approach the steaming pot of pork and beans without performing the necessary ablution". And the culprit meekly complied.

The French Canadians came in great numbers to the large camps in Upper Canada and added to colour of shanty life. One writer called the Scotch, Irish, and French shantymen of those days "splendid specimens of physical humanity". The French Canadians loved to tell stories and these spun along night after night, with variations and additions. Joshua Fraser speaks of other recreations: "Cards, chequers, reading if they have books, . . . an occasional dance, song, and story all accompanied by the merry strains of the fiddle and better than all, a *camaraderie* which pervades the whole—make the long winter evenings pass quickly and pleasantly, until it is time to turn in under the warm blankets, to sleep that sweet, sound, refreshing slumber which only strong men in the redundance of health and animal life, without care or thought of the morrow, can obtain and realize".

After winter in the bush, when the men arrived at the river for the

* Joshua Fraser, *Shanty, Forest and River Life* (1883).

*Picturesque Canada*

PIONEER TIMBER SLIDE, OTTAWA

Willis, *Canadian Scenery* W. H. Bartlett

TIMBER SLIDE AT CHATS LAKE, 1839

spring drive, as one reporter said, "all hell broke loose". There was an eat-drink-and-be-merry attitude, for tomorrow they might die in a tossing crib or among the logs. At the end of the slides or rapids and in the rafting grounds rival gangs might be tied up for weeks, and the taverns and inns swarmed with cleat-shod men of the river, drinking, singing, swearing, wrestling, and brawling. The men lucky enough to complete the timber drive to Quebec could consider themselves veteran shantymen and drivers with prideful justification.

White and red pine square timber and saw logs were manufactured in Lanark, Dalhousie, Sherbrooke, Lavant, Darling, Palmerston, and Canonto townships where the Caldwell and Gillies timber limits extended. At Lanark village the farmers did a thriving trade supplying the shanties with flour, pork, beef, beans, oats and hay. Alexander Caldwell's brother, Boyd, started a woollen mill in 1850 and later moved into lumbering as well, operating on the Mississippi at Carleton Place. In 1850 William Lees built a saw mill at Fallbrook and carried on the manufacture of lumber there for many years. After the 1850s there were many more saw mills thriving throughout the county.

*Illustrated Atlas*, 1880

WILLIAM LEES
Born at Fallbrook, son of pioneer William Lees,
M.P.P. for Lanark, elected 1879.

## CHAPTER XV

# EARLY SCHOOLS AND LIBRARIES

Although the Scottish emigrants were poor in "the things of this world" they were far from impoverished mentally. One might search Lanark County o'er today to find a household—rural or urban—owning, not to say reading, such weighty volumes as Gibbon's *Decline and Fall of the Roman Empire* or the works of Josephus. Yet such works the Scottish settlers, many of whom had been tradesmen, brought with them, and it was to these emigrants that the early settlements owed much in the way of cultural and educational influence.

The mental fare the first libraries offered to those who could read was strong stuff, but highly fortifying for facing the wilderness. The books the settlers brought with them and the letters they received from home were the only links with "civilization". Many could not pay the postage rates charged on incoming letters at the local depot (Perth in the early years) and their letters lay abandoned to be finally destroyed. For them only the books remained as a contact with the world beyond the clearings.

Of these the Bible (many brought Gaelic Bibles with them) was the anchor and mainstay—an encyclopedia containing the answers to all questions. When the first schools were formed the Bible was used most of all books—for reading, memory work, literature, as well as history and geography.

The first school in what now constitutes Lanark County was probably one established in Jesse McIntyre's home in the township of Montague in 1804. This was on lot 20 of the second concession. Later the first schoolhouse was built nearby on lot 24. Lamira Dow was the first teacher in Merrickville.

In 1807 an Act establishing a "Public" (what we call High) school in each of the eight Districts of Upper Canada was passed, granting

£100 per annum for teachers. These were the later Grammar Schools.

The Common School Act was passed in 1816. By it the inhabitants of any town, township, village, or "place" might meet and arrange to build a school. When the building had been erected and provision made for a teacher's salary three people could be appointed trustees. They in turn were to examine the moral character and qualifications of anyone applying to teach. A government grant was divided among the Districts of Upper Canada, more or less on the basis of population, but no more than £25 could be drawn toward the salary of any one teacher. The Lieutenant-Governor appointed District Boards of Education and to these the trustees reported annually. This Act was in effect until 1820.

In 1815 one of the items of emigration assistance offered by Lord Bathurst had been that a school teacher might accompany each group of families desiring to form a community in Upper Canada, and that this school teacher would be paid £50 annually.

As mentioned in an earlier chapter, John Holliday arrived with the first band of emigrants forming the Rideau settlement. He had distinguished himself at Brockville during the winter of 1815 by asking for an additional $2.00 or $2.50 to teach each settler's child, which did not ingratiate him with government authorities.

Arriving in Perth, Holliday proceeded to his location on Lot "A" of North Burgess with the Scotch Line settlers. On his land he built a large log building in the fall of 1816, covering it with a bark roof. Part of it was for the use of his wife and family of seven children, the other part a schoolhouse. Ten years later his log house was replaced by a stone one which is still standing. The school for the Scotch Line was built on lot 21 of the first concession of Bathurst near the junction of the Scotch Line and the Glen Tay road. It was too far from Perth for children there to use, and when the Rev. William Bell arrived in 1817 and proposed to open a village school, Perth officials happily granted him a salary of £50.

Mr. Bell, however, was not aware that henceforth he was considered by government officials as the chosen teacher for the Rideau settlement and that Holliday was being paid nothing. Holliday was meanwhile corresponding with officials in an effort to get his rightful salary, and when two years had passed and he still remained unpaid he appealed to Bell as his last resort, although neither liked the other. Priding himself on being a just man, Bell undertook to see justice done and wrote to the Hon. John McGill at Montreal on behalf of the unfortunate schoolmaster. He received a reply indicating that Holliday would have been paid long ago but that he had charged the parents of his pupils extra and that he had been insolent to government officials. It was also pointed out that Bell was then receiving the salary which would otherwise have gone to Holliday. In March 1818 a Roman Catholic teacher, Murdock by name, arrived in Perth and with the assistance of the superintendent, Daverne, tried to take over Bell's new schoolhouse; but Colonel Cockburn, to whom Bell wrote in haste, squelched these ambitions. Murdock later went to the Lanark depot.

Again in 1819 Holliday resumed his correspondence, writing to Governor Maitland. When he received no reply he again appealed to Bell, who wrote Maitland in December going over the whole case and pointing out that four years had elapsed and still nothing had been paid to Holliday from government funds for his labours as teacher. Moreover, it was stated, the man had a family of twelve children and had had to abandon teaching in order to support them. Bell remarked in his Journal "so ignorant were the government advisors of the District that they confounded the village school with that of John Holliday", and even reprimanded Bell for not realizing that a salary could not be paid out of public funds for both.

Meanwhile the Rev. Michael Harris, an Episcopalian, arrived at Perth. One of his first acts was to take over Bell's school, for the Church of England was then considered the official church of Upper Canada. In December 1819 the governor's military secretary directed Colonel Cockburn to pay John Holliday's salary from the time Bell was removed from office. Harris seems to have had little success with his school, and it appears that Bell continued to teach his own children and some others in his own home until a common school was opened in Perth.

John Holliday resumed his teaching career and continued until 1842. A grandson who attended his school in 1838-1842 described him as a "very severe and even cruel teacher". He was a Cameronian and very active in establishing a Reformed Presbyterian Church in Perth in later years. He died at the ripe old age of 92 and was buried on the old homestead beside his wife. The next school was one in Drummond Township built in 1817 on lot 14 of the seventh concession. Duncan McCormick was the first teacher.

The Common School Act was renewed in 1820 but grants were cut and a monitorial system set up whereby older pupils "listened to" the younger ones and relieved some of the burdens of school teaching, since there was a great shortage of qualified teachers.

In 1820 the Lanark Society settlers arrived to be dispersed in the townships of Lanark, Dalhousie, and Ramsay, with a few families locating in other townships. By December plans were being made at New Lanark (now Lanark Village) to build a schoolhouse which would also serve as a temporary church. The four trustees appointed were: James Hall, Alexander Ferguson, Robert James, and James Thompson. A month later the trustees met at the home of Alex Ferguson with a group of settlers and proceeded to the school lot, where logs were cut sufficient for the building. Nothing further was done until July when a raising bee was organized and a school erected on July 14th; but there was still no schoolmaster to take charge. George Richmond of Dalhousie Township was apparently the only teacher to come out with the first lot of Lanark Society settlers in 1820, and he had been killed by a falling tree during the first winter.

To serve the needs of the Dalhousie families George Easton, located on lot 16 of the third concession, built a schoolhouse near his own dwelling and taught boys and some girls. His only pay was the labour from the boys, who worked for him on Saturdays.

In September 1821 the Lanark Committee wrote to the Rev. Robert Easton at Montreal, requesting both a teacher and a minister in accordance with the conditions of emigration under the Lanark Societies, but not until February 18th, 1822, did Robert Mason hold classes in Lanark.

All Lanark Township settlers holding land, by Mason's terms, might have their children taught gratis, but residents of Lanark village, not entitled to draw land in the usual way, had to pay for English reading and grammar 2s. 6d, and for writing and arithmetic 3s. per quarter.

Robert Mason was a stern "dominie", long remembered in the community. He typified the early teacher of the backwoods who ruled by striking fear and trembling through the hearts of his pupils; whose taws, cane, or other weapon was used readily and without hesitation. But if teachers were sometimes cruel, it must be remembered that the tradition in many a district was to throw a new teacher through the window on the opening day of school.

An eloquent account of Mason's reign as schoolmaster appears in the book *Shanty, Forest and River Life* by the Rev. Joshua Fraser, who attended the Lanark school as a boy.

> For nearly thirty years he taught and thrashed in the little stone schoolhouse of the village. He was a tall, gaunt, raw-boned, beetle-browed Scotchman, an elder in the Kirk, and a true blue Presbyterian

of the hardest and sternest cast. He seldom smiled and when he did it was as if under protest from his grim and iron nature, . . . was just as absolute and upon occasions tyrannical in his sway as an autocrat of the Middle Ages.

His system of education was of the simplest and most rudimental nature. Reading, spelling, writing and 'countin' made up the sum total of his instruction. Grammar, geography, history, composition were tongues unknown. I remember one peculiar theory he held with regard to teaching arithmetic to girls: he gravely maintained that there was not the least use of their going further in 'countin' than the four simple compound rules of addition, subtraction, multiplication and division. Their minds were not capable of rightly grasping anything beyond these . . . .

The boys, however, were soundly drilled (for the old man was thorough as far as he went) up to vulgar fractions, but decimals, and the square and cube root were *terra incognita* to the 'Maister', and of course to his pupils.

His taws were the most horrible instrument of torture that could be imagined. I don't believe that more terrible thrashings were ever inflicted, either in ancient or modern times than what those unhappy youths had to undergo, in that old square stone schoolhouse in the village of Lanark under Robert Mason. . . . Leather was dear and when the taws were stolen, he would scrounge around in a barnyard and find a horse trace thrown away—he would pare down one end so he could wield it from both hands and the other end he would slice into three or four tails, then singe and harden them in the fire to give them more weight and sting. With this awful weapon, perhaps five feet in length, he would go to work as deliberately as a man chopping down a tree. I have seen as many as a dozen pupils ranged before him, each awaiting chastisement . . . after each one had received a dozen or more allotted 'licks', the old man would be somewhat exhausted but I believe it was pleasant exhaustion.

There were about seventy of us, of all ages from the child to the stalwart man of 20 or more, packed into this small building of twenty feet square. The oldest received the same 'licks' as the youngest but sometimes rolling their coat sleeves they would square up to him and cry out "Maister, I'll fecht you". This would cause great excitement and uproar in the school. The 'Maister' was powerful and as good with his fists as the taws and the two would go at it in dead earnest. . . .

Attending the Lanark school at the same time as Joshua Fraser was Charles Mair, son of a village merchant James Mair who came to Lanark village in 1820. Charles Mair was to become a distinguished poet, but not before he absorbed his share of punishment. Mair's greatest offense was playing truant, and he was oftimes returned to the schoolmaster by his father who regarded truancy as one of the deadliest sins. Charles "hated the school with a perfect and undying hatred. I can safely say", says Fraser, "that all the mental and scholastic attainments that he gained during that period were absolutely nil". Mair took every opportunity to run away to the woods, the hills, the riverside. When his father caught him and returned to the school, "it was quite a common thing to see him appear at the schoolhouse door, leading Charlie by the hand and stalking up to the desk with stern aldermanic dignity say: 'There, Maister, tak him and thresh the deevil out of him'".

Charles Mair, in an interview at his home in Victoria in later years, recalled Mason as being "muscular and ungainly with rugged cheeks and a long bristly chin", but although at the time of his childhood often smarting under the threat or descension of the dreaded taws, in reminiscence he conceded no other class of teacher could have controlled the country school of those days.* Robert Mason's subject matter was limited to grammar and the three R's; it was, however, very thorough, and sometimes, Mair said, comical, for not satisfied with his pupils recognizing an adverb or a preposition at sight, he made them memorize a whole series. He liked Pope and he knew Burns well, but he never wandered from his rigid course of study to quote poetry in class.

When Robert Mason died in the 1860s both Mair and Fraser, home on holidays from Queen's University, were present and, "not without a silent tear, helped to lower his coff into the grave". The log schoolhouse in Lanark was replaced by a stone one which stood on a hill on Prince Street between the Presbyterian church and the cemetery.

Records at Middleville indicate a log schoolhouse standing in 1821, and that Robert Mason taught there. Whether he accompanied the 1820 or the 1821 settlers from Scotland is not known, but it seems unlikely that a schoolhouse would be built at Middleville before the one at the Lanark depot. One of the early teachers at Middleville was Rollo, a cobbler, who listened to his pupils' lessons as he cobbled.

In Ramsay Township John Young, one of the 1821 settlers, taught

* *Master-Works of Canadian Authors*, Vol. XIV, edited by John W. Garvin, Toronto, 1926.

school at his Rosedale farm (near Union Hall) and was paid by goods or barter. The Bible was the book used by him and Gaelic the common language, although the surrounding settlers could also speak English. John Gillan, a native of Aberdeen who also came on the *David of London* in 1821, located on lot 9 of the 6th concession of Ramsay and built one of the first schoolhouses on his farm. Here he taught until invited to take over the village school at Ramsayville.

Several records indicate Arthur Lang as the first teacher at Shipman's Mills. He seems to have taught there until 1826, when the first public school was built near the present St. Mary's church. A teacher named Ferguson was put in charge, but the school was so badly run that two or three years later some families banded together and brought Miss Styles from Montreal to open a private school. She was succeeded by Miss Bates.

No precise records of early schools in Beckwith Township exist. One account speaks vaguely of a first school located on a farm owned by Peter McLaren north of the 6th line, and a second built on a Dewar farm near the present Dewar and Kennedy cemeteries in the Derry. When the Rev. George Buchanan arrived in 1822 to be both minister and physician for the community he brought with him classical attainments in Latin, Greek, and Hebrew. He spoke both English and Gaelic and undertook to teach the children of his parishioners in a small log school near his home on lot 14 of the 6th concession, using as his first textbook the Shorter Catechism, until grammars and geographies could be brought from Perth. Mud, wolves, deep snow, and storms could not keep his scholars at home. "Some walked 5 or 6 miles every morning and evening and were never absent or tardy."* Buchanan taught for a number of years in Beckwith, never receiving a penny for his labour. The *Illustrated Atlas* for 1880 speaks of an early school in Beckwith being constructed on lot 24 of the 6th concession with James Leslie as the first teacher, and that a school was opened in Franktown in 1824 with Mr. Kent as teacher. In 1825 the first school to open in Morphy's Falls was "an unsightly log shanty" on the corner of the town line between Ramsay and Beckwith townships and Bridge Street. Mr. Kent arrived from Franktown to be the first schoolmaster.

In Pakenham Township the first school was built on lot 6 of the 8th concession in 1824 (Cedar Hill) with James Connery as the first teacher. The first school in Pakenham Mills was probably at the west

* Campbell, *The Pioneer Pastor* (1900).

end of the bridge, built in the late 1830s. The first school at Balderson on the township line of Bathurst and Drummond townships stood near the Lanark toll gate. The teacher was Peter Stewart, a severe Scot similar in personality to Robert Mason of Lanark.

On November 15, 1822, an Education Board was set up at the Court of Quarter Sessions in Perth, consisting of Drs. Thom and Reade, Wm. Morris, Colonel Josiah Taylor, and Father John McDonald the Roman Catholic priest. The same year Benjamin Tett opened a school in a house.

The Rev. Michael Harris, James H. Powell, George Thew Burke, William Marshall, William Morris, and Henry Graham were appointed the first trustees for the new District Grammar School in 1824. It opened with John Stewart as the first teacher.

The common schools of Perth and the townships were entrusted to a District Board of Education in 1824 consisting of: Mr. Harris, William Morris, Anthony Leslie, Alex McMillan, and Dr. George H. Reade. Benjamin Tett's private school closed in 1825, but was reopened by young John Wilson, law student, who kept it going until 1832 when he abandoned teaching for apprenticeship in James Boulton's law office.

Private schools for young ladies were opening in Perth. Two daughters of the Rev. George Buchanan of Beckwith arrived to open one of the first of these in 1822. Subjects taught varied with the talents of the owners. The Misses Jessop who had a school on the north side of Brock Street between Drummond and Beckwith streets, taught: spelling, reading, writing, arithmetic, and plain needle work for fifteen shillings. Geography, history and ornamental needlework cost £1 per quarter and French, drawing, and music £1 per quarter. This was a boarding-school and board and washing amounted to £6 per quarter while fuel for the season was 5 shillings. The school was later taken over by the Misses Jessop's sister-in-law, Mrs. Jessop, who ran it as a co-educational institution. Mr. Jessop was a gardener. A son of pioneer Alexander Fraser, writing in a 1905 issue of the *Courier*, recalled his experience in the school with nostalgia:

> I can hear now his far-reaching, unmelodious voice shouting to the children to 'keep off the borders!' Mr. Jessop also kept sheep, where I don't know, but I remember the wool we had to tease. I have also a lively recollection of the hooks and eyes we had to cut off, and the old garments to rip; kindergarten was unknown then, but we had it in essence. Mrs. Jessop taught music to the more advanced girls of

the school (boys didn't take music lessons then). I can both see and hear the piano, and the dear prim old lady sitting beside her pupil with a knitting needle in her hand, and very much on the watch for a wrong note, and I think tears were not an uncommon occurrence during what is now called *amusement.* I never got farther than the first book of lessons with Mrs. Jessop. She made no pretence of teaching the higher branches but she taught thoroughly as far as she went, painstaking and conscientious to a fault.*

Fraser later attended the primitive log school between Balderson and Lanark village where the seats were "sections of tamarac trees". Says Mr. Fraser: "I expect we had lesson books of some kind, but what I remember most about it was the rivalry as to who could repeat the greater number of chapters in the New Testament from memory". After lunch, it was the practice to spend the remainder of the lunch hour learning to dance Scotch reels.

Smith Falls had a number of private schools. During the early years, the common school was in North Elmsley, School Section #1, three miles distant from the townsite, but this was too far for children to travel and private schools began to open up. Miss Frances E. Bartlett, a sister of the town treasurer, Russell Bartlett, opened the first in 1831, and another was in operation under one Lane. Neil Dunbar had a private school for young men and women on the north side of Mill Street. The first grammar school was opened by one MacPherson who taught in a room in Dodd's building on Beckwith Street.

A report of Common Schools in Bathurst District for 1838 indicated 84 schools in operation, with 1,154 boys and 936 girls attending. The books used were: *Reading Made Easy*; Mavor's *Spelling*; the Bible and New Testament; English Grammar and English Reader. There were thirty-one pupils attending the only grammar school in the District of Bathurst at Perth. Here subjects of study included Simpson's *Euclid* in mathematics, and Caesar, Ovid, Sallust, Virgil, Cicero, and Horace in Latin. Mr. Morris signed the report and commented: "The school is well conducted by Mr. William Kay who gives a very general satisfaction to the trustees, as well as parents of the pupils".†

By 1842 the School Report for Bathurst District revealed the following:

Bathurst Township: 13 school sections, all occupied except S.S. #12.

* Perth *Courier*, June 30, 1905.

† *Documentary History of Education in Upper Canada*, by J. George Hodgins (1894).

Beckwith Township: 11 school sections, all occupied but S. S. #10.
Burgess Township: 2 school sections, both occupied.
Dalhousie Township: 6 school sections, all occupied but S.S. #4. Teachers for the year were: Dan. Currie, James Brown, Ronald Smith, John Donald, Alex Shanks.
Darling Township: 3 school sections, with S.S. #1 and S.S. #3 vacant. John Dodds teaching at S.S. #2.
Drummond Township: 11 school sections, all occupied.
North Elmsley: 6 school sections, 3 occupied, S.S. #2, S.S. #4, S.S. #6 vacant.
Lanark Township: 12 school sections, all occupied.
Pakenham Township: 4 school sections, all occupied.
Ramsay Township: 13 school sections with S.S. #2, #3, #5 and #6 vacant.
North Sherbrooke: 2 school sections, both occupied.

(sgd) Alex. McMillan, Warden,
Bathurst District.

In pioneer days penmanship, one of the more important subjects, was taught as an art in itself, and among the topics for adult education it held a prominent place. Literature, poetry, and grammar were also taught by visiting instructors. The following notice from a writing-master appeared in an 1834 issue of the *Bathurst Courier*:

> Mr. Heath, Writing Master, informs his friends and the public that he shall spend but a short time longer in Perth, and those who wish to avail themselves of the present opportunity of acquiring a beautiful style of writing by expending a few afternoons or evenings at a trifling expense, will do well to apply soon, else when they seek they'll not find.

In the grammar schools, quill pens were sometimes used for writing. Donald Fraser reminiscing through the *Courier* columns in later years related:

> William Somerville . . . was the ideal dominie—military in discipline and firmness itself in all his decisions. . . . Steel pens were an abomination to him. He prepared the pens (quill) daily. A boy was selected to distribute the pens, and another the copy books to the pupils. When all was ready he gave the word of command—"Dip". Each boy was obliged to shake off the superfluous ink and wait for the next word of command—"Write". We then wrote as though our lives depended upon the beauty and symmetry of our writing. Each line had to be better than the preceding one, and we wrote only three lines during the exercise. The copy books were collected, each

line thoroughly inspected and woe-betide the boy who showed any degree of carelessness. The pen was to be held lightly between the thumb and forefinger, the middle finger three-quarters of an inch from the point of the pen; the handle of the pen pointing to the right shoulder and the knuckles pointing to the ceiling of the room, the whole hand resting lightly on the little finger".*

The early schools were supplemented by pioneer libraries set up to hold the precious volumes carried laboriously from the old country to the new. Probably the first community library was that set up at Watson's Corners in Dalhousie Township by emigrants of the Lesmahagow Society who arrived in 1821.

Thomas Scott, their leader, organized his settlers into a St. Andrew's Society seven years later and made plans for a library. They drew up a petition to send to the Earl of Dalhousie, Governor General, asking for his patronage. The Earl wrote to Colonel Marshall, the Superintendent of settlement at Lanark, and having assured himself that such a library would serve a useful purpose in the community, he issued Marshall with the authority to draw up to £100 from his Quebec bank account for assistance to the proposed library. He also sent a quantity of books including copies of the *Encyclopedia Britannica.* By 1829 a log building had been erected at Watson's Corners to house the library. It was named St. Andrew's Hall, and was to be used for township meetings, social affairs, and as a place of worship. By 1832 there were at least 500 volumes in this library, the surrounding settlers having donated books from their own precious store. The following titles indicate the calibre of books the Highlanders enjoyed:

| | |
|---|---|
| Gibbon's Roman Empire | 6 volumes |
| Hume's History of England | 8 volumes |
| The Works of Josephus, Jewish Historian | 2 volumes |
| D'Aubigne's History of the Reformation | 5 volumes |
| Antiquities of Greece | 1 volume |
| Dr. Cumming's Scripture Readings, Lectures on the Parables, etc. | 16 volumes |
| Blackstone's Commentaries on the Laws of England | 4 volumes |
| Hale's Contemplation | 2 volumes |
| Wilson's Sermons | 2 volumes |
| Scott's Napoleon | 3 volumes |
| The Lives of Nelson and Mary Queen of Scots | 2 volumes |
| The Life of David Crockett, written by himself | 1 volume |
| The Book of Common Prayer | 1 volume |

* Perth *Courier*, dated June 30, 1905.

Macaulay, Carlyle, Dickens, and, of course, Burns and Sir Walter Scott were well represented in this library. There were many books of general information, such as volumes of the "Caledonian Horticultural Society", "Trade and Navigation Returns", "The New York Canals", and seventeen volumes of the *Edinburgh Almanack.*

The settlers eagerly patronized the new library, making long journeys through the woods on Library Day (six times a year, books being kept for 2 months at a time) when the hall was crowded almost from morning to night. The day became a social event as friends exchanged news, gossiped and made their selections for the next two months. By 1843 there were over 800 books in the Dalhousie Library. "Many a discussion at 'bees' and 'raisings' was endorsed by arguments drawn from Howett on 'Priestcraft' or Doddridge on 'Regeneration'. The men of Dalhousie worked hard and meditated deeply on things of Church and State, and their otherwise uneventful lives were given a deep satisfaction out of what, to them at least, were the treasures maintained in the old bookcases of St. Andrew's Hall".*

Inspired by the formation of the Dalhousie Library, a group of emigrants at Shipman's Mills in Ramsay, also Lanark Society settlers, organized a Ramsay Library in 1829. Part of the log schoolhouse at the corner of Main and Country streets was used to house the first volumes donated. An old record shows that most families in the area contributed something. Here are some of the 321 volumes forming the nucleus of the Library:

| | Donor |
|---|---|
| A Geography and an English Collection | Robert Wilkie |
| The Seasons, the Minstrel, St. Pirie, Young's in One Volume | Robt. MacFarlane |
| Wemyss' Essays | James Hart |
| History of England | Peter McGregor |
| Cottages of Glenburnie | John Nielson |
| Robertson's America in Three Volumes | Arthur Lang |
| Life of Franklin | Thomas Mansell |
| Paine's Rights of Man | Findlay Sinclair |
| The Works of Flavius Josephus | William Drynan |
| Dr. Franklin's Essays | Thomas Lowry |
| Goldsmith | Gerald Nagle |
| Picture of London | Alexander Stevenson |
| Ferguson's Astronomy | John Buchanan |

* Haydon, *Pioneer Sketches in the District of Bathurst*, p. 188.

| | |
|---|---|
| Welch's Sermons | Daniel Galbraith |
| Burns on Poor Rates | Allan Gilmour |
| Guthrie's Life, etc. | David Buchanan |
| Allan's Alarm to the Unconverted | Walter Wm. Rae |
| Two volumes of the Misses Magazine | John Gemmill |
| Parable of the 10 Virgins | John Toshack |
| Defence of the Gospel | Greville Toshack |
| The Afflicted Man's Companion | John Shaw |

It will be noted that some of these men were the first settlers in Ramsay—Robt. Wilkie who arrived prior to 1819, and Thomas Lowry, Thomas Mansell, John Gemmill, Arthur Lang, John Shaw. Gerald Nagle was one of Peter Robinson's Irish settlers. Many were located long distances from Shipman's Mills.

The next books donated were:

| | Donor |
|---|---|
| The Life of Joseph Tompkins | Joseph Yuill |
| Young's Night Thoughts | Ebenezer Wilson of North Sherbrooke |
| The Wonders of Nature and Art | James Rae, Sr. |
| The Exiles of Siberia | Wm. McQueen |
| A London Edition of the Devil on Two Sticks | Neil McQuarrie |
| Ossian's Poems | David Snedden |
| Bacon's Essays | Andrew Paul |
| Smollett's History of England | John Gilmour, Sr. |

Entrance fee to the library was 10s. in the coinage of the day. Money was also donated, and the first executive purchased more weighty volumes—Rollin's *Ancient History* in four volumes; Dr. Chalmer's Works in three volumes; and Sir Walter Scott's *Waverley Novels* in 49 volumes. The next packet of donations contained:

| | Donor |
|---|---|
| The Antiquities of Rome | Andrew Paul |
| The Huron Chief and Other Poems by Kidd | Miss Janet Wylie |
| 17 volumes of the Canadian Magazine; 4 parts of the Canadian Review, and the Beauties of Johnston | Alexander Morris of Brockville |
| The Poetic Works of Robert Burns | Malcolm Cameron (Perth) |
| Shakespeare's Dramatic Works—2 vols. | John Armstrong |

Aspect of the Times .................................... Malcolm Cameron
Fenning's System of Geography—2 vols. .... Wm. Morris, M.P. (Perth)

These donations were made in 1831. By this time the Ramsay Library had 142 volumes.

Another early library was the Elmsley Library Association at Smiths Falls, organized in 1837 by Rev. John Romanes and John Ballantyne. At first members arrived at library meetings with baskets of books which they proceeded to exchange with each other. Later a permanent location had to be set up with a permanent stock of books. For a time it was located over William Keith's bookstore on Main Street.

The Carleton Place Library came into existence in March 1846 under the auspices of the Carleton Place Library and Mechanics Institute. Rates were 2 shillings 6 pence entrance and 5 shillings per annum. The Library opened with 16 volumes and by the end of the year had 144 volumes. David Lawson was the first librarian.

# CHAPTER XVI

## PIONEER CHURCHES AND MINISTERS

One of the most colourful figures on the scene was the Rev. William Bell, the first resident minister. Sent out by the Associated Presbytery of Scotland to minister to the needs of the Scottish emigrants, Mr. Bell arrived aboard the *Rothiemurchus* in 1817, a voyage he graphically describes in his interesting and lengthy Journals. The reader of his Journals today would be inclined to feel he was much too harsh in his judgments and that by closing his church doors to families who did not adhere strictly to the doctrine of Christianity, as he interpreted it, he may well have contributed to the indifference and dissipation he continually deplored.

Perhaps, however, his very rigidity of viewpoint protected him from the heartbreak attending the pastor of many a pioneer settlement. In any case his life exemplified his devotion to Christian principle, as he understood it, and neither sickness nor misfortune prevented him from doing whatever he considered to be his duty. From his arrival at Perth in 1817 until his death in the early 1850s, he kept up a constant, tireless round of preaching in Bathurst, Drummond, and all the outlying townships, travelling a circuit from one schoolhouse or home to another until churches could be built. Even after churches had been established throughout the District of Bathurst he continued to hold services in homes along his circuit.

It is illuminating to recount Mr. Bell's experiences. On the voyage across the Atlantic he held services on board ship for the passengers, and during their six days' stay at Quebec he "had the pleasure on the 4th of June" of preaching his first sermon in Canada at St. John's Chapel.

The Bells took the steamboat *Malsham* to Montreal where they met the Rev. Robert Easton and enjoyed the hospitality of his family.

Carriages were provided by the Commissary, Mr. Clarke, to convey them to Lachine and from there they had a bateau for the St. Lawrence voyage to Prescott. Here there was a delay of several days and Bell left his family in charge of another traveller while he went on to Brockville to visit his old friend, the Rev. William Smart. He preached in Mr. Smart's new church, then rode by wagon with John Kilborn for 12 miles toward the Perth military settlement. Then borrowing a horse from his host, he travelled on horseback through the woods as far as he could. Finally he left Mr. Kilborn's horse at a farmer's house, staying overnight at Oliver's Ferry with the Donaldsons. Next morning he completed the eight-mile journey to Perth on foot.

When he arrived at the new settlement on June 24th, 1817, there were only a few houses and shanties including the government storehouse comprising the village.

Within a few days, Bell had visited the Scotch Line settlers, found a house he could rent for his family, and held his first church services. By October he had set out to preach at what he called "The Rideau settlement" which possibly meant the area bordering the Rideau Lakes and river, in the vicinity of Merrickville. Of his first journey he tells of calling upon Archibald Morrison, whose homestead was near Oliver's Ferry, and prevailing upon him to guide him through the wilderness. They travelled 14 miles, past the Pike and Black rivers through which they had to wade, and two bad swamps, reaching Edmonds' house by dark. Here Mr. Gifford, Edmonds' brother-in-law, fed them sage tea, bread, and butter. From there they travelled by canoe down the River Rideau three miles "to a school in Wolford where I was to preach", says Bell. Outside were 20 or 30 horses tied up and a congregation waiting. Bell's account of this experience is somewhat amusing:

> Many of them never having seen a Presbyterian minister before, they regarded me with a curious glance, as if I had been a bear, or some other wild beast. In the house the men sat all on one side, the women on the other. When the service was over, the class leader (for they were nearly all Methodists) invited me to his house, but as I had to go back in the canoe with the rest, I did not remain. In the evening Mr. Gifford, who is from New England, gave me much information respecting the state of religion in that country.

In January Bell visited the third and sixth concessions of Drummond Township, calling on families along the Mississippi River. The same month he went to Bastard and Beverley townships preaching in a schoolhouse at Stone Mills. He also preached at Mr. Kilborn's on his return journey and baptised 13 children. Kilborn was to be a constant friend and assistant whenever Bell travelled through his neighbourhood, either loaning the pastor one of his horses or driving him over part of the journey. During the first year Mr. Bell preached regularly on the Scotch Line and elsewhere in Bathurst, and at Donaldson's near Oliver's Ferry.

Mr. Bell, although brought up in the Established Church of Scotland, had been sent out as a Secession minister and in 1818 he joined with other Presbyterian clergymen in Eastern Upper Canada, William Smart, William Taylor, and Robert Easton to form the Presbytery of the Canadas. By the mid-1820s there were some 10 Secession Presbyterian ministers and five of the Established Church of Scotland resident in Eastern Upper Canada.

At this time a Roman Catholic padré, Rev. Abbé Peter de la Motte of the de Watteville and de Meuron regiments, had settled in Perth and had started a chapel. However, most of his parishioners were in Burgess Township, too far from Perth to support his work and he left the chapel unfinished to be completed by the next Roman Catholic priest, Father John MacDonald.

Early in 1819 a group of Beckwith settlers arrived at Perth to learn from Bell how they might obtain a minister for their district. In April Bell made his first visit to Beckwith to look the situation over, travelling in Mr. Adamson's "train" (horse-drawn sleigh), leaving his horse at Franktown, and walking five miles to Mrs. Ferguson's "shantie". Here he preached and baptised 2 children. On his return journey he preached "in Spratt's kitchen" and baptised more children. It was a debilitating journey. Spring rains were beginning, and Bell had to plod home well soaked although snow was still on the ground. Journeys of this sort were his lot until rough roads took the place of tracks through the forests.

In October 1819 the first Church of England minister arrived—the Rev. Michael Harris, an M.A. from Trinity College, Dublin, who had been ordained at Montreal. This good man proceeded to take over Mr. Bell's schoolhouse, since he represented the official church of Upper Canada. This act began a long struggle between the Church of England and the Church of Scotland in the District of Bathurst which did not end until the Clergy Reserves were secularized and official recognition accorded other Protestant denominations.

Mr. Bell temporarily ignored the intruder and went about his busy round of the outlying settlements. In January 1820 he went to Beckwith again to preach and baptise children, borrowing a horse from Angus Cameron for the trip.

> When I left home [he wrote] the morning was fine and sleighing tolerable; before I proceeded half-way it began to rain and continued heavy all day and all the following night, and the air being warm, travelling soon became extremely difficult. But it was necessary to return home before I slept even if I should travel all night. On my return, my horse had no less difficulty getting through than I did. The snow being half melted, he sank to the bottom at every step. Between 12 and 1 next morn, I reached home as wet as if I had been drawn out of the river, having waded a good part of the way to the knees in snow, while the rain poured copiously. Had I waited till the rain was over, my return for some time would have been difficult if not impossible. The snow melted so fast that in two days the swamps were all covered with water, and the river had over-flown the banks. In a short time the Tay had risen to such a height that it carried away the bridge built by the settlers in 1816 and we were forced to travel for about two months between the north and south side of this town in boats and canoes.*

By December 1820 Mr. Bell was extending his mission to Lanark and the Lanark Society settlers who had arrived that August. On the 18th he preached in Lanark village at Mr. Hall's house and baptised children.

In January 1821 he extended his mission to Wolford in the area now known as Easton's Corners. Travelling 28 miles through the woods he preached in the schoolhouse and lodged with Captain Burritt. In June again he went to Lanark, this time holding service in the upper storey of Henry Glass's house. After this service a church was organized and arrangements made for building a suitable house of worship. The 1821 Lanark Society settlers were then arriving, and wagons with emigrants daily passed through Perth. Duncan McInnes came with his family, bringing Bell letters from Scotland. In September Bell again went to Lanark, preaching in Mr. Fraser's house and dining with Capt. Leech. On this occasion he married Henry Glass to Christina Cameron, daughter of his elder, Angus Cameron, who kept the Inn on the Lanark road. The next day Bell ventured into Dalhousie Township for the first time, travelling up the Mississippi River through the woods and eventually reaching a "dark, smoky shantie" belonging to

* Bell, *Hints to Emigrants* (1823).

Duncan McInnes, where he preached to about 30 people and baptised three children.

In June 1820 Bell had written to Dr. Peddie asking that an ordained minister be sent out for the Beckwith settlers, but it required a petition of the settlers themselves in 1821 before Dr. George Buchanan was persuaded to leave his church in Edinburgh and emigrate to the wilderness of Beckwith to become preacher, teacher, doctor, and consultant to the demanding Scots.

In February 1822 Bell went to Beckwith and organized a church admitting 90 members. He held communion services in the upper storey of the Franktown Inn (presumably Nowlan's). This service inaugurated the Beckwith Presbyterian Church; but when the Rev. George Buchanan arrived in June of the same year nothing had been prepared for him by the settlers. James Wall, a generous Irishman, offered the Buchanans, including 7 girls and 2 boys, his own newly built log house. Here they remained for 6 weeks until the settlers could erect a house for them. Winter was setting in before the settlers built a small log church which Mr. Buchanan's daughter, Mrs. Campbell, described in *The Pioneer Pastor* as "cold, smoky, and exceedingly uncomfortable in winter". Alex. Dewar, John Carmichael, John Ferguson, and Duncan McDonald were the elders.

In September Mr. Buchanan journeyed to Perth to assist Bell at the communion service held the second Sunday of the month. It was a great occasion for folks who had not heard a sermon preached in Gaelic since they left Scotland, and Highlanders flocked into Perth from the surrounding townships.

> Groups of people on foot [Mrs. Campbell wrote], with here and there a man or woman on horseback, thronged the roads leading to Perth. The church would not hold them and scores stood around the door and the open windows. Father preached in the morning from the words: 'The harvest is past, the summer is ended, and we are not saved'. He then served the first table in Gaelic, and Mr. Bell served the others. At that period communicants left their pews and sat at long tables—rough boards covered with white cotton—in the aisles to receive the sacrament. The ministers would address each set which was called 'fencing the tables', and hand the bread and wine to the elders to distribute to the members. After another short address those at the tables would return to their seats to make room for the next lot, continuing in this way until all had communed who wished. Everything was decently and in order with no unseemly haste, communion services generally lasting several hours. Usually

Courtesy Jessie Buchanan Campbell

THE FAMILY OF REV. GEORGE BUCHANAN, BECKWITH

> 5 or 6 tables were served at Perth, and 4 or 5 at Beckwith. . . . In the afternoon . . . Father conducted the entire service. He preached with great effectiveness from the text: 'All power is given unto Me in heaven and on earth'. Tears flowed down the cheeks of hoary listeners to whom the service and language brought back vividly the scenes of their youth in Scotland. Every heart was stirred and every eye moist.

The young Buchanan ladies found life in Beckwith distressing, and Mrs. Campbell says "we formed a sorrowful group and ardently wished ourselves in Edinburgh". Their experiences typify the backwoods areas of Upper Canada at this time.

> Foxes, owls and wolverines helped the wolves make the nights hideous. Hunger sometimes drove the wolves to extremes. People could not venture far from home without risk of meeting a band of them. At noon one day 15 walked past our yard, heading for the sheep. Rattling tinpans and blowing a horn frightened them off. . . . In the winter Father hired men to clear several acres of ground and take out timber for a new house. They worked hard until spring, hewing logs for a two-storey building and sawing lumber for floors and partitions with a cross-cut saw. We had a large garden. Two cows were bought in April, the good women sent a fowl occasionally and we got along nicely. The new house was ready in September 1823. It had plank floors, a stone chimney, a number of rooms and a cellar. . . . This house was our home until Father exchanged it for a mansion in the skies, the children settled elsewhere and Mother removed to the eastern section of the province. . . . Two of my sisters, shortly after our arrival in Beckwith, went to Perth and opened the first school in the country taught by ladies. If anxious to see them, two or three other sisters would rise early, take a lunch and a small Bible along, rest on some grassy plot to eat and learn a chapter, and complete the walk to Perth by 2 or 3 o'clock. My first trip of this sort was in my eleventh year. Two more taught school in Montreal and one at Richmond, leaving sad gaps in the happy family.*

Helen married John Ferguson of Perth but died in her 26th year in 1830. Margaret married John Dewar, a "thrifty" farmer of the Derry, not long after the Buchanans took up residence in the township. Elizabeth married Archibald Campbell of Rideau Ferry, who trafficked in freight and owned a wharf and warehouse at the Ferry. He died

* Campbell, *The Pioneer Pastor* (1900).

of cholera in 1832 and his wife carried on the business for many years. Jessie married Duncan Campbell, also of Rideau Ferry.

One of Mr. Buchanan's staunchest supporters was his sheep-dog Oscar whom Mrs. Campbell considered

> wiser than many a two-legged creature. He knew when Sunday came and observed it scrupulously. Awhile before service, he would stand in front of the building and watch the people gathering for worship. Anyone who walked past he would seize by the clothes and endeavour to turn towards the entrance. He would station himself near the pulpit during service, stand up during the prayers and, like numbers of human beings, sleep during the sermon. Nor would he hunt squirrels or game on the sacred day.*

Mr. Buchanan's salary was paid by his congregation since he had not been part of any government emigration scheme. Each family paid $3 a year or $1 and two bushels of wheat. A few Irish settlers who were Protestant and members of the Anglican church also attended Mr. Buchanan's services, since no provision had as yet been made for Anglicans residing in Beckwith. These settlers also called Mr. Buchanan in case of sickness or a death in the family.

Caring for the sick was another of Mr. Buchanan's duties. "Frequently he was aroused at midnight to attend a poor woman in childbirth", writes Mrs. Campbell, "or relieve a case of sudden illness, walking miles on logs set lengthwise to reach the scene of distress". During his ministry he visited McNab, Horton, and the back townships to preach, baptise infants, and marry young couples; often Mrs. Buchanan accompanied him. Occasionally he preached at Richmond and Smiths Falls. "His mission-field comprised nearly the entire country between Perth and Ottawa, in which section he was long the only minister".

The 1820-21 Lanark Society settlers had been accompanied by a minister who was also a doctor, the Rev. Dr. John Gemmill. Dr. Gemmill came with his family aboard the *David of London* in 1821. He had been sent out by the London Missionary Society for field work, for the Established Church of Scotland remained aloof in early Upper Canada and made little attempt to establish itself. It sent itinerant missionaries who made reports, but did not set up congregations or churches as a result.

During his voyage Gemmill had preached on Sundays with the

* Campbell, *The Pioneer Pastor.*

assistance of Hugh McEwen, Sr. Arriving in Lanark, the pastor, who was also a printer and a doctor, set himself up in business. Meanwhile the board of trustees had appealed to the Presbytery in Montreal, asking that a Presbyterian minister be supplied in keeping with the original terms of settlement. Mr. Bell met the Rev. Dr. Gemmill and after satisfying himself as to the doctor's suitability, recommended him as minister for Lanark.

Dr. Gemmill held his first service in the log schoolhouse at Lanark village in 1823. It is doubtful if the government provided him with the usual salary accorded ministers who accompanied emigrants, for in 1824 the congregation informed him that they could no longer pay his salary, having just built a stone church. Sustained by his printing business and whatever he collected as a physician, he continued to hold church services until 1829.

About this time the three clergymen—Buchanan, Bell, and Gemmill—began a joint communion service which was to continue for many years. In 1830 the Rev. William McAllister arrived at Lanark from the Established Church of Scotland to replace Dr. Gemmill, who continued to preach at St. Andrew's Hall, Watson's Corners, until a week before his death in 1844 at the age of 83. Sometimes Dr. Gemmill accompanied Bell on his trips through the townships, sharing church services with him.

Early in the 1820s Mr. Bell had asked his Presbytery for a supply of German Bibles and Testaments for the de Fencible and de Meuron discharged soldiers in the Burgess settlement and these arrived in 1823 to be joyfully received. Bell's ministry in the early years continued to expand to include Morphy's Falls, Smiths Falls, Lanark, Watson's Corners, Rideau Ferry, and Lombardy. A typical weekly itinerary is this March 1823 entry in his Journals:

> On Tuesday married Patrick Campbell and Ann Gray. On Wednesday preached at Beckwith. On Thursday went to Richmond, preached in the schoolhouse, dined with Mr. McLaren and returned to Duncan Stewart's where I stayed all night. Saturday preached at Lanark. Stayed the night at Alex Ferguson's. Sunday preached in their schoolhouse and administered sacrament to 70.

Wading through streams, bitten by mosquitoes, and plagued by conditions of trail and climate, Mr. Bell doggedly followed his missionary course, preaching to Presbyterians and non-Presbyterians alike. Here is a typical journey from the 1830s:

> As summer came on and the roads passable I again resumed my visiting, preaching to congregations from 20 to 100 and never getting as much for it as would pay for horse shoes.
>
> Going on foot, having left my horse at Wm. Andison's where I preached the night before, Mr. A. came with me two miles to Clarke's. Then came swamps for two miles. At Mud Creek I had to take off my shoes and stockings and wade to the bridge. After I passed the creek, it was all jumping from one log to another for about a mile of newly laid corduroy.
>
> I got along dry shod until I got to the borders of Beckwith where passing a creek, I stepped on a round stick which rolled and threw me in the water where I imbibed water and mud. I had to undress and dispense with my indispensables till I squeezed the water out of them. The day was hot and mosquitoes numerous, coming round in thousands. . . . My clothes had to dry on me as I went which was soon done, the sun being hot.
>
> In another half mile, a beaver meadow where I had to strip my lower half and wade again. The day was warm and my feet were refreshed by the cold water. A walk of two miles brought me to a hut . . . four children were the occupants. The eldest sang a hymn and I gave her all the coppers I had. I rested here an hour. It was two miles to the next house and a herd of cattle ran after me, greatly excited till I left them at a high fence.
>
> I next came to the house of Mr. McNabb, the Baptist preacher, where the good man was busy with his loom. We had a long talk. They insisted on my staying to dinner. I had a comfortable meal in spite of two spoiled and squalling children. At six I preached at Mr. Buchanan's in Beckwith to a small congregation for they are not used to attending week-day preaching.

Some of his experiences were comical:

> I came to the house of Mr. P. Mrs. P. and one of her neighbours were seated by the fire visiting together rather slovenly in dress. On opening the door a dog belonging to the visitor which had been kept out to prevent his fighting with another inside, got in and they flew at each other. In the struggle they came too near a cat, nursing her family in the corner. She flew at the strange dog and scratched him unmercifully, repeatedly returning to the attack. The dog finally flew at her till she yelled murder, ran through the fire, which was on the floor, and up the corner by the logs of the house, missed her hold and fell into a barrel of flour. Again making a dash for the

> wall she reached a small shelf on which lay a cheese and she sat on top of this. Meanwhile a hen which had been quietly seated on her nest in a corner, got alarmed and flew across the fireplace, so filling the house with a shower of ashes. All the while sticks and umbrellas were employed on the dogs to bring them to reason. Tranquility being restored, I proceeded to discharge the duty for which I had come.

And there were trying incidents:

> At P.N's, I was much annoyed while preaching by a great dog trying to get at some pigfeed behind me, to get at which he had to pass between my legs. The noisy squabbling of a mischievous child whose mother allowed her to run loose also disturbed me greatly. P.N. was laid up with a bad cut in his foot. His great toe split in two with an axe. But he stuck it together with plaster and it got well without a doctor.

The only rivals which Bell had in his missionary circuit came from the Methodist camp, for the Anglican ministers stayed close to their own firesides once established, and there were few of other denominations. The Rev. William Brown was the first Methodist preacher to approach the Rideau settlement, having Smiths Falls and Merrickville in his circuit. Early in the twenties near Merrickville Joseph Cox had built a chapel on his farm, probably the first house of worship in Montague Township; he later deeded the chapel to the Methodists.

In 1822 a Methodist minister, the Rev. John Griggs Peale, arrived in Perth and proceeded through the townships holding camp-meetings and organizing groups. Meanwhile the Rev. Ezra Healey, an American appointed to Montague, Beckwith, and Goulbourn townships had travelled to Morphy's Falls where he preached at "Brother Wallace's" and at Mr. Mansell's in Ramsay. The Pooles, James, Boultons, Richeys, Boyds, Bradens, Mansells, Greenleys, McGraths, and Stedmans appear in Methodist records. At Perth Philander Smith arrived and was "well received by Canadian families such as the Boultons and Adams". He replaced the Rev. John Peale for a few weeks, and then Franklin Metcalf arrived. Metcalf had an assistant, Solomon Waldron, and together they established a "society" of over 100 Methodists in Perth. During the following year Waldron travelled regularly through Ramsay, Lanark, and Pakenham townships.

Bell found Metcalf "a very sensible, decent, good man", although their opinions on scripture differed. They agreed to differ and at the same time unite their efforts in establishing a Sunday School for children of all denominations. After much bickering over inconsequential details, a Union Sunday School opened at Boulton's Mills on the 10th Concession of Bathurst. This Sunday School was still operating in the 1850s, by which time they had a library of 275 volumes besides "tracts and monthly publications".

Although Mr. Bell got along reasonably well with the Methodists, he took exception to his Anglican rival on several counts. Bell *never* read a sermon while Harris, trained as an Army chaplain, *always* read his and could not preach without the written text. If perchance he forgot his text, consternation reigned as on one occasion when preaching at Balderson. When the loss was dicovered Mr. Boulton who had come with him had to hurry back to Perth with his horse and sleigh to retrieve the sermon. As he had a spirited horse he was gone only an hour and a half during which time Mr. Harris read prayers. Mr. Bell wryly commented in his Journals: "The people wondered at the devotional spirit of their pastor". Although Mr. Harris arrived in 1819 it was some time before he began collecting Anglican families in the township and holding church services. In 1823 the Beckwith Anglicans who had been attending Dr. Buchanan's church sent a petition to Mr. Harris asking that the government storehouse lying vacant at Franktown be given them for services. Harris wrote to the Lieutenant Governor's military secretary at York, enclosing the petition signed by 82 names, and specifying that he had been holding service once a month in Pat Nowlan's tavern at Franktown because no other building was available. He pointed out that the tavern was scarcely suitable for services of worship. Permission to use the storehouse was granted.

Photo by the author

ST. JAMES ANGLICAN CHURCH, FRANKTOWN

Completed in 1827, it is the oldest church now in use in Lanark County.

At the same time plans were made to dispose of the government storehouse now vacant at Perth, and the funds from the sale to be used to build an Anglican church at Franktown. The Hon. William Morris bought the Perth storehouse and the officials handed the money over to Mr. Harris. The result was that by 1827 an Anglican Church was completed at Franktown. This is now the oldest church continually in use in Lanark County. The Rev. Richard Hart, a missionary priest, was appointed to the Franktown station in 1829 and remained until 1833, when he was succeeded by the Rev. Richard Flood.

In 1821 the Rev. Father Sweeney had succeeded Abbé de la Motte at Perth, to be followed by the Rev. John MacDonald in 1823. Father MacDonald set up a mission among Robinson's Irish Catholic settlers in Ramsay and Pakenham. By 1825 a parish had been established in Perth.

John Ryerson and Samuel Belton were appointed to the Methodist circuit in 1825. In 1826 William H. Williams had charge at Perth and the Mississippi, having as his assistant Colonel Andrew Playfair who owned and ran several mills at Playfairville. Colonel Playfair had been impressed by Methodist enthusiasm and converted to Methodism early in its Rideau history, but he was a man much in the public eye and was finally disqualified as a preacher because he inadvertently violated Methodist principles by being present at a Sunday dinner party where some young people were dancing. The fact that his host was a Roman Catholic and that Playfair left the premises as soon as he was aware of the dancing did not excuse him in Methodist eyes. He continued to support the cause of Methodism in Canada. The Methodists were the first to build a church in Carleton Place. It opened in 1829 and was designated the Mississippi Methodist Episcopal Registrar of Baptisms, Births, Marriages, and Deaths, all of which were kept by Sam Boyd from 1829 to 1843.

Meanwhile in September of 1827 Mr. Bell and Dr. Buchanan toured Upper Canada in the interest of Presbyterianism, "to visit ministers and their congregations and to ascertain the state of religion among them". They also hoped to awaken interest in establishing a Home Missionary Society and a religious publication for their parishioners. Bell was looking forward as well to hearing his son Andrew ordained at York. The two men travelled on horseback to Brockville, and from there by steamer to Kingston and York. They visited Bell's son, Robert, who ran the printing office of the Gore *Gazette* near Ancaster. They also called on John Galt of the Canada Company before returning to York, where Andrew was ordained and sent off to his first mission at Streetsville.

In the 1820s Duncan McNabb, a farmer and weaver of Beckwith, had established a Baptist missionary circuit going as far as Bathurst township to preach occasionally in the homes of settlers. A Baptist congregation was organized in Carleton Place in 1825 but it is not known when the first Baptist church was built there. Mr. McNabb moved to North Elmsley in 1833 and organized a Baptist congregation in his own home with a membership of five. Much later a Baptist Church was built in Smiths Falls. It was due to the efforts of McNabb that Baptist congregations formed and churches were built in Beckwith, Carleton Place, Drummond, and Smiths Falls.

There were also Baptist services held in North Sherbrooke in the 1820s. The Rev. Andrew McAlpine, who accompanied the Lanark Society settlers, held services occasionally at the home of Josias Davies, and sometimes Mr. Bell preached there.

During the winter of 1830 an itinerant Cameronian preacher from New York State, one McKee, preached in several parts of the settlement, "especially Ramsay", as Bell noted in his Journals. At this time in Ramsay Township were a group of Cameronians* or Covenanters as they were called, mostly Lanark Society settlers. They held prayer services at Bennies Corners prior to 1830. In 1830 the Gardners, Lindsays, MacQueens, Moirs, Raes, and a few others belonging to this sect were organized by the Rev. James Milligan from Vermont into a congregation with James Rae and William Moir as elders. In 1834 they built a log church on the 8th line of Ramsay with the Rev. James McLachlin as their first minister. In 1835 another Cameronian church was built near Clayton.

There were also Cameronians at Perth, some like John Holliday, the first school teacher, having come out with the first Rideau settlers. These petitioned the Ramsay church in 1835 for part of their minister's time, and it was finally agreed that Mr. McLachlin would preach every fifth Sunday at Perth. By 1836 an official congregation had been organized at Perth with John Brown and John Holliday as ruling elders and about 30 members attending.

The Church of Scotland at this time decided to send a minister to Perth in answer to some Presbyterian dissension in Mr. Bell's con-

* The term *Cameronian* derives from a leader called Cameron, hunted and killed by soldiers in Scotland, whose followers had broken from the Established Church of Scotland.

Courtesy Wilfred Snedden

REFORMED PRESBYTERIAN (CAMERONIAN) CHURCH, ALMONTE

gregation. The Rev. Thomas Wilson arrived and held his first services in the Court House until St. Andrew's church was built for him. Mr. Bell called upon him and recorded in his Journals:

> The discipline of our church had been offensive to some of our gentry who wished to live just as they liked and they determined to have a minister from the Church of Scotland who, they expected would be more indulgent to their foibles. When he arrived in Perth and learned how matters stood, he seemed somewhat discouraged. Two days after his arrival I called upon him and in a friendly way had some conversation. I told him if he had come for the purpose of opposition, we of course could not cooperate but if he had come for the purpose of promoting pure and spiritual religion, he would find me a willing fellow labourer.

With the arrival of Mr. Wilson a change came. Other settlers who had been members of the Established Church of Scotland began to desire a freedom and friendly climate to continue their religious views in Upper Canada, and Mr. Bell lost many of his congregation to the new church. In Beckwith Mr. Buchanan's congregation were split by the same issues. Dr. Buchanan was asked to change his ways and join the Auld Kirk of the Established Church of Scotland. Then in his 71st year, he refused and in 1831 the parishioners applied for a minister of the Established Church. Mr. Bell, on a trip to Beckwith in January that year, held service in "the miserable shanty they have for worship" and commented in his Journals that the Synod should see the "House of Worship" they provided:

> An old shanty in such a state of ruin that cats and dogs might pass between the logs . . . here they were sitting in a miserable log hut, the wind whistling between the logs, the thermometer down to zero. Yet they will neither repair the place nor send firewood lest it might make *the minister* comfortable! Though they knew he was sick, not one of them called to see him, excepting his son-in-law.

Apparently the Synod did not investigate the conditions under which Dr. Buchanan had had to labour, and he was dismissed before he could enjoy the pleasure of preaching in the handsome new stone building erected in 1833 on the 7th Concession of Beckwith. He continued to hold services in the largest room of his house for the few who remained loyal to Free Church views. Three years later in 1836 he died at the age of 74. The Rev. John Smith was sent to Beckwith from Scotland, remaining until 1851, and conducting services in both English and Gaelic.

In Ramsay another congregation of the Established Church of Scotland was formed in 1834 and a stone church built on the 8th line in 1836. The Rev. John Fairbairn officiated until his return to Scotland in 1842. Many Presbyterians from Pakenham Township travelled to this Ramsay church until the 1840s, when a Presbyterian church was built in Pakenham village.

Courtesy Wilfred Snedden

AULD KIRK, RAMSAY
Built in 1836.

Photo by the author

SCOTTISH BARONIAL CHURCH, FRANKTOWN

At Smiths Falls, the Rev. George Romanes, also from the Established Church of Scotland, arrived in 1833, but a church was not built until 1835. The Presbyterians at Lanark had applied for a minister and in 1830 the Rev. William McAllister was sent out. His charge included Dalhousie and Lanark townships. Subscription for a Presbyterian church at Balderson was started in 1834. Both Bell and Wilson served here. The Anglicans had already built a church at Balderson in 1832, and here Mr. Harris held services.

The Methodists extended their services to Ramsay after building a church at Carleton Place, erecting a chapel on the 8th line of Ramsay in 1835. It was near the Presbyterian "Auld Kirk". The Rev. William McFadden and John McIntyre officiated. Methodists from Pakenham and Huntley townships came to this chapel, travelling as far as 15 miles, often on foot, carrying children and food with them, attending a morning and afternoon service and then returning home. At Smiths Falls a Methodist church was built on Market Street in 1838. This stone edifice was enlarged in 1858 and served the congregation for 47 years.

At Merrickville an Anglican church was built in 1837 on the site of the present Anglican church. Anglicans in Smiths Falls used the government storehouse near the canal for their meeting-place. Anglicans and Methodists both used a log building at Boyd's Corners, near Innisville, prior to the 1830s, but in 1834 or 1835 St. John's Anglican Church was erected at Innisville.

In 1836 a Mormon preacher named Page spent several months at Perth and converted a few families to the Mormon faith. When he left they went with him, travelling in covered wagons to Naiwoo, Illinois.

Since the arrival of Mr. Wilson at Perth Mr. Bell's congregation had dwindled. A telling notation of his position appears in his Journal of 1838 when he remarks that there were many small congregations in Upper Canada at this time destitute of ministers, and that he was sometimes tempted to supply somewhere else as he received very little from his congregation financially. At the same time he felt strongly attached to his few faithful followers of more than 20 years and remarks "I would feel lonely if removed from them". He went so far as to apply to the Governor and Council for assurance that his salary would continue should he go elsewhere. Despite this assurance he heeded the advice of his friends and with his "ever increasing infirmities", for he was now 59 years of age, he remained in Perth.

In 1832 Roman Catholic churches were built in both Merrickville and Smiths Falls. Smiths Falls had had a Roman Catholic mission since 1829 with 30 members. The St. Francis de Sales church was built in 1832 on Church Street and services held three times a year until the Rev. Philip O'Reilly arrived in 1846.

In the 1840s the Anglicans extended their ministry to Pakenham, building a church in 1841 just outside the village at the top of a hill on the road to Arnprior. The Rev. Hannibal Mulkins was the first minister. Another Anglican church was built at Clayton in 1840 and christened St. George's. It was a log structure where the present cemetery now stands, and the Rev. Charles Harris officiated.

At Almonte the first Anglican service was held in a log schoolhouse in 1843, by the Rev. E. I. Boswell of Carleton Place, but a church was not built there until 1863. At Lanark an Anglican church was built in 1842, the Rev. Michael Harris of Perth extending his charge.

The Roman Catholics at Merrickville replaced their small wooden church with a stone one in 1845. Father McDonough succeeded Father John MacDonald at Perth in 1838, where he remained until 1845, following the circuit MacDonald set up, including Pakenham and Almonte. Father Terrance Smith, a missionary in Huntley in 1837, included Almonte in his charge from 1845 to 1848, and Father Edmund Vaughan from Mayo County, Ireland, followed him in 1849.

The Presbyterians built a church at Pakenham village in 1842, and Mr. Bell was the first minister to preach there. An Established Church of Scotland minister was sent out for this charge—the Rev. Alexander Mann, who remained at Pakenham for over 40 years. His grave is in the cemetery of the Auld Kirk on the hill.

Late in the 1840s a group of families residing near Middleville and Rosetta in Lanark Township left the Presbyterian church over some disagreement with the pastor and joined the Congregational denomination, later applying to the Congregational College at Toronto for a minister. In 1850 James Hay was sent to them as student minister.

In 1843 a further split occurred in the Presbyterian denomination, and "Free" churches were formed in many communities. In Ramsay a "Free' church was built kitty-corner from the Auld Kirk on lot 15 of concession 8. Another "Free" church was established in Smiths Falls with the Rev. William Aitkin as minister. A frame building to house this congregation was built on William Street in 1846. Knox Church built at Black's Corners in 1846 was another "Free" church.

In 1851 the Perth Cameronians further divided into two groups and formed the First Cameronian and Second Cameronian churches, but there were not sufficient members to support the second church and it disbanded before the end of the 1850s.

The two pioneer pastors, Michael Harris and William Bell, died within a year of each other—Harris in 1856 at the age of 61, and Bell in 1857 at the age of 78.

It is rather interesting to compare the religious origin of the Lanark population with affiliations when the pioneer period was drawing to a close. The Lanark County census for 1851 revealed that there were more Irishmen by then than any other nationality, although in the early days the Scots predominated:

| | |
|---|---|
| England and Wales | 586 |
| Scotch | 3,740 |
| Irish | 5,798 |
| Non-French Native | 16,448 |
| French | 378 |
| United States | 217 |
| N.S. and P.E.I. native | 11 |
| New Brunswick | 6 |
| Newfoundland | 3 |
| West Indies | 5 |
| East Indies | 2 |
| Germany and Holland | 10 |
| France | 9 |
| Spain and Portugal | 4 |
| Russia and Poland | 3 |
| Switzerland | 9 |
| Channel Islands | 2 |
| Others | 22 |

The religious affiliation of the population was reported as follows:

| | |
|---|---|
| Church of England | 7443 |
| Church of Scotland | 6549 |
| Roman Catholic | 5393 |
| Free Church Presbyterian | 2721 |
| United Presbyterian | 349 |
| Wesleyan Methodist | 2573 |
| Baptist | 792 |
| Reformed Presbyterian | 71 |
| Congregationalist | 254 |
| Universalist | 99 |

| | |
|---|---|
| Quaker | 11 |
| Mormon | 11 |
| Unitarian | 4 |
| Adventist | 3 |
| No church | 50 |
| Unknown | 10 |

Despite the missionary efforts of the Presbyterians and Methodists, the Church of England predominated at the close of the pioneer period.

Sketch by the author

REV. JOHN FAIRBAIRN
He was the first Free Church minister
in Ramsay Township.

# APPENDICES

## A. Towns, Villages, and Postal Points

### *Almonte*

A town on the Mississippi River in Ramsay Township. A United Empire Loyalist, David Shepherd, was the first settler where Almonte now stands. In 1819 he received a concession to construct a saw mill and grist mill. The saw mill, partially completed, was destroyed by fire in 1820 and the concession passed to another "Yankee" from Brockville named Boyce. Daniel Shipman, a son-in-law of Boyce, proceeded to Ramsay and built a saw mill on the property in 1821, adding a grist mill later. In 1825 Daniel Shipman was the only licensed innkeeper in Ramsay Township, and his son Sylvanus ran the only distillery in the township. The first carding mill was operated by I. K. Boyce, a brother-in-law of Shipman, and the first planing mill and waggon-making shop was operated by John M. Haskin. In 1840 Edward Mitcheson erected a three-storey flour mill on the east side of the falls; it was later sold to J. B. Wylie and James H. Wylie. Almonte was one of the principal wool manufacturing towns of the Ottawa Valley in later years. The first woollen mill was erected in 1850 by the Ramsay Woollen Cloth Manufacturing Company. The village was successively named Shepherd's Falls, Shipman's Mills, Ramsayville, Waterford, and finally Almonte, after a Mexican general who had served as Ambassador to Washington and distinguished himself by standing up for the rights of his country against American aggression.

### *Carleton Place*

A town situated on the Mississippi River in Beckwith Township, 28 miles from Ottawa. It was founded in 1818 by Edmond Morphy and his sons, William, John, and James of Tipperary, Ireland, who located on the Mississippi River at this point (Lots 14 and 15, Con. 12). One Coleman arrived in 1820 and purchased water power along the Morphy farm with the understanding that he would build a mill within six months. When he found himself unable to do so, he sold his rights to Hugh Bolton who completed the grist mill within the allotted time. Later Bolton added an oatmeal mill. William Moore opened a blacksmith shop and Robert Barnett a cooperage shortly afterward. In 1821 Alex. Morris began the manufacture

Public Archives of Canada Philip Boyce

ALMONTE
This watercolour shows the Anglican Church.

*Illustrated Atlas*, 1880

RESIDENCE OF J. MENZIES, ALMONTE
Mr. Menzies was registrar of North Lanark. His house beside the bridge is still used as a dwelling.

Walling's *Directory of Lanark and Renfrew*, 1863

VICTORIA WOOLLEN MILLS, ALMONTE, IN THE 1860s

Courtesy Wilfred Snedden

SCOTTISH STONE BRIDGE, ALMONTE

Built in 1863, it was recently demolished.

of potash, later adding a tannery, store, and "groggery" to his enterprises. John Loucks opened a store in 1822. The village was first called Morphy's Falls. Captain Thomas Glendinning acquired 400 acres of Glen Isle, near the village, locating there in 1820. In 1829 Robert Bell, son of the Rev. William Bell of Perth, opened a general store. He was among the most influential men in the village through his interests and activities—from Chairman of the Loyal Village Guards to Member of Parliament for North Lanark in later years. In 1830 a post office was opened and the name Carleton Place given to it. Caleb S. Bellows was the first Postmaster. Napoleon and Francis Lavallee, natives of Hochelaga, Lower Canada, arrived in 1830. Napoleon opened a cooperage, and later operated an inn called the Carleton House which became a favourite rendezvous for meetings and celebrations. He later ran the Mississippi Hotel which still stands.

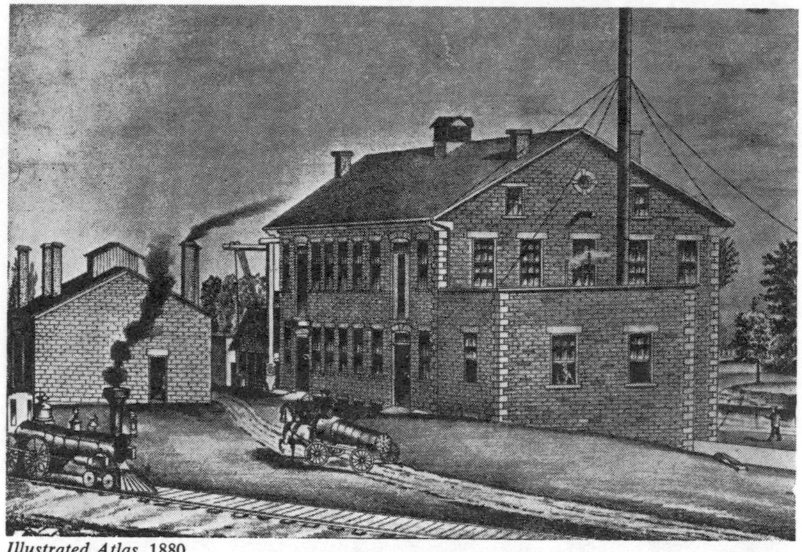

*Illustrated Atlas*, 1880

GILLIES & BEYER'S MACHINE WORKS, CARLETON PLACE

*Smiths Falls*

A town on the boundary line of North Elmsley and Montague. In 1823 Major Thomas Smyth, a British officer and veteran of the American revolutionary war, arrived to take possession of land he had been granted there in 1784. With his sons Terrance and Henry, his nephew William Merrick, and Thomas Waterman and Alex. McCrea he began to build a saw mill and dam on the Rideau River. The saw mill was built on Lock Island in 1823. However, his land had been mortgaged to a Boston merchant, Joseph Sewell, in return for some ready cash in 1810, and when the debt

*Illustrated Atlas*, 1880

WILLIAM WYLIE,
CARLETON PLACE

had not been paid in 1825 Sewell brought action for foreclosure. The land was sold at a Sheriff's sale in Brockville and went to Charles Jones for £105. Next year Jones sold it to a lumberman from Maitland, Abel Russell Ward, for £600. Ward reconstructed Smyth's saw mill and erected a log house beside it. By 1827 Wardsville, as the location was called, was still only a small clearing surrounded by forest. James Simpson, a young surveyor working on the construction of the Rideau Canal, described it as follows:

> When I came to Smith's Falls or Wardsville in 1827, the place had no roads leading to it. It was an entire wilderness with the exception of an old saw mill newly rigged up by Abel Ward for the purpose of sawing lumber to build with, and his own dwelling, a log house nearby. The saw mill had hardly commenced operations when by an order of Colonel By, the officer in charge of the entire works, I removed it to make way for a dam for the canal. I came on with about twenty men and with teams, and we opened a road from Smith's Falls to the Bytown road, a distance of 8 miles; also a road towards Perth, about 9 miles; also a road to Dack's Tavern on the post road to Brockville, and a road of 5 miles from the Falls to the Rose settlement.

Colonel By awarded Ward £1,500 in damages for removal of his saw mill, the largest settlement made to any mill-owner along the canal route, and Ward rebuilt his mill on another part of the island. Mactaggart, the Scottish engineer who wrote at length about canal building in Upper Canada, described the Smyth falls as the "most appalling" met anywhere, since they fell over beds of hard bastard marble rock, 36 feet in less than a quarter of a mile. James Simpson bought two-thirds of the property belonging to

*Illustrated Atlas*, 1880

ABEL RUSSELL WARD
He was the first settler in Smiths Falls.

*Illustrated Atlas*, 1880

CAPTAIN
JOHN McGILL CHAMBERS
He settled in Smiths Falls in 1828 and commanded a steamboat on the Rideau from 1828 to 1840.

Ward in 1827, and together they became joint owners and proprietors of the site for Smiths Falls. Ward opened a tavern colourfully called "Bucket of Blood", a name probably earned during the canal construction when the hostelry yard was often the scene of battles. Ward later built grist, shingle, carding, and oat mills. The first store was opened by Simpson and George C. Middleberger in 1828. In 1829 the property was surveyed as a townsite by John Booth, deputy provincial land surveyor, and the owners assisted him in clearing and laying out streets. About this time Obediah Read, a waggon-maker, built the first hotel (on Beckwith Street), which became

*Illustrated Atlas*, 1880

FRANCIS T. FROST
SMITHS FALLS

Archives of Ontario — Thomas Burrowes

SMITHS FALLS

Walling's *Directory of Lanark and Renfrew*, 1863

FROST & WOOD MACHINE SHOP, SMITHS FALLS

the favourite stopping-place for government employees on the canal. Settlers flocked in while the canal was under construction. Three locks were built across the river, and the potential water power was later used for factories, eventually turning the location into a trading centre.

*Illustrated Atlas*, 1880

GARRETT'S BLOCK, BECKWITH STREET, SMITHS FALLS

*Allan's Mills*

A village in North Burgess Township on Grant's Creek, 6 miles from Perth. Situated near the Scotch Line. The original owners of the land were absentee United Empire Loyalists. In later years W. Allan purchased Lot 12 of the 10th concession and built saw and grist mills on Grant's Creek. He later opened a general store.

*Andrewsville*

A village at the southeast corner of Montague Township called after Rufus Andrews who bought land from William Merrick and located there in 1843. Later he built a shingle mill and a village grew up around it. There was a canal lock here, with J. Richardson one of the early lockmasters.

*Appleton*

Located in Ramsay Township on the east side of the Mississippi River between Almonte and Carleton Place, and first called Apple Tree Falls. Joseph Teskey, son of John Teskey, one of Peter Robinson's settlers of 1823, from Rothkeale, Ireland, located near the falls and with his brother Robert built a saw and grist mill. Around this grew a village called for some years Teskeyville. The land on which Appleton now stands was once Indian camping ground and farmers living in the area have uncovered Indian artifacts while plowing. A post office opened here was named Appleton and the village subsequently changed its name.

*Ashton*

A village on the Jock River, partly in Goulbourn and partly in Beckwith Township. It was first laid out and settled by John Sumner who opened a general store. In the early years it was called Mount Pleasant or Sumner's Corners. In 1840 a post office was established and the name was changed to Ashton, after the Sumner family estate in England. John Sumner was appointed first postmaster.

*Balderson*

A village on the town line between Drummond and Bathurst Townships, 5 miles from Perth. Sergeant John Balderson from Lincoln, England, located here with his wife, Annie Hewitt (daughter of Sir Robert Hewitt), in 1816. Other early settlers were John Publow, Lieut. Gould, and John Robinson. Peter Stewart was the first schoolteacher. By 1850 the village contained two churches, two general stores, a school, a hotel, a cheese factory, a pump factory, and several mechanics shops.

*Bennies Corners*

Once a village in Ramsay Township near the Pakenham and Ramsay township line. Founded by James Bennie, a Lanark Society settler of 1821, who located on lot 26 of the 8th concession. William and John Baird arrived in 1830 and built a flour mill along the nearby Indian River (the "Mill of Kintail" is now the Tait McKenzie museum). Stephen Young, further down the Indian River where it joins the Mississippi, built a barley mill. William Phillip opened a blacksmith shop at the crossroads corner in the 1840s. By 1851 Bennies Corners had a population of 75. Alex. Leishman kept a general store and the post office. Today nothing remains of the village but S.S. #10 schoolhouse at the crossroads corner.

*Black's Corners*

A village in Beckwith Township now on the main highway from Smiths Falls to Carleton Place, named after John Black an early settler. Knox Presbyterian church was built here in 1846. A municipal hall for the township was built at this crossroads in 1857 and here the Beckwith Township council held its meetings. A post office was later established.

*Blakenay*

On the Mississippi River in Ramsay Township. Originally called Norway Pine Falls because of the abundance of red pine here; later called Snedden's Mills because the land was originally taken up by Alexander Snedden in 1822. He built a saw mill, timber slide, grist mill, and inn. The inn was situated on the 9th line of Ramsay. Along the Mississippi River, Alex. Snedden built a residence in 1834, which was later used as a cheese factory (the ruins of this building are still standing). In the 1850s the name was again changed, this time to Rosebank. A post office was opened in 1874 and named Blakenay, though Rosebank was retained popularly, and the railway station just outside the village was designated (and still is) Snedden.

*Bolingbroke*

A village on Bob's Lake in South Sherbrooke Township. John Currie operated flour, saw, shingle, and planing mills here, and George Currie was his miller. There was a post office by 1868.

*Brightside*

In Darling Township on the town line between Darling and Lanark townships. Abraham Cohen ran a general store and William Lochead was postmaster in the late 1880s. This village is no longer in existence.

*Cedar Hill*

Situated in Pakenham Township. Around the first schoolhouse which James Connery built on his farm (con. 8, lot 6) after 1824, grew a community called Upper Pakenham. The name Cedar Hill was registered in 1861 as a postal station on the property of Samuel Dickson (con. 7, lot 5), and Mr. Dickson was first postmaster.

*Clayton*

On the Indian River in Ramsay Township, 27 miles from Perth. Called Bellamy's Mills in the early days after Edmund Bellamy of Vermont who built a grist mill here in 1824. Later the name Clifton was given the village for postal purposes, but later renamed Clayton.

*Elphin*

The only village and post office in North Sherbrooke Township. Robert Smith, Jr., seems to have been the first occupant of land now part of the village. George Wilson had a licensed inn there in 1825 and was later postmaster. In the 1880s there was a population of about forty with a general store, and tailor, blacksmith, and carpentry shops.

*Fallbrook*

A village in Bathurst Township, situated on Bolton Creek near the point where it flows into the Fall River. William Matheson and Wentworth Winslow (from Nova Scotia), both early settlers of Perth, were the first landowners at this point. William Bolton purchased land and built one of the first grist mills in Bathurst Township. Later he added a saw mill. William Lees who came to Canada from Roxburghshire, Scotland, aboard the

*Illustrated Atlas*, 1880

STORE AND RESIDENCE OF JOHN FUMERTON, FALLBROOK

*Rothiemurchus* in 1817, located on the Mississippi River near here in 1818 (con. 11, lot 25). His son, William, became a Conservative M.P. for South Lanark in later years. A later resident of Fallbrook, Robert Anderson, ran a nursery business with his son John, and developed the Lanark Greening apple.

*Ferguson's Falls*

A village on the Mississippi River and the road from Lanark village to No. 7 highway, situated in Drummond Township. Named after a nearby early settler, Captain John Ferguson, who received a deed for his land in the 1820s, it was first registered as Millford for postal purposes. Thomas McCaffrey of the 1815-16 settlers was the earliest locatee of the site, settling on the southeast side of the present bridge. In the 1850's Robert Blair built a dam across the river and created an artificial falls. Using this power he built a saw mill on the north bank of the stream and a grist mill on the south bank. John Boyle and Charles Hollinger later ran hotels here. Hollinger was also in beef- and pork-packing business. Robert Hicks was postmaster and kept a general store. John Hollinger was village constable.

*Flower Station*

The most northerly community in Lavant Township. It was a postal point in the 1880s with Gilbert White as postmaster and general merchant. This wild country nurtured Lanark County's most famous centenarian, "Granny" Majury, who in 1953 celebrated her 102nd birthday by taking an aeroplane ride from the Carp airport. She was born in Darling Township in 1851, her father being Joseph Crawford, an Irish immigrant. She married

Harry Majury in 1870 and moved to Flower Station. At 99 she was still quilting, knitting, and making bread. On her 100th birthday she step-danced with an 80-year-old "lad" from Fallbrook in Lanark Township. She died at the remarkable age of 105. She attributed her longevity to "hard work, plenty of sleep, and smoking a pipe".

*Franktown*

A village in Beckwith Township on the main highway from Smiths Falls to Carleton Place. A government storehouse was built at this point in 1818 or 1819 to accommodate the discharged soldiers for the Richmond military settlement and the settlers of neighbouring townships. A townsite was laid out in 25-acre blocks in 1821. Patrick Nowlan, a storekeeper, opened the first tavern in 1820 and Thomas Wickham an inn. Both men were operating licensed inns by 1821. Dr. George Nesbitt, physician and surgeon, arrived about this time. Owen Quinn, a surveyor, was another first settler, along with Joseph Sutton, John Conboy, John Nesbitt, Peter and John Fullan, Daniel Ferguson, Stephen Redmond, Josiah Moss, John Moorhouse, Andrew Houghton, and Thomas Armstrong. Later Owen and Charles McCarthy bought townsites. James Burrows was another early settler, and later kept a hotel. The early inns owned by Pat Nowlan and Thomas Wickham are still standing.

*Gillies Corners*

West of Franktown on the early government road between Richmond and Perth in Beckwith Township. Archibald Gillies, who located here in 1819, ran a licensed inn from the 1830s to the 1850s. A few houses and an abandoned church now constitute the one-time village.

*Hall's Mills*

Once a village on the Indian River on the town line between Darling and Lanark townships, it was named after William Hall who owned a saw mill there and became postmaster in the 1880s. By 1885 the post office had been discontinued and the neighbourhood was serviced by rural mail delivery. Daniel Munro was an early village blacksmith.

*Harper*

A village northwest of Glen Tay in Bathurst Township. Archibald Campbell, an 1818 settler, was the first to locate in this area, on lot 21 of the 7th concession. The village was named after Joseph Harper who bought forty acres of land on lot 21 of the 6th concession in 1840.

*Hopetown*

A village situated on a tributary of the Clyde River in the township of Lanark, 18 miles from Perth. Robert Cannon, a Lanark Society emigrant of 1820, was the first settler in the vicinity. He took up land on lot 17 of the 2nd concession of Lanark Township, adjoining Little Lake. Here he later built a hotel on lot 18, con. 2. He was the first postmaster and also kept a cooperage. John Robertson, another Lanark Society settler of 1820, located next to him on lot 18 of the 2nd concession. Robertson later moved to Middleville. James Horn located on nearby Horn Lake. Alex Horn, his son, carried on a lumbering business at Hopetown in the 1850s.

*Huntersville*

Onetime village in Ramsay, near Clayton. An old map shows it on lot 18 of the 4th concession. Here James and Alex Hunter established a woollen-mill on a tributary of the Indian River, employing about 20 people. In 1873 it was destroyed by fire. John Speirs rebuilt it. He lived in the former Hunter house.

*Innisville*

A small village on the Mississippi River and No. 7 highway in Drummond Township. The land where the village now stands was first deeded to Capt. Noah Freer, one of the discharged officers of the Perth military settlement of 1815-16. It was first called Freer's Falls, though Freer never lived there but moved to Montreal shortly after 1818. Early settlers in the vicinity were: Henry Ruckle and Michael McCabe from Ireland (1820); Thos. Williams and Green Willows (from England) and Thomas Dawson (1819). James Ennis, after whom the village was later named, built the first mill—a grist mill—apparently about 1825. He later built an oat mill and saw mill and ran the Ennisville Hotel. Woollen mills were later built here by Abram and George Code, and James Ennis and James Jackson.

*Kilmarnock*

A lock village on the Rideau river. It was Lock station No. 24 on the Rideau Canal. James Maitland was the first settler, and the lockmaster for many years, retiring in 1849 when he was replaced by George Newsome.

*Lavant*

A village in Lavant Township near Robertson Lake. John and Archibald Browning and George Molyneux took up 50 acres of land on the same lot where later the village and a postal station took shape.

*Lanark*

A village on the Clyde River in Lanark Township, 18 miles from Perth. First located as the Lanark supply depot in 1820 for the Lanark Society settlers in the townships of Lanark, Dalhousie, Ramsay, and North Sherbrooke. Colonel Marshall superintended the depot, with J. A. Murdock as storekeeper and James Shaw as clerk. It was called New Lanark in pioneer days, David Bowers building the first log dwelling. Capt. Alex. Ferguson from Perth opened a store in his own log house and built a grist mill on the Clyde in 1821. James Hall, Peter McLaren, Capt. Matthew Leech, and William Gordon located here in 1820. John Hall and Henry Glass opened stores by December 1820. A schoolhouse was built in 1821 with Robert Mason as teacher. The Rev. John Gemmill arrived in 1823 with his family. It is believed Mrs. Gemmill died shortly after arrival at Lanark. A daughter, Grizel, married John Hall. John G. Gemmill, a son, became a printer in the office of the first newspaper at Perth, the *Examiner*. He later founded the Lanark *Observer* in 1850, but after two years moved to Port Sarnia where he established the Lambton *Observer*. Dr. Gemmill was the first printer in Lanark County, doing job printing on a press which he brought with him from Scotland. Other early Lanark village settlers were: Francis Hall (an engineer), James Wilson, William Kirkpatrick, and William Craig. A post office was opened in 1824 with J. Murdock as postmaster for 28 years.

In the early years the Mair family were prominent members of the community. James Mair arrived from Scotland with his family and father, John Mair, Sr., in 1820. John Mair was a shoemaker, and James opened a general store. In later years he also had a store in Perth, and was engaged in the lumbering business with his sons, Holmes and James. Charles, who became a well-known poet, was born at Lanark in 1838. In an interview during his sunset years in Victoria, B.C., where he was living with his daughter, he recalled the Lanark village of his boyhood as a romantic panorama of beautiful hills, valleys, and woods. One of the highlights was Training Day when the men were called out and put through exercises by some "old retired officer", says Mair, "the only one in uniform":

> The men were of all conditions and in every variety of garb—in bare feet, or shoe packs, or with straw ropes for belts, and indescribable hats. It was a comical crowd. Drawn into long lines for drill on the field, it was grotesque in some of its features but the men were thoroughly in earnest. They were no poltroons but hard workers who loved the flag and would have died for it. To us boys it was an inspiring day and I well remember my neat little jacket, leather belt and sword of painted lath, and the proud strut with which I headed my little band of loyal urchins as we marched up and down the village street. Woe to the Yankee boy, had he appeared among us then! The day ended in a glorious carouse, of course. Whiskey was only one shilling a gallon, but there was far less abuse of it in those days in proportion to the population than I have seen in more recent times. Our pastimes were swimming, quoit-play, wrestling, racing and games of all kinds and in winter shinny, an old Scotch game played on ice, resembling hockey. There was skating, snow shoeing, sleighing with girls and dancing.*

* *Master-Works of Canadian Authors*, Vol. XIV, edited by John W. Garvin (1926).

*Illustrated Atlas*, 1880

A. G. DOBBIE
ONE-TIME REEVE OF LANARK

*Illustrated Atlas*, 1880

MILLS AND RESIDENCE OF BOYD CALDWELL, LANARK

*Leckie's Corners*

Once a village in Ramsay township near Almonte. It is believed to have been established in the late 1830s or early '40s. Thomas Leckie had a general store at this crossroads; also a dressmaking and millinery establishment run by Margaret and Elizabeth Waddell, daughters of pioneer James Waddell of Pakenham Township. Robert Yuill was the village tailor. The village never acquired postal status, and nothing remains now but the old tannery building once operated by Thomas Mansell.

*McDonald's Corners*

A village on the Mississippi River in Dalhousie Township, 26 miles from Perth. John and Robert McDonald first located on property where the village now stands. Duncan and Allan McInnes were later nearby settlers. By 1857 a Free Church had been built with the Rev. James Geggie as minister. Hugh McLean was first postmaster.

*McPhail*

A post village in Drummond Township on the same road as Tennyson, six miles from Perth. Peter McPhail from Perthshire, Scotland, located on this site in 1817. Donald McPhail was first postmaster and also ran a cheese factory.

*McGarry*

Situated between the 6th and 7th concessions of Drummond Township, 7 miles from Perth, and named after James McGarry, the first settler. A discharged soldier from the Glengarry Light Infantry he located on land here in 1816. A post office was established with Alex. McGarry as postmaster in later years.

*Merrickville*

A village on the Rideau River, half in Montague Township and half in Wolford. It was founded by William Merrick and his sons in 1794—the earliest village in what now constitutes Lanark County. Merrick built a grist mill and located on the north bank of the Rideau in Montague Township. Other United Empire Loyalists arrived shortly after the Merricks. John Chester opened a store, and Sam Dow a blacksmith shop. The village was called Merrick's Mills in early days (in some records it is spelled Mirick's). Dr. Basil Church was another early arrival, serving the community as physician for many years. He was still practising in the 1850s. By 1817 there was a community of about 300 people. During the building of the Rideau Canal in the late 1820s and early '30s, mechanics and others flocked in and after completion of the canal many remained, finding employment in the Merrick mills. The blockhouse at Merrickville was used for various functions (since it was never needed for defence purposes) including the lockmaster's dwelling and as a hall for church services in the 1830s. The lockmaster wore a British uniform until 1854. For many years two shifts were required on the canal, day and night. William Merrick, Sr., died in 1844 and his enterprises—two grinding mills, a carding mill, and a saw mill—passed to his sons. A new section was built as a woollen factory in 1848. One of the first textile mills in Ontario, it was operated for 106 years, producing tweeds, blankets, and rugs. When it was forced by economic depression to cease operation in 1954 it was the oldest mill in Ontario.

*Maberley*

A village in South Sherbrooke Township on the Fall River. Isaac Currie had a saw mill, grist mill, and shingle mill here. In the 1860s John McGregor was postmaster. In the late 1880s the village boasted general stores, a hotel, blacksmith shops, a town hall, and a cooperage. John Buchanan, on whose land Maberley grew into a village, was making boots and shoes, Michael Flood was manufacturing carriages, and Robert Cannon was providing the community with barrels and wooden containers.

*Middleville*

A village near the centre of Lanark Township close to the Clyde River. John Campbell from Paisley, Scotland, an independent emigrant of 1820, purchased land from the Crown and located where Middleville now stands. He later sold part of his land as town lots and as a site for the Presbyterian church. Matthew Laurie located on land adjoining that of Mr. Campbell on lot 15 of the 6th concession. John Anderson and Kennedy Baxter from Ireland came to the next lot in 1821. The same year James and William Borrowman and their families arrived from Glasgow aboard the ship *Canning*. Borrowman located on the east half of lot 15 of the 5th concession. Daniel Glossop, from Saltcoats, Ayrshire, was the pioneer shoemaker of the village, and George Dorset had an early cooperage. Mrs. Dorset was famous for her herb cures. Peter Morris ran an inn, a candy shop, and a tinsmith business, and also wove carpets. William Scott was a wheelwright by trade and made spinning wheels, reels, and spindles for the neighbouring Scots. He was later schoolteacher and clerk of the township.

*Montague*

A village in Montague Township, now known by the railway station Rosedale in honour of Ezekial Rose, the first settler. The village bore the name Roseville for many years, even after 1859 when a post office was opened and called Montague. John Telford was the first postmaster. The Montague Township Agricultural Society held its fairs here.

*Pakenham*

A village in Pakenham Township on the Mississippi River. James Harvey from Brockville was the first settler, arriving in 1823. He cleared land and erected a saw mill and potash works in partnership with John Powell of Perth. Another settler, Hume, arrived about the same time and opened a store near the mill. Later Harvey & Powell built a grist mill. The village was called "Pakenham Mills" in the early days, after Sir Edward Pakenham, brother-in-law of the Duke of Wellington. William McAdam built the first inn, Norway House. Owen Quinn, a surveyor from Franktown, located near the village, working from there on the survey of Renfrew County. In 1831 Harvey & Powell sold their mill rights to Andrew Dickson, from Nova Scotia, then living near Galetta. Dickson moved to Pakenham and as his enterprises grew the village became known as Dickson's Mills. Postal service came to the village in 1832 and Dickson became the first postmaster, the post office being called Pakenham Mills. The municipal council for the township first met here in 1836. Andrew Dickson became Sheriff for Bathurst District in 1844. By 1842 Pakenham village contained 250 inhabitants with three churches, Episcopal, Presbyterian, and Methodist, post office, grist mill, saw mill, carding machine, and cloth factory, four stores, a tannery, two taverns, and a number of shops.

Courtesy Vera Ross McGiffin

ANDREW DICKSON
PAKENHAM

Courtesy Mrs. John McGill, Sr.

5-SPAN STONE BRIDGE, PAKENHAM
Believed to be the only one in Canada.

*Playfair*

Situated on the Mississippi River close to Fallbrook in Bathurst Township. It was called Playfair Mills in pioneer days after Lieut. Andrew W. Playfair who located there in 1816, building first a saw mill and later grist and fulling mills. Playfair had been born in Paris and had served as Ensign and Lieutenant in the 32nd and 104th Regiments from 1806 to 1813. He was commissioned Colonel in the Lanark Militia in 1818. "Colonel" Playfair, as he was called, espoused Methodism and was one of the lay preachers in Lanark County. He stood as candidate for several elections and was member for South Lanark in 1858. In later years saw mills were also operated by John Johnson, A. W. Playfair, Jr., and John Playfair along the Fall River at this point. Playfair often preached at the Methodist church in the village, built in 1860. The Playfair cemetery nearby is one of the early family cemeteries of Lanark County.

*Poland*

Once a village in Dalhousie Township. James Paul was the earliest settler in this area, coming to Canada as a Lanark Society settler in 1821. Moses Paul was an early shoemaker and weaver, and Poland actually developed on his property. Moses Paul was later postmaster.

*Port Elmsley*

Located in Elmsley Township and originally called Barbadoes and then Pike's Falls. The railway station was still called Pike's Falls Station in the 1880s. Near here was the Rideau Ferry bridge joining the counties of Lanark and Leeds. The village at one time boasted a woollen factory, grist mill, 2 saw mills, a hotel, general stores, church, some minor shops, and the town hall of Elmsley Township.

*Prospect*

A village near the Derry in Beckwith Township. James Conn is the first recorded settler on land where Prospect now stands; he later moved to Ashton. The earliest recorded burial in the Prospect cemetery was that of Hugh Conn who died in 1830 at the age of 39. On property next to the later village site was located William Kerfoot from Kilkenny, Ireland, in 1819. He donated land to build the Prospect Methodist (later United) church. Next to the Kerfoots settled Hugh Conn and John Poole, and other Pooles located near Prospect. The Alcocks were among other early settlers. In the 1850s John Burrows was the postmaster.

*Rideau Ferry*

Originally called Oliver's Ferry after Captain Oliver who ran a ferry service across Rideau Lake and later operated an inn. The road from Brockville to Perth later crossed the lake at this point. In the 1840s there was a small tavern, wharf, and storehouse here.

*Rosetta*

A village in Lanark Township about 3 miles from Middleville. The family of James Dick, a Lanark Society settler of 1821, first located here on lot 13, concession 9. James Dick was drowned at Lachine en route to Lanark but Mrs. Dick and her 11 children took up the allotted land. By the end of 1821 Mrs. Dick had also died. John, the eldest boy, took over the homestead at the age of 17. Kind neighbours helped the orphans establish a home and clear their land. Rosetta was given its name in 1854 when a post office was established here for the first time. John Dodds was first postmaster. The only Congregational church in the county was built here during the latter half of the century.

*Stanleyville*

A village in North Burgess Township near Pike Lake, 9 miles from Perth on the old Kingston road. The Devlins, Shields, McFarlands, Kibbes, Murphys, Donleys, Lappins, McVeighs, Jackmans, Byrnes, Killeens, Coopers, Quigleys, Quinns, Dunns, McGuiggans, Kennedys—Irish settlers of the 1840s—located in this area. The village was named after Michael Stanley who located on lot 15 of the 8th concession. By 1863 the village had a town hall, a schoolhouse, and a few dwellings.

*Tatlock*

Once a village in Darling Township. John Coulter ran one saw mill and Marsden & Robb another in the 1860s. In 1864 Tatlock had a post office with James Guthrie as postmaster.

*Tennyson*

A village on the road from Blacks Corners to Perth, in Drummond Township, about 10 miles from Perth. Two half-pay officers, John and Duncan McNaughton, Jr., were the first settlers on this land. A post office was later established with D. McGregor as postmaster.

*Watson's Corners*

A village in Dalhousie Township, 19 miles from Perth. Robert Cumming and James and Alex Park, Lanark Society settlers, located here in 1820. The village which grew up at this crossroads was called Granny Cumming's Corners in the early days. In 1829 St. Andrew's Hall was built and a library established from settlers' private collections of books brought from the Old Country. The hall was a log building covered with shingles, and was used as well for church services and township meetings. Thomas Scott, head of the Lesmahagow sponsored settlers of 1820, who located near here, was largely responsible for establishment of the library and the St. Andrew's Society hall. He left for Western Ontario in 1854.

*Wilbur*

Once a village near Caldwell Lake in Lavant Township. It existed while the Caldwell iron mine was operating in the nearby area. In the 1880s there was a post office here.

THE AUTHOR'S MATERNAL GRANDPARENTS
John Arthur of Blakenay with his wife, Jessie Stewart, and daughter Margaret (the author's mother).

## B. Statistical Data on Scotch Line Settlers Interviewed by Robert Gourlay in July 1817

*Peter McPherson* from Callendar, Perth County, Scotland, 6 children, no wife. Original profession "a farm grieve". Has erected house 18 x 20 feet. "Well satisfied."

*William McPherson,* his son (now 19). Also "well satisfied".

*James McLaren,* a weaver, from Callendar, Scotland. Wife and 5 children. Has erected house 21 x 18½ feet. "Well satisfied."

*James Taylor,* dyer and clothier from Lanark County, Scotland, parish of Carronwath. Wife and 5 children. Has erected a house of 26 x 21 feet. "Satisfied."

*John Simpson,* a shoemaker from Rothes parish, Murray County, Scotland. Wife and 5 children. Has erected house 20 x 18 feet.

*James Miller,* shipmaster, from Kilbride parish, Ayrshire, Scotland. Wife and 3 children. Has erected house 21 x 17 feet.

*Hugh McKay,* a weaver, from Glasgow Parish, Lanark County, Scotland. Wife and 5 children. Has erected house 25 x 20 feet.

*William Spalding,* a mason, from Dundee parish, Forfar County, Scotland. Wife and 1 child left at home. Has erected a house 26 x 19 feet.

*William Rutherford,* a millwright from the same location. Bachelor. Built a shanty 12 x 10 feet.

*John Hay,* farm labourer from St. Virgin parish, Forfar Co., Scotland. Not married. Has built 18 x 15-foot house.

*Thomas McLean* and *Archibald Morrison,* both unmarried, each having half of a house they built 29 x 22 feet. McLean, a stone mason, from Dunscore parish, Dumfries Co. and Morrison, a ship-carpenter, from Glasgow, Scotland.

*John Halliday,* schoolmaster, from Hutton parish, Dumfries Co., Scotland. Wife and 8 children. Has built house 33 x 19 feet. "Well satisfied."

*Alex. McFarlane,* a farmer from Kilbirnie parish, Ayrshire Co. Wife and 5 children. Has built house 23 x 16 feet.

*James McDonald,* a whitesmith from New Greyfriars, Edinburgh Co., Scotland. Unable to write. Has built house 22 x 14 feet.

*John Ferguson, Sr.,* farmer. No wife, 7 children, From Callendar parish, Perth County. Has built house 24 by 21 feet.

*John Flood*, weaver, from Glasgow, Lanark County, Scotland. Wife and 2 children. Has erected house 21 x 18 feet.

*William McGillevry*, a farmer from Glasgow, Lanark Co. Wife and 6 children. Has house 22 x 18 feet.

*John Brash*, a farm labourer from Glasgow parish, Lanark Co., Scotland. Wife and 3 children. Has house 18 x 16 feet.

*Ann Holderness*, widow of William Holderness. 6 children. From Boobwith parish, Yorkshire Co. Has house 22 x 20 feet.

*John Miller*, farm labourer. Bachelor. From Coldenholm parish, Berwickshire Co. His house has burned down.

*William Old*, shopkeeper from Canongate parish, Edinburgh Co. Wife and 1 child. House 16 x 16 feet.

*Francis Allan*, a clerk in property tax from Corsdorfin, Edinburgh. Wife and 1 child. House 18 x 13 feet.

*Thomas Cuddie*, a gardener from Corsdorfin, Edinburgh Co. Wife and 1 child. Erected a house 18 x 12 feet.

## C. Ship Lists*

(1) Settlers Located by Alexander McDonell, Superintendent, 18th June, 1816.

| SHIP | TOWNSHIP | CON. | LOT |
|---|---|---|---|
| *Baltic Merchant* (1815) | | | |
| Alexander Kidd | Bathurst | 1 | 18 |
| Robert Gibson | Bathurst | 1 | 15 |
| Robt. Wood | Drummond | 3 | 7 |
| | | | |
| *Atlas* (1815) | | | |
| Thos. Barber | Burgess | 10 | 8 |
| John Brash | Burgess | 10 | 3 |
| John Flood | Bathurst | 7 | 23 |
| Alexander Simpson | Elmsley | 10 | 29 |
| Thomas McLean | Elmsley | 6 | 23 |
| Alexander McFarlane | Burgess | 10 | 1 |
| Archibald Morrison | Elmsley | 6 | 23 |
| Robt. Gardner | Burgess | 10 | 4 |
| John Miller | Burgess | 10 | 4 |
| John Kerr | Bathurst | 1 | 21 |
| James Holdsworth | Bathurst | 1 | 19 |
| John Farrier | Burgess | 10 | 7 |
| Wm. Holderness | Bathurst | 1 | 21 |
| Wm. Old | Bathurst | 1 | 20 |
| Sam Pardie | Bathurst | 1 | 12 |
| James McDonald | Burgess | 10 | 1 |
| James Taylor | Elmsley | 10 | 28 |
| James Brice | Bathurst | 1 | 13 |
| David Oliphant | Burgess | 9 | 1 |
| Thos. Borries | Bathurst | 1 | 8 |
| John Johnston | Burgess | 10 | 2 |
| John Ritchie, Jr. | Bathurst | 1 | 10 |
| Heirs of Wm. Wallace | Burgess | 7 | 10 |
| | | | |
| *Dorothy* (1815) | | | |
| James Drysdale | Burgess | 10 | 6 |
| James McLarren | Elmsley | 10 | 28 |
| John McDonald | Elmsley | 4 | 16 |
| Donald McDonald | Elmsley | 3 | 14 |
| Alexander McDonald | Elmsley | 4 | 16 |

* Only partial ship lists available in Crown Land Papers, Ontario Archives.

| SHIP | TOWNSHIP | CON. | LOT |
|---|---|---|---|
| Thomas Manion | Bathurst | 3 | 18 |
| Wm. McPherson | Elmsley | 10 | 27 |
| Went. Winslow | Drummond | 12 | 8 |
| | | | |
| *Eliza* (1815) | Bathurst | 2 | 2 |
| John Christie | Bathurst | 2 | 4 |
| George Gray | Bathurst | 3 | 21 |
| Robt. Mutton | Bathurst | 2 | 4 |
| John Gray | | | |
| | | | |
| *Alexander* (1816) | | | |
| Thos. Robinson | Bathurst | 6 | 23 |
| James Wilson, Sr. | Bathurst | 15 | 22 |
| James Wilson, Jr. | Bathurst | 15 | 22 |
| Edward Topping | Bathurst | 6 | 23 |
| Henry Montgomery | Bathurst | 8 | 23 |
| James Montgomery | Bathurst | 8 | 23 |
| Archibald Kennedy | Drummond | 3 | 12 |
| Sam Craig | Drummond | 3 | 12 |
| Thos. Fullen | Bathurst | 9 | 16 |
| Jos. King | Bathurst | 9 | 12 |
| John McWhinnie | Bathurst | 9 | 13 |
| Abraham Dickey | Drummond | 4 | 2 |
| Thos. Lemmon | Drummond | 4 | 3 |
| John Currie | Bathurst | 9 | 16 |
| Pat. Little | Bathurst | 9 | 12 |
| Wm. Adams | Bathurst | 1 | 22 |
| | | | |
| *Fame* (1815) | | | |
| Wm. Taylor | Drummond | 9 | 8 |
| Mathew Jackson | Drummond | 9 | 7 |
| Wm. Simpson | Drummond | 8 | 2 |
| Thos. Richardson | Drummond | 10 | 6 |
| George Miller | Drummond | 7 | 3 |
| John King | Drummond | 7 | 3 |
| Richard Ellis, Sr. | Drummond | 8 | 4 |
| Richard Ellis, Jr. | Drummond | 8 | 6 |
| Edward Ellis | Drummond | 8 | 4 |
| Thomas Taylor | Drummond | 9 | 8 |
| Duncan McNaughton | Drummond | 6 | 25 |
| Duncan Robinson | Drummond | 6 | 23 |
| James Robinson | Drummond | 6 | 25 |
| John McNaughton | Drummond | 6 | 24 |

| SHIP | TOWNSHIP | CON. | LOT |
|---|---|---|---|
| Robert Potty | Drummond | 4 | 11 |
| Ronald McDonell | Drummond | 4 | 7 |
| Thomas Morner | Drummond | 7 | 27 |
| *Lavinia* | | | |
| Wm. Webb | Bathurst | 9 | 21 |
| *Aide* | | | |
| Robt. Coulthard | Drummond | 11 | 10 |
| Ralph Story | Drummond | 11 | 10 |
| *William & Ann* | | | |
| Wm. Reid | Drummond | 11 | 8 |
| John Reid | Drummond | 11 | 8 |
| *Elvira* (1815) | | | |
| Thos. Donaldson | Elmsley | 5 | 22 |
| David Donaldson | Elmsley | 5 | 23 |
| Andrew Donaldson | Elmsley | 4 | 23 |
| John Donaldson | Elmsley | 3 | 22 |
| James Donaldson | Elmsley | 3 | 22 |
| Henry Watts | Bathurst | 9 | 25 |
| Angus Campbell (1816) | Bathurst | 9 | 25 |
| *Caledonian* | | | |
| Robt. Ferguson | Bathurst | 4 | 23 |
| John McLaren | Bathurst | 1 | 14 |
| John McClesh | Bathurst | 9 | 23 |
| John Ferguson, Jr. | Bathurst | 4 | 23 |
| John McNee | Bathurst | 1 | 14 |
| John McDougall | Bathurst | 9 | 26 |
| Hugh Pedan | Bathurst | 9 | 26 |
| *Trader* | | | |
| Christopher Leggo | Drummond | 10 | 8 |
| Hopineas Ayton | Drummond | 10 | 8 |
| *Diana* | | | |
| James Tate | Bathurst | 3 | 21 |
| John Thompson | Drummond | 11 | 11 |
| *Fancy* | | | |
| John McAllum | Elmsley | 3 | 14 |

| SHIP | TOWNSHIP | CON. | LOT |
|---|---|---|---|
| *Spartan* | | | |
| Henry Hurstwait | Drummond | 10 | 14 |
| James Hurstwait | Drummond | 10 | 14 |
| | | | |
| *Royal Sovereign* | | | |
| John Thornton | Drummond | 1 | 8 |
| James Nicholls | Drummond | 4 | 1 |
| | | | |
| *Brig Sirias* | | | |
| Henry Bradfield | Drummond | 10 | 6 |

(2) Settlers Located by George Fowler, Superintendent, after July 1, 1816.

| SHIP | TOWNSHIP | CON. | LOT |
|---|---|---|---|
| *Brig Ann* | | | |
| John Robson | Drummond | 1 | 14 |
| John Ferguson, Jr. | Drummond | 1 | 14 |
| Sam Wilson | Bathurst | 1 | 15 |
| | | | |
| *Greenfield* | | | |
| Duncan McTavish | Drummond | 1 | 10 |
| Alexander McTavish | Drummond | 1 | 12 |
| Robert Jameson | Drummond | 1 | 10 |
| James Chambers | Drummond | 2 | 13 |
| Angus McKennon | Drummond | 5 | 25 |
| John McKennon, Jr. | Drummond | 5 | 25 |
| Edward Richards | Drummond | 7 | 7 |
| Christopher Flintoff | Drummond | 6 | 19 |
| Alexander McDonald | Drummond | 5 | 26 |
| | | | |
| *Morning Field* | | | |
| Alexander Cameron | Burgess | 10 | 2 |
| John Cameron | Drummond | 2 | 14 |
| William Fraser | Drummond | 2 | 14 |
| Donald McLelland | Beckwith | 7 | 3 |
| John McDonald | Beckwith | 6 | 6 |
| Archibald McDonell | Beckwith | 7 | 3 |
| | | | |
| *Lord Wellington* | | | |
| Robt. Thompson | Drummond | 1 | 13 |

| | TOWNSHIP | CON. | LOT |
|---|---|---|---|
| *Lady Delavale* | | | |
| James McMillan | Drummond | 1 | 13 |
| *Clifford* | | | |
| George Wilkinson | Drummond | 1 | 12 |
| Alex. Sutherland | Drummond | 4 | 11 |
| Duncan Cameron | Drummond | 7 | 14 |
| John McMillan | Beckwith | 3 | 15 |
| Alexander Campbell | Beckwith | 4 | 9 |
| *Commerce* | | | |
| James Deacon, Sr. | Drummond | 5 | 10 |
| *Sophia* | | | |
| Theophile Bartlett | Bathurst | 9 | 19 |
| *Hariot* | | | |
| Wm. Hamilton | Bathurst | 9 | 22 |
| James Ward | Bathurst | 9 | 22 |
| *John* | | | |
| Benjamin Rathwell | Drummond | 4 | 15 |
| Henry Watkins | Drummond | 3 | 18 |
| John Connor | Drummond | 4 | 15 |
| John Tattlock | Drummond | 3 | 19 |
| Thos. Kelly | Drummond | 3 | 19 |
| James Deacon, Jr. | Drummond | 4 | 8 |
| Richard Leach | Drummond | 3 | 18 |
| John Gibbons | Drummond | 11 | 11 |
| John Codd | Drummond | 4 | 19 |
| *Mary & Betty* | | | |
| Thomas Burke | Drummond | 2 | 19 |
| Moses Murphy | Drummond | 7 | 18 |
| Wm. Stedman | Drummond | 2 | 17 |
| Nathaniel Stedman | Drummond | 2 | 17 |
| John White | Drummond | 8 | 6 |
| *Brig Charles* | | | |
| Thomas James | Drummond | 2 | 19 |
| William James | Drummond | 2 | 18 |
| John James | Drummond | 2 | 18 |

| | TOWNSHIP | CON. | LOT |
|---|---|---|---|
| *Lady of the Lake* | | | |
| Donald Campbell | Drummond | 6 | 3 |
| Duncan Campbell | Drummond | 6 | 3 |
| Alexander McDonald | Beckwith | 8 | 4 |
| Richard Immerson | Drummond | 1 | 8 |
| *Golden Grove* | | | |
| Stephen Redmond | Beckwith | 3 | 10 |
| *Nancy* | | | |
| William Clarkson | Beckwith | 3 | 10 |
| William Hunter | Drummond | 7 | 19 |

(3) Settlers Located by George Fowler, Superintendent, in 1817.

| | | | |
|---|---|---|---|
| *Prompt* | | | |
| Peter McLaren | Drummond | 6 | 8 |
| Alex. McPherson | Drummond | 2 | 14 |
| Thos. Finlay | Burgess | 8 | 15 |
| Robt. Dibbs | Burgess | 8 | 4 |
| Richard Finlay | Burgess | 8 | 15 |
| John Dibbs | Burgess | 9 | 4 |
| Peter McPherson | Drummond | 2 | 15 |
| John Wilson | Drummond | 3 | 5 |
| *Harmony* | | | |
| Malcom Campbell | Beckwith | 2 | 16 |
| John McNaughton | Beckwith | 2 | 15 |
| Alex. Campbell | Beckwith | 1 | 16 |
| Jas. Anderson | Beckwith | 1 | 16 |
| Duncan McKerkir | Beckwith | 2 | 15 |
| Donald McNaughton | Beckwith | 1 | 15 |
| Jas. Anderson (2nd) | Beckwith | 2 | 17 |
| Hugh McOwen | Beckwith | 10 | 24 |
| John McOwen | Beckwith | 2 | 18 |
| Alex Crerar | Beckwith | 1 | 18 |
| Peter Crerar | Beckwith | 1 | 8 |
| Peter Cameron | Beckwith | 1 | 15 |
| Donald Crerer | Beckwith | 1 | 8 |
| John Berry | Beckwith | 5 | 8 |
| Wm. Power | Beckwith | 5 | 8 |
| Jos. Catley | Elmsley | 7 | 28 |

| *Maria* | | | |
|---|---|---|---|
| Geo. Merrett | Bathurst | 4 | 13 |
| John Campbell | Beckwith | 4 | 2 |
| Jos. McEntire | Beckwith | 4 | 2 |
| Francis Bennett | Beckwith | 3 | 5 |
| Lachlin McLaghlin | Drummond | 2 | 22 |
| Jos. Seagers | Elmsley | 7 | 28 |
| Wm. Dennison | Elmsley | 7 | 29 |
| Ed. James, Sr. | Drummond | 2 | 9 |
| Ed. James, Jr. | Drummond | 1 | 19 |

(4) Ships carrying Lanark Society Settlers, 1820-21.

*Brock* (1820)
Robt. Johnston
Peter McLaren
Angus McCallum
Robt. McNeil
Thos. Orr
John Turnbull
Thos. Whitelaw
Jas. Baird
John Gunn
Jas. Hannah
John McLachlan
Chas. McClean
Robt. Urquhart
Geo. Waddell
James Blain
Andrew Boss
Neil Campbell
John Moulton
Wm. Morris
Geo. Codd
John Flinn
John Fair
John Lawrin
Jos. Lamont
John McLeland

*Prompt* (1820)
John Clymie
Duncan Clymie
Wm. Granger
Jas. Hood
Wm. Hood
Jas. Jack
Wm. Jack
John Lamb
Wm. Muir
Jas. McNiden
Jas. Lightbody
Jas. Muir
Robt. Penman
Jas. Rogers
Robt. Rogers
Robt. Scouler
Thos. Scott
Jas. Watson
Wm. Tatlock

*Commerce* (1820)
John Turriff
Wm. Turriff
James Reed
Duncan MacPherson
John McNicoll
Wm. Gibbons
John Grahame
Wm. Morrison
James McArthur
Robt. Monday
Wm. Anderson
Robt. Anderson
James Anderson
James Blackwood
Wm. Bennett
Kennedy Baxter
Wm. Walker
Wm. Yule
John Cumming Sr. & Jr.
Thos. Davidson
Robt. Drysdale
Jas. Drysdale
John Douglas
George Douglas
Alex. Ferguson
Wm. Ferguson
Geo. Gold
Henry Gold
Henry Glass
Jas. Hall, Sr.
Jas. Hall, Jr.
John Hay
Henry Hammond
John Ireton
Wm. Brown
Thos. Bullock
David Ballantyne
Jas. Bulloch

David Bower
Peter Barr
Daniel Cumming
Archibald Cumming
Paul Cumming
Jas. Colquhoin
Robt. Cannon
Robt. Ferguson
Gilbert Forgie
John Galbraith
Thos. Gammell
David Hamilton
John Henderson
Chas. Esdale
Robt. James
Matthew Kirkwood
Jas. Lindsay
Wm. McIntyre
John Mair
Peter Munro
Alex. McInnis
John Robertson
Jas. Braiden, Sr.
Jas. Braiden, Jr.
Sam. Boyd
John Boyd
Henry Bertram
Wm. Bertram
Jas. Forsyth
Chas. Fleming
Wm. Francis
Mich. Foley
Hugh Gahan
Ed. Hopkins
Noble Graham
Henry Hammond
Jas. Maloney
John McMannis

*George Canning* (1821)

Wm. McEwan
John McPherson
Duncan McInnes
Jas. Braidwood
Jas. Yuill, Jr.
Jas. Paul
Jas. Borrowman
Walter Black
John Kilpatrick
Robt. McLaren
Jas. Aitkenhead
Walter Bain
Andrew Brown
Jas. Patterson
Thos. McLaren

*David of London* (1821)

Sam. Stevenson
John Blair
David Young
Geo. Bremner
Arch. Paterson
Wm. Drynon
John Robertson
John Young
Arch. McKechnie
Wm. Beattie
Peter McGill
Walter Gardiner
David Leckie
Jas. Rae
Jas. Bowes, Sr.
Robt. Whitton
Thos. Bowes
Jas. Bowes, Jr.
John Gillan
John McKerecher
Thos. Pollock
Jas. Pollock
John Gammil
Jas. Wilson
Robt. Smith
Donald McLean
John Hughes

**D.** List of Emigrants from the South of Ireland who embarked on board the *Stakesby* for passage to Quebec, Cove of Cork, July 8, 1823.*

* Peter Robinson Papers, Ontario Archives, Microfilm. Note: only those who located in the District of Bathurst are included in this list.

| NAME | FORMER RESIDENCE | AGE | TOWNSHIP |
|---|---|---|---|
| Martin Ryan | Six-Mile Bridge, Clare | 36 | Ramsay |
| Margaret Ryan | | 30 | |
| Michael Ryan | | 12 | |
| Mort. Ryan | | 10 | |
| Martin Ryan | | 8 | |
| John Ryan | | 6 | |
| Katharine Ryan | | 4 | |
| James Ryan | | 2 | |
| Thomas Boyle | Clonmeen, Clare | 30 | Pakenham |
| Mary Boyle | | 32 | |
| Henry Boyle | | 20 | |
| William Boyle | | 8 | |
| Mary Boyle | | 5 | |
| Charles Boyle | | 4 | |
| Esther Boyle | | 1 | |
| Timothy O'Brien | Liscarrol, Cork | 32 | Ramsay |
| Katharine O'Brien | | 28 | |
| Pat O'Brien | | 9 | |
| Joanna O'Brien | | 8 | |
| Jeremiah O'Brien | | 5 | |
| Julia O'Brien | | 2 | |
| John Benson | Charleville, Cork | 32 | Ramsay |
| Mary Benson | | 28 | |
| William Benson | | 7 | |
| Francis Benson | | 5 | |
| Robt. Benson | | 3 | |
| John Benson, Jr. | | 1 | |
| Thomas Hennissy | Castlewrixon, Cork | 43 | Ramsay |
| Thos. Hennissy, Jr. | | 19 | |
| Honora Hennissy | | 16 | |
| Mary Hennissy | | 15 | |
| Elisa Hennissy | | 12 | |
| John Green | Castletownroche, Cork | 32 | Pakenham |
| Katharine Green | | 22 | |
| Thomas Green | | 30 | Pakenham |

| NAME | FORMER RESIDENCE | AGE | TOWNSHIP |
|---|---|---|---|
| Bustard Green | | 25 | Pakenham |
| Anne Green | | 23 | |
| Rose Green | | 24 | |
| William Green | | 22 | Pakenham |
| George Green | | 20 | Pakenham |
| Abigail Green | | 25 | |
| Pat Sullivan | Mallow, Cork | 32 | Pakenham |
| Mary Sullivan | | 30 | |
| Mary Sullivan, Jr. | | 8 | |
| John Barry | Mallow, Cork | 32 | Ramsay |
| Fanny Barry | | 19 | |
| Denis Galvin | Mallow, Cork | 19 | Ramsay |
| Timothy Quinn | Rathcormac, Cork | 40 | Ramsay |
| Mary Quinn | | 28 | |
| Katharine Quinn | | 5 | |
| John Quinn | | 3 | |
| Margaret Fitzgerald | Rathcormac, Cork | 22 | |
| Robert Shea | Mallow, Cork | 36 | Lanark |
| Mary Shea | | 28 | |
| Simon Shea | | 2 | |
| John Sullivan | Watergrasshill, Cork | 31 | Pakenham |
| James Flynn | Cork | 31 | Ramsay |
| Margaret Flynn | | 28 | |
| William Flynn | | 10 | |
| John Flynn | | 8 | |
| Daniel Flynn | | 3 | |
| Thomas Madden | Cork | 38 | Ramsay |
| Ellen Madden | | 32 | |
| Jeremiah Madden | | 16 | |
| Mary Madden | | 9 | |
| John Madden | | 7 | |
| Thomas Madden | | 5 | |
| Bart. Murphy | Clogheen, Cork | 22 | Ramsay |
| Michael Corkery | Carrigrohan, Cork | 39 | Ramsay |
| Pat Corkery | | 16 | |
| Michael Corkery | | 3 | |

| NAME | FORMER RESIDENCE | AGE | TOWNSHIP |
|---|---|---|---|
| Ellen Corkery | | 20 | |
| Elisa Corkery | | 18 | |
| Bridget Corkery | | 10 | |
| Daniel Ryan | Kanturk, Cork | 37 | Ramsay |
| Mary Ryan | | 35 | |
| Mary Ryan, Jr. | | 12 | |
| Bridget Ryan | | 8 | |
| Con. Ryan | | 6 | |
| John Ryan | | 2 | |
| Richard Wynn | | 27 | Ramsay |
| William Leahy | Michelstown, Cork | 27 | Ramsay |
| John Leahy | | 25 | Ramsay |
| Mary Leahy | | 22 | Ramsay |
| William Leahy | | 30 | Ramsay |
| William Drake | Kildorrery, Cork | 23 | Ramsay |
| Michael Lynch | Castletownroche, Cork | 25 | Pakenham |
| Julia Lynch | | 22 | |
| John Ahern | Castletownroche, Cork | 28 | Pakenham |
| Bridget Ahern (died Aug.6) | | 27 | |
| Thomas Ahern | | 3 | |
| Jane Ahern (died 29 July) | | 3 | |
| James Sayward | Castletownroche, Cork | 21 | Pakenham |
| William Gubbins | Castletownroche, Cork | 40 | Ramsay |
| Florance Carey | Ballyhooly, Cork | 25 | Ramsay |
| John Mantle | Rathcormick, Cork | 45 | Huntley |
| Ellen Mantle | | 40 | |
| James Mantle | | 18 | |
| Mary Mantle | | 16 | |
| Ellen Mantle | | 12 | |
| Margaret Mantle | | 10 | |
| Robert Mantle | | 6 | |
| Katharine Mantle | | 2 | |
| Jeremiah Abbot | Rathcormick, Cork | 25 | Lanark |

| NAME | FORMER RESIDENCE | AGE | TOWNSHIP |
|---|---|---|---|
| Pat. Healy | Fermoy, Cork | 40 | Ramsay |
| Abbey Healy | | 40 | |
| Mary Healy | | 20 | |
| Denis Healy | | 18 | |
| James Healy | | 14 | |
| Margaret Healy | | 5 | |
| John Thomson | Fermoy, Cork | 30 | Ramsay |
| Margaret Thomson | | 22 | |
| Martha Thomson | | 2 | |
| John O'Brien | Kanturk, Cork | 34 | Ramsay |
| John French | Mallow, Cork | 24 | Pakenham |
| Mary French | | 24 | |
| Sarah French | | 2 | |
| John Deleurey | Mallow, Cork | 24 | Ramsay |
| Biddy Deleurey | | 20 | |
| William Riordan | Mallow, Cork | 20 | Ramsay |
| John Nunan | Mallow, Cork | 22 | Huntley |
| Katharine Nunan | | 22 | |
| Mary Nunan | | 3 | |
| Tim. Kennedy | Charleville, Cork | 25 | Pakenham |
| Denis Shanahan | Charleville, Cork | 21 | Pakenham |
| Anniver Cusick | Charleville, Cork | 29 | Pakenham |
| Edmond Barry | Mallow, Cork | 41 | Darling |
| Henry Mahony | Mallow, Cork | 26 | Pakenham |
| Bridget Mahony | | 30 | |
| Pat Donaghue | Mallow, Cork | 44 | Ramsay |
| Anne Donaghue | | 40 | |
| Katharine Donaghue | | 7 | |
| Margaret Donaghue | | 4 | |
| Mary Donaghue | | 2 | |
| Patrick Nelligan | Doneraile, Cork | 23 | Huntley |
| John Phelan | Killmore, Tipperary | 37 | Ramsay |
| Katharine Phelan | | 35 | |
| Denis Phelan | | 14 | |
| Michael Phelan | | 9 | |

| NAME | FORMER RESIDENCE | AGE | TOWNSHIP |
|---|---|---|---|
| Ellen Phelan | | 7 | |
| John Phelan, Jr. | | 4 | |
| Joanna Phelan | | 5 | |
| Pat Phelan | | 2 | |
| Michael Nagle | Mallow, Cork | 35 | Bathurst |
| Mary Nagle | | 32 | |
| David Nagle | | 10 | |
| Ellen Nagle | | 8 | |
| Mary Nagle | | 6 | |
| Morris Nagle | | 3 | |
| James Roche | Michelstown, Cork | 39 | Ramsay |
| John Ruby | Mallow, Cork | 17 | Ramsay |
| John Roche | Charleville, Cork | 27 | Lanark |
| Charles McCarthy | Rathkeal, Limerick | 27 | Ramsay |
| Maurice Buckley | Fermoy, Cork | 35 | Ramsay |
| James Brown | Lismore, Waterford | 19 | Ramsay |
| William Brown | | 16 | Ramsay |
| Maurice Bresnehan | Buttevant, Cork | 24 | Ramsay |
| John Young | Adare, Limerick | 41 | Ramsay |
| Katharine Young | | 39 | |
| Rachel Young | | 19 | |
| Margaret Young | | 18 | |
| Letitia Young | | 17 | |
| Dorah Young | | 15 | |
| Katharine Young | | 13 | |
| Maryanne Young | | 5 | |
| Harriet Young | | 3 | |
| William Gregg | Conna, Cork | 34 | Pakenham |
| Fanny Gregg | | 34 | |
| William Gregg | | 5 | |
| Mary Gregg | | 4 | |
| Eliza Gregg | | 1 | |
| Michael Gregg | | 23 | |
| Michael Regan | Mallow, Cork | 28 | Ramsay |
| John Leahie | Conna, Cork | 20 | Ramsay |

| | | | |
|---|---|---|---|
| John Mara | Rathcormick, Cork | 42 | Ramsay |
| Joanna Mara | | 36 | |
| Mary Mara | | 15 | |
| John Mara | | 12 | |
| Joanna Mara | | 8 | |
| Bridget Mara | | 6 | |
| Thomas Mara | | 5 | |
| Ellen Mara | | 3 | |
| Pat Quinn | | 1 | |
| Mary Corkery | | 3 | |
| Thos. O'Brien | Mallow, Cork | | Ramsay |

**E.** List of Emigrants from the South of Ireland who embarked on board the *Hebe* for passage to Quebec, Cove of Cork, July 8, 1823. (No ages were given in this List. It may be assumed the woman's name after the male head of the family was usually his wife, but in some cases it may be a sister or daughter. See Peter Robinson Papers, Ontario Archives, Microfilm; also *Pakenham: Ottawa Valley Village 1823-1860*, by Verna Ross McGiffin, 1963.)

| NAME | FORMER RESIDENCE | TOWNSHIP |
|---|---|---|
| Robert Armstrong | Kilfinnane, Limerick | Ramsay |
| Margaret Armstrong | | |
| Jane Armstrong | | |
| Janny Armstrong | | |
| Sophia Armstrong | | |
| Rebecca Armstrong | | |
| Elizabeth Armstrong | | |
| Thomas Armstrong | | |
| Michael Horan | Mallow, Cork | Ramsay |
| John Sullivan | Doneraile, Cork | Pakenham |
| Mary Sullivan | | |
| Bess Sullivan | | |
| John Sullivan | | |
| Mary Sullivan | | |
| Margaret Sullivan | | |
| John Doherty | Churchtown, Cork | Pakenham |
| Jude Doherty | | |
| Pat Doherty | | |
| Edward Doherty | | |
| Daniel Doherty | | |
| David Ward | Newmarket, Cork | Ramsay |
| Ally Ward | | |
| Mary Ward | | |
| Nora Ward | | |
| Bess Ward | | |
| Tim. Clahan | Churchtown, Cork | Pakenham |
| Margarette Clahan | | |
| Joanna Clahan | | |
| Catharine Clahan | | |
| John Carey | | |

| NAME | FORMER RESIDENCE | TOWNSHIP |
|---|---|---|
| Matthew Tuskay | | Ramsay |
| Tim. Sheehan | Liscarrol, Cork | Ramsay |
| Mary Sheehan, Sr. | | |
| Mary Sheehan, Jr. | | |
| Joanna Sheehan | | |
| Maurice Sheehan | | |
| Honora Sheehan | | |
| Cornclius Sheehan | | |
| John Evans | | |
| William Ryan | Croom, Limerick | |
| William Hickey | Michelstown, Cork | Ramsay |
| Pat Foley | Castlelyons, Cork | Ramsay |
| Helen Foley | | |
| Mary Foley | | |
| John Foley | | |
| David Foley | | |
| Pat Foley | | |
| Michael Foley | | |
| Helen Foley | | |
| Francis Jessop | Kilfinnane, Limerick | Ramsay |
| Patrick Rourke | Newcastle, Limerick | Ramsay |
| Ellen Rourke | | |
| Pat Dahill | Newmarket, Cork | Ramsay |
| Tim Rahilly | Newmarket, Cork | Ramsay |
| Mary Rahilly | | |
| Jeremiah Rahilly | | |
| Pat Rahilly | | |
| Jeremiah Millane | Ballygibblin, Cork | Ramsay |
| Joanna Millane | | |
| James Ray | Doneraile, Cork | Ramsay |
| Mary Ray | | |
| Margaret Ray | | |
| Michael McGaurin | Liscarros, Cork | Ramsay |
| William Hickey | Michelstown, Cork | Ramsay |

| NAME | FORMER RESIDENCE | TOWNSHIP |
| --- | --- | --- |
| Denis Sweeney | Buttevant, Cork | Ramsay |
| Mary Sweeney | | |
| Margaret Sweeney | | |
| Kitty Sweeney | | |
| Joanna Sweeney | | |
| Robert Sweeney | | |
| Pat Sweeney | | |
| Cornelius Sweeney | | |
| Denis Sweeney | | |
| Cornelius Roche | Doneraile, Cork | Pakenham |
| Bridget Roche | | |
| John Roche | | |
| Denis Roche | | |
| Garret Nagle | Fermoy, Cork | Ramsay |
| Honorah Nagle | | |
| Garret Nagle, Jr. | | |
| Richard Nagle | | |
| John Nagle | | |
| Pat Nagle | | |
| Michael Nagle | | |
| James Nagle | | |
| Maryanne Nagle | | |
| Pat Slattery | Clogheen, Cork | Pakenham |
| Helen Slattery | | |
| Katharine Slattery | | |
| Mary Slattery | | |
| Pat Slattery, Jr. | | |
| Patrick Lynch | | Ramsay |
| Garret Dulmage | | Ramsay |
| Sarah Dulmage | | |
| Margaret Dulmage | | |
| Richard Dulmage | | |
| Lawrence Dulmage | | |

**F.** Payment for services on government projects was often in the form of land grants. The following is a typical grant given for services:

Grant to Josiah Taylor of the town of Perth in the County of Lanark in the Bathurst District, Esquire. Captain in the Canadian Regiment, employed in cutting a road through the wilderness in the communication to Penetanguishene, all that parcel of land in the township of Pakenham in the County of Carleton in the Bathurst District being the south-westerly half of Lot No. 26 in the 4th Concession; the south-westerly half of Lot No. 7 in the 9th Concession; the south westerly half of Lot 20 in the 11th Concession, that is to say commencing where a post has been planted, etc.... containing 400 acres more or less (Reserving all navigable waters within the same with free access on beach by all vessels, boats and persons).

For which allotment of 57 acres and 1/7 is made for a Protestant Clergy in Lot No. 10 in the 2nd concession of said township of Pakenham (also) Order in Council 15 day March 1815 and Ticket of Location, Land Board, Bathurst District, 12 June 1823. Under the Administration of Sir Peregrine Maitland, K.C.B., Lieutenant Governor, for 700 acres of Land.

(signed) T. Ridout

Under the Regulations of 6th July 1804

Warrant No. 2546 Land Officer

fees paid Description No. 8133

A.G.O. No. 9536<br>25 Sept. 1827 } The settlement duty performed

Surveyor-General's Office, York. 20 September 1827.

**G.** The Militia.

*Officers of the 3rd Lanark Militia 1822-24*

Colonel Josias Taylor

Lieut. Col. Ulysses Fitzmaurice

Major Donald Fraser

Captains: Thomas Glendinning
John Robertson
Julius Lelievre
John Ferguson
Thomas Wickham
George Nesbitt
Duncan Fisher
William Naughty

Lieutenants: Robert Ferguson
Israel Webster
James McFarland
John Cram
John Fulford
William Baird
Peter McGregor

Ensigns: John Nesbitt
Alex Dewar
John Dewar
Manly Nolan
Daniel Ferguson
Joseph Fullan
Peter Fullan
Owen Quinn
John Donaghue

**H.** Statement of Imports and Exports Through Tay Canal, Summer 1835. (*Bathurst Courier*, 1835)

| *Exported* | *Imported* |
|---|---|
| Potash—1504 bbls. | Gypsum—5 bls. |
| Butter—753 firkins | Fine Flour—9 bls. |
| Whiskey—3 bb. | Whiskey—89 bls. |
| Saw logs—1340 | Oats—20 bu. |
| Flour—16 bbs. | Wheat—40 bu. |
| Salted Fish—30 bls. | Firewood—40 cords |
| Beer—116 bls. | Ploughs—24 |
| Fanning Mills—8 | Apples and plums—29 bls. |
| Oak staves—57,154 | Household furniture—11 tons |
| Oak timber—181,550 ft. | Merchandise—199,318 tons |
| Soft timber—19,765 ft. | Salt—807 bls. |
| Pine boards—141,170 ft. | Boards—11,976 ft. |

J. McKay, Perth-Tay Navigation Company.

## I. Health and Longevity of Lanark County Pioneers.

There is a prevalent belief that early settlers in Upper Canada did not usually live to a ripe old age, that few reached the age of 90, and many died at 18. This does not seem to have been the case with Lanark County pioneers many of whom lived to a greater age than their descendants of this century.

Many did die from malnutrition, and tuberculosis was a dreaded scourge as were ague, cholera, and scarlet fever. The interminable swamps and dense forests were breeding grounds for hordes of mosquitoes. Lack of roads made the importation of food to vary the diet almost impossible, even if the settler could afford the price, which most could not. Dampness in summer and lack of sunshine in winter contributed to disease.

Many pioneers lived, however, to not only a good age but to an unusually old age as evidenced by obituaries in newspapers, pioneer cemeteries, and other records. One of these records was a Doomsday Book, extant in the Perth Museum, and once belonging to Dr. Wilson of Perth. It was begun in June 1857 and covered a period of some fifteen years, recording births, deaths, and causes of deaths.

The most common causes given were: consumption, whooping cough, and croup. Anyone dying over 70 was recorded as dying of "natural decay". Such was the death of the Rev. William Bell, pioneer clergyman, who died in August 1857 at the age of 78. Other diseases carrying off victims were: heart disease, dropsy, water-on-the-brain, ulcer on stomach, delirium tremens, inflammation of the lungs, "inward complaint", brain fever, sore throat, sore leg, diphtheria, cancer on the face. There was only one entry of "asthma".

The oldest death recorded in this book was that of "Old Grannie Marshall" who died at Graham, Bathurst Township, of "Old Age" on November 10th, 1870, age 105.

Other entries include: Mrs. Kelso who died in December 1857 in Bathurst Township, age 89; Mrs. McLenaghan, Drummond Township, May 1, 1858, age 88; and Andrew Mitchell, no date, age 96.

According to the Rev. Bell's Journals many discharged Army officers who lived in Perth from the beginning of the settlement died of drunkenness, and whenever he believed that this was the cause of death he proceeded to deliver a funeral oration on the evils of drink. The establishment of temperance societies in the county in the 1830s probably decreased the number of confirmed alcoholics.

The following information is recorded on tombstones in the county's cemeteries. It is chosen at random and does not include, of course, all who lived to be 80 years or more, but it does indicate longevity:

*Elmwood Cemetery, Perth*

Sophia Cherry
Wife of Andrew Playfair, M.P.
Died July 10, 1881
Age 89.

Peter McTavish
1800-1881.

John Brown
Died September 14, 1904
Age 85.

His wife Mary Ann Rose
Died August 22, 1894
Age 86.

Robert Bell
Born 1808
Died April 1894.

*Craig Street Cemetery, Perth*
(Earliest Cemetery in Perth)

Thomas Morris
Died July 1861
Age 87.

In memory of James Bryce
Died April 1866
Age 94.

*Allan's Mills, Burgess*

Thomas Moodie
Died 1880
Age 96.

His wife Christena Drysdale
Died 1872
Age 83.

John Wilson, Sr.
Died 1888
Age 86.

*Stanleyville, Burgess*

Henry McVeigh
Died 1889
Age 100.

Thomas Lappin
Died 1880
Age 97.

*Campbell's (Family) Cemetery, Drummond*

William Fraser
Age 89.

*Auld Kirk Cemetery, Ramsay*

John Jeffries
Died August 10, 1866
Age 83.

Alfred Mansell Greig
1848-1936.

Anne Marg Nielson
1852-1926.

Hugh Metcalfe
Died May 7, 1902.
Age 81.

His wife Jean McLean
1824-1920.

Marion Aitken
Wife of Alex. Turner
Died 1885
Age 85.

Josephine Frances Mansell
Wife of James Greig
Died March 24, 1908
Age 96.

John Arthur
1822-1904.

*Union Hall Cemetery, Ramsay*

Henry Rath
Died 1883
Age 84.

John James
Died 1897
Age 87.

*Boyd's Settlement Cemetery*
(between Innisville and Perth)

Agnes Dunn
Wife of Wm. Shaw
Died 1890
Age 85.

Sarah McCulloch
Wife of John McCulloch
Died 1893.
Age 87.

Hugh Keys
Died 1873
Age 82.

Catherine
Wife of Peter McPhail
Died 1873
Age 82.

Mary McLaren
Died 1871
Age 90.

*Scotch Corners Cemetery, Beckwith* (Known as the "Sinclair cemetery")

John Sinclair
Died 1869
Age 80.

His wife Sarah Black
Died 1879
Age 80.

Thomas MacDonald
1834-1923.

His wife Elizabeth McNaughton
1839-1927.

*Middleville Cemetery, Lanark*

Janet wife of John Taylor
Died 1878
Age 81.

James Gillies
Died 1851
Age 86.

Peter Reid
Died age 80.

Margaret Scott
Wife of James Watt
Died 1886
Age 83.

Robert McArthur
Died 1866
Age 88.

William Scott
Died 1883
Age 81.

Don Munro
Died 1851
Age 81.

*Pakenham Presbyterian Cemetery, Pakenham*

Elizabeth Forbes
Wife of Andrew W. Dickson
1796-1885.

John Grant
Died 29 March 1862
In his 80th year.

*Ashton Cemetery, Beckwith*

John Shore
Died 1808
Age 89.

Andrew Fleming
Died 1864
Age 84.

Thomas Garland
Died 1880
Age 80.

*Dewar's Cemetery, Beckwith*

Findley McEwen
Died 1868
His wife Mary McLaren
Died 1861
Age 84.

*Prospect United Church Cemetery, Beckwith*

Thomas Poole
Died 1886
Age 83.

Elizabeth Kerfoot
Wife of William Kerfoot
Died 1858
Age 93.

*St. John's Anglican Cemetery Drummond*

James Stewart
Died 1891
Age 85.

Peter Nolan
Died 1890
Age 86.

Thomas Hopkins
Died 1861
Age 98.

*Crawford's Cemetery, North Sherbrooke*

Hugh Weir
Died 1917
Age 80.

Robert Love
Died 1862
Age 84.

David Brownlie
1793-1877.

John Gilmour
Died 1846
Age 81.

James Gilmour
Died 1853
Age 83.

Mary Dunlop
Wife of Robert Brownlie
Died 1902
Age 89.

MR. AND MRS. JOHN McGILL
The author's grandparents. John McGill came to Canada in 1848 from Ireland and settled in Pakenham township. He died in 1934 at the age of 92.

# BIBLIOGRAPHY


## Primary Sources

I *Manuscripts*

Bathurst District Papers, Ontario Archives.

Bell, William: A History of the Christian Church in this Settlement, Douglas Library, Kingston.

Bell, William: Journals, Vols. 1 to 17, Douglas Library.

Bell, William: Letters, Douglas Library.

Blue Books: District of Johnstown, Return of Sales by Crown Land Agent 1840-45, 1847-55, Ontario Archives.

Carleton Place Library Association Catalogue 1846-50.

Crown Land Papers, Ontario Archives:

Assessment Rolls of Elmsley, Montague and Marlborough, and Smiths Falls.

Bathurst District Return of Inspector, 1838, 1840, 1844.

Census of Montague 1797.

Census of Montague and Marlborough 1821, 1822.

Census of Burgess and Elmsley 1817, 1819.

Lanark Society Settlers to whom stores were issued 1821-1828.

Military Settlement of Soldiers and Emigrants 1816-1828.

Reports of Surveyor General 1795-1799, Vol. 5.

Returns of Irish Immigration 1823, located by Peter Robinson.

Returns of Irish Immigration 1825, located by Peter Robinson.

Settlers located by Alexander McDonnell, George Fowler, Major James Powell 1816-1820.

Settlers located by Major Powell and Captain Marshall 1820-21.

Crown Land Papers, Q. 155, Public Archives of Canada.

Doomsday Book, Record of Births, Deaths, and Causes of Deaths at Perth from 1857 to 1872, Perth Museum.

Doomsday Books, Land Patents Office, East Block, Parliament Buildings, Toronto.

Fiats of Rideau Military Settlement, Microfilm, Ontario Archives.

F. J. French Papers: "Sketch of Upper Canada Military Establishment, District of Bathurst", Ontario Archives.

Historical Documents, Papers, and Deeds, Perth Museum.

Land Patents Granted Prior to 1850, Microfilm, Ontario Archives.

McNicol, Donald: A History of Dalhousie Folk from Pioneer Days, Watson's Corners Library, Dalhousie.
Minute Book of Presbyterian Church, Lanark, Perth Museum.
Minutes of Upper Canada Land Board, Vol. S: Return of Lanark Society Settlers, dated July 28, 1836, Ontario Archives.
Morris, Alexander: Papers, Ontario Archives.
Morris, William: Papers, Douglas Library, Kingston.

Peter Robinson Papers, microfilm, Ontario Archives.
Peter Robinson's Settlers 1823-1825, Ontario Archives.

Record Book of Letters from 1815, written by Alexander McDonnell, Superintendent of Perth Military Settlement, Perth Museum.
Returns of Schools in Bathurst District for 1838, 1842, 1843, Ontario Archives.

Sailing Lists of Ships: Atlas, Baltic Merchant, Dorothy, Lady of the Lake, Golden Grove, etc. 1815-1816, Ontario Archives.
Sailing Lists of Ships: Commerce, Brock, Prompt, George Canning, and David of London, 1820-21, microfilm, Ontario Archives.
Surveyors Diaries: W. Conger (1817), John Booth (1817), Reuben Sherwood (1816), John B. Demers (1816), Ontario Archives.

Tweedsmuir Histories, Women's Institutes of Lanark County.

Upper Canada Sundries, Public Archives of Canada.

## II *Newspapers*

Almonte Gazette
Bathurst Courier
Bathurst Independent Examiner
Brockville Gazette
Canadian Annual, Brockville
Canadian Churchman, Merrickville
Canadian Illustrated News
Carleton Place Central Canadian
Carleton Place Herald
Family Herald
Illustrated London News
Kingston Chronicle
Kingston Spectator
Lanark Herald
Mirickville Chronicle & Weekly Advertiser
Ottawa Citizen
Ottawa Tribune

Perth British Standard
Perth Courier
Perth Expositor
Perth Weekly Despatch—Commercial and Agricultural Advertiser
Rideau Gleaner, Smiths Falls
Smiths Falls Review

III *Books, Pamphlets, and Periodicals*

Alfred, Rev. Bro.: *Catholic Pioneers in Upper Canada,* Toronto, 1947.

Almonte Congregation of Reformed Presbyterian Church Centennial Booklet.

Anglican Church Records: *Third Annual Report of the Incorporated Church Society of the Diocese of Toronto* for year ending 31st March 1845, printed at the Diocesan Press, Cobourg, 1845: "Facts and Particulars Relating to the Case of Morris vs Cameron Recently Tried at Brockville".

Annual Reports of the Agents of Emigration in Canada for 1841, Appendices 7 and 11, London, 1842.

Annual Report of the Normal, Model and Grammar, and Common Schools in Upper Canada for the year 1864, Perth Museum.

Bedore, B. V.: *The Broad Valley of the Ottawa,* Arnprior.

Belden, H. & Co.: *Illustrated Atlas of the Dominion of Canada,* Toronto, 1880: "Historical Sketch of the County of Lanark".

Bell, William: *Hints to Emigrants,* article appearing in *The Canadian Review,* December 1824.

Bradstreet Report for Province of Ontario 1871.

Campbell, C. T. *Pioneer Days in London,* London, Ont., 1921.

Campbell, Jessie Buchanan: *The Pioneer Pastor,* Toronto, 1900.

Canada Post Office Records.

Canadian Almanac for 1858.

Canadian Farmer's Almanac for 1862, 1863, 1865, 1868, 1873, 1876.

Canadian Historical Society Papers, Vol. XXX, 1934: "Journal of the Hon. Wm. Morris's Mission to England in the Year 1837" transcribed and edited by E. C. Kyte.

Carroll, John: *Case and His Cotemporaries.* 5 vols., Toronto, 1867-77.

Centennial Booklets: Almonte, Arnprior, Carleton Place, Lanark, Perth, Smiths Falls.

Cornish, George: *Handbook of Canadian Methodism,* Toronto, 1867.

Directories:
Canada Directory 1857-58.
City of Ottawa and Lanark County.

Counties of Leeds, Grenville, Lanark and Renfrew Directory, 1866-67.
Mitchell's Ottawa and Carleton County Directories 1864-1902.
Morrey's Directory of 1897.

Easton, George: *A History of the Easton Family* (booklet).
Education Proceedings of Upper Canada Legislature in 1823, Legislative Library, Toronto.
Foley, E. T.: *Seventy Years—The Foley Saga*, 1945.
Fraser, Alexander: *The Last Laird of MacNab*, Toronto, 1899.
Fraser, Joshua: *Shanty, Forest, and River Life in the Backwoods of Canada*, Montreal, 1883.
Fraser, Marjorie J. F.: "Feudalism in Upper Canada 1823-1843" in Ontario Historical Society *Papers & Records*, Vol. 12, 1914.

Gard, A. A.: *Pioneers of the Upper Ottawa and the Humors of the Valley*, 1906.
Garvin, John W., ed.: *Master-Works of Canadian Authors*, Vol. XIV, The Radisson Society of Canada, 1926.
Gould, Alice Kathryn: *By the Rideau—A Tale of Smiths Falls in Song and Story*, 1932 (booklet).
Gourlay, John L.: *History of the Ottawa Valley*, 1896.
Gourlay, Robert: *A Statistical Account of Upper Canada*, Vols. 1 and 2, London, 1822.
Grant, G. M. (Ed.): *Picturesque Canada*, 1879.
Guillet, Edwin C.: *The Great Migration*, Second Edition, Toronto, 1963.
Guillet, Edwin C.: *Pioneer Inns and Taverns*, Vol. II, Toronto, 1956.

Hart's Almanacs for 1860 and 1862, Perth, Perth Museum.
Haydon, Andrew: *Pioneer Sketches of the District of Bathurst*, Toronto, 1925.
Hodgins, J. George: *Documentary History of Education in Upper Canada from the passing of the Constitutional Act of 1791*, Vol. I: 1790-1830, Toronto, 1894.
Hodgins, J. George: *Schools and Colleges of Ontario 1792-1910*, Toronto, Vol. I, .
Holliday, Clarence: *John Holliday* (booklet), Cobourg.

Jackson, Joseph A.: *The Leckie Clan* (booklet).
Jamieson, E. L.: *The Story of Lanark and District*, Lanark, 1962.
Jones, Robert Leslie: *History of Agriculture in Ontario 1613-1880*. Toronto, 1946.
Journals of Education, Upper Canada, 1865, Perth Museum (booklet).
Journals of the Legislative Assembly of Upper Canada, Legislative Library, Toronto.

Kidd, G. E.: *The Story of the Derry*, Vancouver, 1943.

Lamond, Robert: *A Narrative of the Rise and Progress of Emigration from the Counties of Lanark and Renfrew to the New Settlements in Upper Canada*, Glasgow, 1821.

Leavitt, T. W. H.: *History of Leeds and Grenville from 1749 to 1890*, Brockville, 1879.

Legget, Robert: *The Rideau Waterway*, Toronto, 1955.

Lett, W. P: *Recollections of Bytown and Its Old Inhabitants*, Ottawa, 1874.

Lowry, Edna Gardner: *A Family Record of Pioneer Scottish Families in Lanark County and Their Descendants* (booklet).

McCaskell, Kenneth: Knox Presbyterian Church Centennial Booklet, McDonald's Corners, 1845-1945.

Mactaggart, John: *Three Years in Canada: An Account of the Actual State of the Country in 1826-27-28*, 2 Vols., London, 1829.

M'Donald, John: *Narrative of a Voyage to Quebec and Journey from thence to New Lanark, Upper Canada*, London, England, 1823.

McGiffin, Verna Ross: *Pakenham, Ottawa Valley Village 1823-1860*, Pakenham, 1963.

Maps of the Counties of Lanark and Renfrew, Canada West, from actual surveys under the direction of H. F. Walling, Prescott, 1863.

May, John: "Bush Life in the Ottawa Valley 80 Years Ago" in Ontario Historical Society *Papers and Records*, Vol. 12, 1913.

Minutes and Reports of the Municipal Council of the District of Bathurst, 1848, Perth Museum.

Morris, J. M.: *A Kerfoot History* (Canadian Branch) (booklet), 1953.

Morris, William: *Correspondence of the Hon. William Morris* with the Colonial Office as the delegate from the Presbyterian body in Canada, Niagara, Upper Canada. Perth, 1837.

Morris, William: *Reply of William Morris, Member of Legislative Council of Upper Canada* to 6 Letters addressed to him by John Strachan, D.D., Archdeacon of York. (Pamphlet) Toronto, 1838.

Ontario Agriculture Commission Report, Appendix I, 1881.

Pakenham Township Council Minutes 1836-1901.

Perth Almanac for 1859, Perth, Perth Museum.

Playter, George F.: "An Account of the Founding of Three Military Settlements in Eastern Ontario—Perth, Lanark, and Richmond 1815-1820", Ontario Historical Society *Papers and Records*, Vol. 20, 1923.

Richardson, R. L.: *Colin of the Ninth Concession*, Toronto, 1903.

St. Andrew's Centenary, Lanark Village 1821-1921.

St. Paul's Church Centennial Booklet, Almonte, 1863-1963.

Shaw, R. W.: "The Treaty Made with the Indians at Kingston May 31,

1819, for the Surrender of Lands", Ontario Historical Society *Papers and Records*, Vol. 27, 1931.
Smith, Josephine: *Perth-on-the-Tay*, Ottawa, 1901.
Smith, W. H.: *Canadian Gazetteer*, Toronto, 1836.
Spragge, George W.: "Elementary Education in Upper Canada 1820-1840", Ontario Historical Society *Papers and Records*, 1951-52.
Statutes of Ontario for 1867-1868.
Strachan, John: *Strachan's Letter Book* (1853-54), Ontario Archives.

Talman, James J.: "Agricultural Societies in Upper Canada", Ontario Historical Society *Papers and Records*, Vol. 27, 1931.
"The Principal of Free Grants in the Land Act of 1841", *Canadian Historical Review*, December 1933, Perth Museum.

Western Ontario Historical Notes, September 1949: "Fractional Currency Instituted by W. & J. Bell, Perth, U.C. in 1837", by Archibald Campbell.
Whitton, Charlotte E.: *A Hundred Years A-Fellin', 1842-1942*, Ottawa, 1943.
Wild, Roland: *MacNab, the Last Laird*, London, England, 1938.
Willis, N. P.: *Canadian Scenery*, 1842.
Women's Canadian Historical Society of Ottawa *Transcriptions*, Vol. XI, 1954, "A Pioneer Community in Beckwith Township, Lanark County, Upper Canada, 1818, locally known as the Derry", by B. R. MacKay.

**Secondary Sources**

Chesshyre, H. T. N.: *Canada in 1864, a Handbook for Settlers*, London, 1864.
Cooney, Percival: *Kinsmen* (novel), Toronto, 1916.
Cowan, H. I.: *British Emigration to British North America*, Toronto, 1961.

Davis, Nicholas Flood: *The Irishman in Canada*, 1877.
Dent, John C.: *Canada Since the Union of 1841*, Toronto, 1881.
Dent, John C.: *The Canadian Biographical Dictionary and Portrait Gallery of Eminent and Self-made Men*, Ontario Volume, Toronto, 1880-81.
Dent, John C.: *Canadian Portrait Gallery*, Vol. 4, Toronto, 1881.

Fraser, Alexander: *A History of Ontario*, Toronto, 1907.

Guillet, Edwin C.: *Early Life in Upper Canada*, Toronto, 1933.
Guillet, Edwin C.: *The Pioneer Farmer and Backwoodsman*, 2 Vols., Toronto, 1963.

Innis, Harold: *Settlement and the Mining Frontier*; and Lower, A. R. M.: *Settlement and the Forest Frontier in Eastern Canada* (one volume), Toronto, 1936.

Mackenzie, Alexander: *The Life and Speeches of the Honourable George Brown*, Toronto, 1882.

Morgan, Henry J.: *Canadian Men and Women of the Time*, 2nd edition, Toronto, 1912.

Morgan, Henry J.: *Sketches of Celebrated Canadians and Persons Connected with Canada from the Earliest Period of History*, Quebec, 1862.

Read, David B.: *The Lives of Judges of Upper Canada and Ontario from 1791 to 1888*, 1888.

Roberts, Charles G. D. and Tunnell, Arthur L.: *A Standard Dictionary of Canadian Biography*, Vol. I and Vol. II, 1934.

Rose, George McLean, ed.: *A Cyclopedia of Canadian Biography*, 1888.

Shortt, Adam: *Canada and Its Provinces*, Vol. 17, Toronto, 1914.

Wallace, W. Stewart: *A Dictionary of Canadian Biography*, 2 Vols., revised edition 1945.

Weaver, E. P.: *The Story of the Counties of Ontario*, Toronto, 1913.

(In addition to the foregoing, material was gleaned from personal interviews or correspondence with descendants of pioneers, family scrapbooks, family and other cemeteries.)

# INDEX